Lamb in Command

By the same author

Lieutenant Lamb
First Lieutenant

Lamb
in Command

Chapter 1

Lamb sighed and carefully manoeuvred a pebble over the edge of the harbour wall with his toe, gazing down with apparent deep interest as the little disturbance smoothed itself on the dirty, gently heaving water. He raised his eyes and stared gloomily at the mass of shipping in the harbour, reflecting without enthusiasm that if a man was forced to kick his heels in idleness then Jamaica was as good a place as any and a damned sight better than some he had known.

It was that perfect time of the year between the light rains of spring and the wet, sweating months of mid-summer, the time when the colours of the sea, sky and hills are strong and vibrant and the Caribbean air sings clean and clear, neither too warm by day nor too cool by night. Behind Lamb, the town of Kingston melted into the lower slopes of the mountains rushing magnificently upwards to brush against a flawless sky, their flanks clothed in rich, dark green; to his front the sun danced on the blue, sheltered water of the harbour, cradled to the east and south by a long, curving tongue of land.

Lamb was unmoved by the splendour of his surroundings; after three weeks of enforced idleness he would willingly have exchanged the warmth and beauty of the island for the deck of any ship, no matter how small or where bound. There was little chance of that, he thought morosely, drowning another pebble; after well and truly blotting his copy-book in the eyes of the Commander-in-Chief he could count himself fortunate that he was not on his way back to England and a permanent, bleak existence ashore.

He cast a cautious glance at the sun. It was almost noon, time to meet his fellow idlers in the Blue Boar. He turned away from the water, thinking that if the *Adroit* did not very soon return he would become a regular sot.

A young naval officer propelled himself into the street by cannoning off the door post as Lamb reached the inn. Lamb fended him off and then grabbed him by the arm to prevent him falling backwards. The sweet smell of port was almost tangible.

'My God, Sandy, you – ' Lamb's chuckle died as his eye took in the bright, new epaulette adorning the officer's left shoulder. He felt an immediate stab of deep envy; Sandy Smith, yesterday a lieutenant, was today a commander, one step short of a post-captain's glory and entitled to the honour of a boatswain's pipe. His envy, however, was overlaid with genuine pleasure at Smith's good fortune; the two officers had struck up a firm friendship in the past two weeks and it was with true warmth that he pumped Smith's hand.

'I had not heard. Congratulations, Sandy – *sir*, I should say.'

Smith beamed and waved a deprecatory hand. He staggered a pace sideways and clutched at Lamb's shoulder for support.

'No, no, Matthew, today I shall remain Sandy to my friends. Tomorrow I shall expect you to prosh – prostrate yourself at my feet but today everyone is my very good friend.' He twisted his neck to cast a loving, swimming-eyed look at his epaulette. 'Don't it look grand, sitting there? I can't wait for it to become faded.' He belched loudly and covered his mouth with a belated hand. 'Pardon me, my dear fellow. Yes, I received the news this morning. Commander into *Audacity*.' Happiness bubbled out of him. 'You should have been here to help me wet my epaulette,' he added, shaking an admonishing finger.

Lamb grinned. 'You appear to have done that remarkably well without my help.'

'Oh, the day is young yet, Matthew. Do not imagine you have escaped your responsibilit – ities in that direction. I have some arrangements to make this afternoon but I shall be back in this honest inn this evening and if I find you absent from your duties you shall feel the full weight of my wath – wrath. No, better still, I have to pass your lodgings: I shall collect you on my way.'

'Aye aye, sir,' said Lamb gravely, touching his hat.

Smith beamed at him, swaying somewhat, his face brick red, eyes dancing. Lamb felt the joy emanating from him and was happy for him but his own thoughts lay in a more selfish direction. Smith's feet were not the only ones on the ladder and

2

an upward move for him meant a certain amount of shuffling for those below. One lucky lieutenant would be taking command of Smith's little gun-brig and if he had stepped up from a schooner or a cutter then there would be a vacant command for another officer. This possibility had flashed into Lamb's mind the instant his eye had registered Smith's epaulette and, while he consciously refused to allow himself to speculate as to whose feet might be taking that upward step, a tiny bubble of hope had risen within him. Smith's next words brutally pricked it.

'Howard Dean takes over from me. Do you know him?'

Lamb gave a bright smile. 'Howard Dean? Yes, we have met once or twice – a likeable fellow.'

Dean was first lieutenant of the *Resistance*, a third-rate. His going would mean no more, probably, than a move up for each of her lieutenants and perhaps promotion for a lucky midshipman.

Smith was not so drunk as to be completely insensitive to Lamb's thoughts and he was not at all deceived by Lamb's brave smile. He gave him a comforting slap on the shoulder.

'Your turn will come, old fellow. I must go. I'll call for you at your lodgings at seven.'

'Steady as she goes,' cautioned Lamb as the new commander made his erratic way along the road with careful regard to the heaving ground.

Lamb hesitated at the open door of the tavern, listening to the rumble of laughter and loud buzz of masculine chatter coming from the cool, dark interior and fingering the coins in his pocket. It was barely half-way through the month and he had been spending too fast. If he was to pay his way tonight without counting the pennies then it would be better to give his customary midday hour in the Blue Boar a miss now. He turned away and strode determinedly in the direction of his lodgings, suddenly eager for the beef stew and dumplings that had been promised him earlier.

Mrs Mainwaring will be pleased when I see her this afternoon, he thought. She had taken to complaining of late that she suspected him of finding more pleasure in a glass than in her company and that too much liquor not only offended his breath but also detracted from his ardour. He sucked his teeth, debating, not for the first time, if it was not high time he and the wife of the Superintendent of the Navy Yard went their separate ways. Not only was their liaison becoming increasingly dangerous – it must surely be only a matter of time before Captain Mainwaring was the only man on the island not given to winking and nudging whenever Lamb hove into view – but his enthusiasm seemed to be declining in proportion to Mrs Mainwaring's increasing demands on him. He gave a wry smile of admiration of her; modesty and shame were not allowed to compete in the smallest way when her lust was at its height. Severing their relationship would not be easy, he suspected; she was usually sweetness itself towards him but she had demonstrated that she could ply a wickedly vicious tongue on occasion and he suspected that vindictiveness would give her more pleasure than pain. Lamb was uncomfortably aware that his own cowardice played a large part in their continuing alliance – but not wholly; Mrs Mainwaring possessed a sharp intelligence, a bright wit and, pleasures of the flesh apart, was an amusing companion with whom to while away some of the otherwise weary afternoons. He was not captivated but he was grateful.

He reached his lodgings with the question still unresolved and he thrust it firmly to the back of his mind as he ducked through the low doorway and caught the delicious smell of bubbling stew. The inn was small but clean and run by strict Navy standards of scrubbed boards and fresh paint. It was owned by an old seaman who had invested his carefully hoarded prize money in the building and much of his energy into fathering a great many pale brown children. Several of these scampered towards the kitchen as Lamb entered, from where they peeped out with eyes wide and mouths firmly stoppered with thumbs.

'When you are ready, Bates,' called Lamb with one foot on the stair.

'Aye aye, sir,' came the shout from the depths of the kitchen. 'You'm a mite early today: she'll be ten or fifteen minutes yet, sir.'

'I shall allow you no more than ten, not a second longer. Are my shirts done?'

4

'Aye, sir, you'll find 'em in your drawer, whiter than new, sir.'

Lamb bounded up the stairs. The stew's aroma had aroused his stomach juices and he felt ravenous. His earlier gloom had quite vanished; the prospect of a satisfying tumble with Mrs Mainwaring was suddenly very appealing, and after that lay a boisterous evening in the Blue Boar. He bent over his shirt drawer, whistling.

Captain Mainwaring had dined long and well with the captain of the *Resistance* and his contented snores rumbled gently throughout his office for close on an hour after his return to the Navy Yard. His clerk was well acquainted with his habits and a pot of tea was on the captain's desk within one minute of the abrupt cessation of snoring. With the tea came a small, pink envelope.

'It was left on my desk while I was out, sir,' said the clerk. 'It is addressed to you, marked "Personal, by hand", sir.'

'I can read, damn it,' grunted Mainwaring. He lifted the envelope from his desk and stared at it suspiciously. The writing was unknown to him but it was clearly in a female hand. And why had his name been penned in full – Captain Charles Thomas Mainwaring? He sniffed at it; scented paper, by God! Who would write personal notes to him on scented, pink paper? Thirty years ago, perhaps . . . He looked up and caught his clerk's interested eye.

'Are you quite certain you'll be able to read it properly from that angle, Atkins?' he enquired pleasantly.

Atkins blushed and retreated hastily to his own small office.

'Nosey little turd,' muttered Mainwaring as he slit the envelope. He read the few lines on the single sheet of paper with a puzzled frown and then murmured them aloud.

> *A mouse will play*
> *When Tom's away;*
> *In the absence of Chas*
> *What fun a lamb has!*

He tossed the letter onto his desk. 'Damn, damn, damn,' he said quietly, pouring himself a cup of tea. But he let it grow cold

5

while he leaned back in his chair, stared at the ceiling and thoughtfully drummed his fingers, a frown of pain and concern on his round, red, pleasant face.

The captain had married late in life, to a woman some thirty years younger, and the physical aspect of their marriage had become increasingly less important to him in the last few years, a condition upon which he was uncomfortably aware his wife did not look kindly. Mainwaring was no fool; he had long accepted that she looked elsewhere for comfort, but providing she conducted her affairs discreetly he was quite prepared to play the part of the ignorant husband, recognizing that much of the blame for such a situation rested on his shoulders. Today's missive, however, could not be ignored; one such spark of tattle amongst his wife's circle of female acquaintances could be quickly fanned by eager tongues into a flame of gossip that would sweep the island. He sighed. Sadness, not anger, was his immediate reaction; he had met Lamb on several occasions and thought him a pleasant, likeable young officer. Action must be taken, nevertheless, covert action that would not be laid at his door, as much for Lamb's good as his own. He rose from his chair, tucked the note into his pocket and reached for his hat.

'I am off for a walk,' he announced to his startled clerk, who was more accustomed to hearing the captain complain bitterly if he had to walk as far as the mast-pond in the yard.

Mainwaring left the Navy Yard and paced slowly along the waterfront, hands behind his back, head bowed deep in thought. A boat was pulling towards the steps, a common enough sight and one to which he would not normally give a second glance, but this was the hospital boat and on the chest of the figure stretched along the thwarts was an officer's cocked hat. He paused to watch as the stretcher was man-handled up the steps. The officer's eyes were closed, his face pale and beaded with sweat. Mainwaring recognized him as Lieutenant Pardoe, elderly commander of HM packet *Heron*, which he had seen entering the harbour as he was leaving the *Resistance*. He crooked a finger at the youthful lieutenant hovering anxiously beside the stretcher as its black attendants prepared to carry it away.

'You, sir, Mr – er – ?'

The lieutenant hastened over and touched his hat.
'Jamieson, sir.'
'Yes, of course. What is the trouble here, Mr Jamieson;'
Jamieson was not sure, sir. The captain had been taken ill a
couple of days back and this morning he had been unable to
leave his cot, complaining of severe stomach pains. He was
running a high fever, sir, and Jamieson hoped to obtain a little
more information at the hospital.
Mainwaring nodded sympathetically. 'Poor fellow. Thank
you, Mr Jamieson.'
The officer saluted and ran off after the stretcher. Mainwaring stood in thought for a moment and then turned and strode
determinedly on short, stout legs in the direction of the Navy
Office. Lieutenant Pardoe's incapacity could not have occurred
at a more opportune moment; a quiet word in the ear of his
friend the Chief of Staff would not come amiss.

Lamb lay flat on his back and gazed at the ceiling of Mrs
Mainwaring's bedroom, giving half his mind to the task in
hand and the other half to the pitiful state of his wardrobe.
Above him Mrs Mainwaring whimpered and hissed and
grunted as she drove herself to that point of bliss for which she
so often strived, the perspiration flying from her nose and chin
and the points of her jouncing breasts, the light from the
lowered jalousies throwing bright, shifting bands across her
pale, slim body.
    Much of Lamb's clothing had been left on the frigate *Adroit*
when he transferred to the prize brig and most of that which he
had taken with him was lost when the prize had caught fire,
exploded and sunk beneath him. He had arrived at Port Royal
with not so much as a razor or comb to call his own and he had
been forced to accept the loan of a few guineas from the
commander of the sloop which had plucked him from the sea.
Clothes were very expensive in Kingston but it was clear that if
he was not to be shortly reduced to a scarecrow he must dig
deep into his small store of money. He began to review his list of
priorities, absently fondling a small breast as it swung and
bounced above him. It was best, he had discovered, to allow
Mrs Mainwaring to dictate the pace of their coupling; her need

7

and endurance were considerably in excess of his own and by adopting the simple stratagem of allowing his mind to wander he had found he could adequately meet her demands with little danger of bringing matters to a premature end. As he was gravely assessing the relative importance of new shoes to that of a new hat Mrs Mainwaring's sighs began to deepen and her clutch to tighten. Recognizing the signs, he abandoned his clothing list and set himself earnestly to the more immediate priorities.

'Was that not wonderful, Mr Lamb?' breathed Mrs Mainwaring breathlessly into his ear as she settled down at his side, pulling herself close and throwing a possessive leg over his thigh. He answered by way of a friendly pat on a damp buttock, amused as always by her insistence on the use of the formal title even at moments such as these. It was, she averred, safer for them both. Why, supposing she talked in her sleep or, becoming too familiar with the use of 'Matthew', spoke of him as such to her husband? Lamb closed his eyes and listened to the gradual slowing of his thudding heart beat, his sweat cooling in the pleasant, flower-scented breeze from the slatted window. He would dearly have loved to drift off into sleep but he knew there was little chance of that; Mrs Mainwaring was always at her most talkative after love-making, as if the act had stirred her brain and loosened her tongue.

She gave a contented sigh and kissed his ear. It had been so nice for her these past two weeks, she murmured, having him to herself and not forever busy about his duties on the *Adroit* at the beck and call of that dreadful Captain Slade, never knowing when she would see him again. It was lovely to think that the *Adroit* would be on patrol for at least another month. They must make the most of the time together – discreetly as ever, of course: they must not arouse Charles's suspicions. She had been so busy in the garden this morning – she was making a new shrubbery in the far corner, had she told him? She was so happy – was he happy, too? She knew he had been sad about losing his prize ship but he must not blame himself; it had not been his fault and she was sure the Commander-in-Chief did not hold it against him. Once he was back on his frigate he would get more prizes, she was quite certain, and make his

8

fortune and become a grand post-captain in no time at all. He was very quiet; what was he thinking?

Lamb turned his head and kissed the tip of her nose.

'I was thinking that I must buy myself new shoes and that I would call in on the way to my lodgings for a fitting.'

She sighed and snuggled closer. 'Nobody could ever accuse you of being too romantic, Mr Lamb. Now give me a proper kiss and then you must go before Charles gets home. Oh, these afternoons go far too quickly!'

Lamb received his fitting and a short monologue from the shoe-maker on the price of leather and was still wincing at the cost he would have to pay when he reached his lodgings. The sun was low over the hills to the west but the air was still warm and he was sweating from his long trudge from Captain Mainwaring's house, downhill though it had been. Bates was sitting on the bench beside the door, taking the evening air and helping it down with a tankard of beer held in his huge fist. Long years of duty on a man-of-war brought him to his feet as Lamb approached and ingrained habit brought his knuckle to his forehead, tankard and all.

'You look a mite warm, sir,' he observed.

'I feel a mite warm, Bates. Would you have any more of that beer in the kitchen?'

'Not above three or four barrels, sir. Hold fast just a second.'

The beer was cool and bitter and refreshing and Lamb swallowed it gratefully as he sat and conversed companionably with the old seaman in the lengthening shadows of the evening. Bates had lost his arm while manning a gun on the *Monmouth* in the battle with Admiral D'Estaing's fleet off Grenada in 1779, when Admiral Byron's ships received a drubbing after finding themselves between the French guns on the island and the French fleet on their lee. The movements of the two fleets were etched indelibly on the old man's memory and there was nothing that gave him greater delight than recounting the action. Lamb listened and nodded and smiled, the shadows grew longer and at length the battle and the beer were finished. He left the old gunner sitting on the bench with the empty tankards beside him, staring into the gathering gloom while his

9

ancient, scarred head rang to the sound of long-gone gunfire.

Lamb peered into his mirror, ran a questioning hand over his chin and decided that his shave of the morning still held good. He stripped off his damp shirt, hurled it into a corner, and washed. The sound of voices came up from below his window as he was buttoning his fresh shirt; one of them he recognized as belonging to Smith, the other was a low mumble. The stairs thundered to the sound of the commander's feet and Lamb's door burst open.

'What's this? Not ready yet?' exclaimed Smith, striding in and collasping heavily on Lamb's bed. 'Seven o'clock I said and it must be almost a minute past now.'

'I shall not keep you a moment,' said Lamb, bending his knees to bring the reflection of his stock into his mirror. 'Who was that you were talking to downstairs?'

'Oh, nobody very important, just a messenger from the Navy Office, asking for a Lieutenant Lamb. I sent him packing with a flea in his ear.'

'What? Asking for me?'

Lamb whirled round. Smith held a large envelope, heavy with embossed seals, between finger and thumb as though it was an object of dubious cleanliness.

'It is only a letter from the office of the Chief of Staff,' said Smith casually, tossing the envelope onto the bed. 'It can hardly be urgent. Let it lie there until the morning.'

'You dog!' said Lamb, snatching it up. He sprang to the wash-basin stand, seized his razor and slit the wax seals.

Smith shook his head sadly. 'Tut-tut. You will ruin the edge of your blade.'

Lamb did not hear him. His eyes were dancing over the contents of the letter. He reached the signature, glanced up at Smith with a broad grin and read the words again.

'Good news?' enquired Smith.

Lamb passed him the letter. 'Temporary command of the packet *Heron*. Her own commander is ill. I am to proceed to Antigua and Barbados on the fourth – what's today, the second?' He sat on the side of the bed and chuckled.

'I am pleased for you, my dear fellow,' said Smith, from whose newly-exalted position in life the command of a mail-packet was marginally favourable to that of steersman in a bum-boat. 'Now put on your coat and let us be off to the Blue Boar before I shrivel with thirst. I have a mouth like a Portagee's bilge.'

Lamb's thoughts were some way from the Blue Boar. 'Beg pardon?' he murmured absently. 'Oh, yes. See here, Sandy, would you think it very unfriendly of me if I did not . . .'

'Indeed I would,' cut in Smith, jumping up from the bed and reaching for Lamb's coat. 'There is nothing you can do on the *Heron* tonight except blunder about with a lantern and irritate the bosun. Leave it until the morning when you can go aboard in style and take stock in daylight.' He shook the coat in front of its owner's nose. 'Stir yourself. Tonight we both have cause to celebrate.'

Lieutenant Jamieson, a square, stocky, very muscular young man, possessed a dark, hard face which belied his true nature. In actuality, as Lamb was to discover, he was a most agreeable youth, given to laughter at the smallest provocation. Today, however, his face was carefully grave as he touched his hat to the tall, thin figure of the new captain, conscious of certain apprehensive flutterings in his stomach. Receiving a new commander was always a testing time on any ship; it was the moment that the new man would often choose to stamp his authority firmly over his subordinates and set the manner of the future relationship, a matter of no small concern in a vessel the size of the *Heron*. He was relieved when the lofty officer smiled warmly, put out his hand and said : 'How do you do? My name is Lamb. You must be Mr Jamieson.'

'Yes, sir,' said Jamieson, crushing his commander's fingers bloodless. 'Welcome aboard, sir. I am sorry the deck is in such disarray but you have caught us at an awkward moment, sir.'

Lamb glanced about him. The main hatch-cover had been removed and forward of the mast a number of water casks were in the process of being scrubbed in readiness for the water-hoy. Sacks of vegetables were piled against the hatch-coaming, boxes, kegs and coils of rope were heaped about the deck and beside the mast a crate of noisy hens protested their confinement and thrust their red heads through the bars. Lamb

11

disregarded the confusion, the normal state of any vessel preparing for sea, and looked instead at the fabric of the ship – the cordage, deck, guns, timber and paintwork. He was not displeased by his brief glance; it was clear that Pardoe had run a taut, clean, well-preserved vessel.

'Not at all, Mr Jamieson,' he said. 'I am pleased you have things well in hand.'

Jamieson covertly studied the captain as he looked about the deck. He did not look well, he thought; after that initial smile of greeting his face had taken on a drawn, frowning look of pain and his eyes were shadowed, bloodshot and narrowed against the light of the early sun. He winced suddenly and momentarily closed one eye. Jamieson realized with a flash of insight and much inward amusement that Lamb was suffering from a hangover, and from the look of him one that had cost a deal of time and money to acquire.

'Send the steward to my cabin, if you please,' said Lamb. 'I shall read myself in shortly.'

'Aye aye, sir.'

Jamieson watched Lamb's hat disappear below deck level as he descended the aft companion and allowed himself a little chuckle. He would not care to have the new commander's head at the moment, he thought. He was not surprised Lamb had not read himself in straightaway; the chances were that his vision would not allow him.

'Sylvester!' he called to an ancient, tiny seaman working beside the hatch. 'Report to the captain's cabin. Mr Snow, send a man below with the captain's gear, if you please.'

Lamb entered his cabin and made his way with carefully lowered head to the chair behind the tiny table, feeling that if his skull should merely brush against one of the low deck beams it would instantly explode. He was certain he had never felt so wretchedly ill; his head throbbed and pounded with a sickening, monotonous rhythm, he had a deep, blinding, stabbing pain over his left eye and his stomach writhed and heaved as if it was home to a nest of adders, all of them intent on exploring his throat. He was only slightly comforted by the thought that Smith must be suffering a good deal worse than he. The commander had drunk with immense zest and enthusiasm and

Lamb had assisted in carrying his unconscious body up the stairs to one of the Blue Boar's beds. He remembered only little of his own activities after that; snatches filtered through – an officer dancing on the table minus his breeches; talking with great seriousness about God to one of the tavern's whores; linking arms with two others and the three of them singing loudly through the dark Kingston streets; Bates bending anxiously over him and wiping his face with a damp cloth while Mrs Bates hovered at the door with her dressing gown clutched to her throat and a look of concern on her handsome, black face.

Lamb shuddered with remorse and closed his eyes, opening them again with a wince as a loud double knock on the panel of the open door sent a brief shaft of agony through his head. A small, slight, elderly individual stood before him, a cheerful grin unashamedly revealing much in the way of gums but less as regards teeth.

'Sylvester, sir, captain's steward and passengers' steward, too, when we has 'em. Your gear is on its way down, sir. Shall I stow it for you?'

Lamb made the mistake of shaking his head. He quickly stilled it.

'No, I can manage that, Sylvester.' He had no wish to arouse the man's pity or scorn at the paucity of his wardrobe. 'What I would like you to do is to bring me a pot of coffee, as strong as you like.'

'One pot of coffee, aye aye, sir. Missed our breakfast, did we, sir?'

'Yes,' said Lamb, with a good deal of truth.

'I could make you a nice bacon sandwich, sir,' offered the little man. 'Fresh bread today, sir,' he added temptingly.

Lamb's stomach heaved at the thought. 'Just the coffee, if you please.'

'Aye aye, sir.'

The steward vanished, giving way to a burly seaman who gave a tap at the door and held up Lamb's single canvas bag in one massive hand.

'Your gear, sir.'

'Thank you. Leave it there. What is your name?'

'Selby, sir.'

'Very good, Selby.'

Lamb sat in his chair and briefly inspected his cabin while he waited for his coffee. He could see little in the way of Pardoe's personal effects apart from a few books on a shelf and a set of tarpaulins hanging behind the door, and he guessed that the remainder of his things had been taken ashore. The cabin was small and sparsely furnished, and its one low cupboard was locked, but compared to the tiny kennels which had been his lot for the past few years it was spaciousness itself and in spite of feeling one short step from death he experienced a glow of pride and pleasure.

The coffee arrived, strong, steaming and reviving, and the first delicious cupful washed the filth from his tongue, quietened the snakes in his stomach and did much to reduce the pain in his head. He refilled his cup and leafed through the punishment book while he sipped. The entries were sparse, well spaced in time and contained none concerned with flogging, he was pleased to note. Apart from the inevitable drunkenness, the occasional idleness and one entry for fighting, the book showed the crew of the *Heron* to be an uncommonly well behaved set of men. He put the book aside and took up the muster book, discovering that his crew consisted of twenty-six men and two boys; he took note of the names of the boatswain, Snow, and the carpenter, Mee, the *Heron*'s two standing officers. The cutter was too small to entertain a sailing-master, surgeon or purser; these duties would be filled by Lamb and Jamieson.

With the entire contents of the coffee-pot inside him Lamb made his way up to the deck feeling considerably more alive than when he had left it. Jamieson was leaning over the hatch-coaming berating an unfortunate seaman below and Lamb waited patiently for him to finish his lengthy diatribe. His eyes wandered slowly around the deck, taking in the length and breadth of his command. The *Heron* was armed with six four-pounder long guns and two nine-pounder carronades, the smallest he had ever seen. Anything heavier, he presumed, would have been too much for the cutter's timbers. The single mast, stepped well forward, towered naked into the air crossed by the short topsail yard. The long mainsail boom extended low over the deck and well out beyond the stern. He was pleased

14

with what he saw and he was suddenly eager to be at sea, to put the *Heron* through her paces. The fore-and-aft rig would enable the packet to lie nearer to the wind than the square-rigged ships in which he had served and she should be able to show a clean pair of heels to all but the speediest of ships, he guessed.

Jamieson removed his head from the hatch-way and Lamb hailed him.

'Pipe the hands aft, if you please, Mr Jamieson.'

Jamieson gave a bellow, the boatswain's pipe split the air and the hands pattered aft, most of them bare-footed, with a few – the petty officers and senior hands – in shoes. Men scampered up from the hold and swarmed down from their slush-pots aloft. The cook, patch-eyed, one-eared, the side of his head an ugly pucker of old scar tissue, emerged from his galley. Jamieson turned to Lamb, touched his hat and reported all hands present and correct.

Lamb took his orders from his pocket and read them aloud, part of his mind looking on and listening to his voice with something close to astonishment, recalling how often he had yearned for this moment and scarcely able to believe it had arrived. His command might be only temporary, his tenure of authority brief, but nevertheless, the moment was one to be savoured with great pleasure. He folded his papers and slipped them back into his pocket. The hands, he thought, looking at their faces, seem remarkably unimpressed by the majesty of the moment; what the occasion needed to give it a due sense of importance was a roll of drums and the crash of gunfire. Well, perhaps not the guns, not this morning.

He nodded to Jamieson. 'Dismiss the hands. Mr Snow, Mr Mee, stand fast, if you would.'

The hands drifted away.

'Right, gentlemen,' said Lamb briskly, 'let us take a turn round the ship.'

Chapter 2

'Ease the sheets, Mr Snow,' ordered Lamb. 'Let her sail free, quartermaster.' He moved away from the tiller as the mainsail was hauled square to the wind and crossed to the weather rail. The tortuous business of threading through the reefs that lay off the entrance to Port Royal had demanded all his attention for the past hour or so and it was with a feeling of relief of sailing in clear water at last that he gazed at the dark green slopes of Jamaica's southern flank creeping past to larboard.

The past twenty-four hours had been a busy time; stores and water had been stowed below and sacks of mail for Antigua and Barbados were under lock and key together with two leather pouches of official mail collected at the last minute from the Navy Office. Lamb had sent Sylvester ashore with almost the last of his money to purchase a few luxuries with which to supplement the ship's stores – and to deliver a note to Bates for conveyance to Mrs Mainwaring together with a shilling to speed the infant Bates's legs.

The passengers had arrived – Lamb had delegated their reception to Jamieson – and been assigned their little cabins below. There was a Lieutenant Fox, a slim, slight, greying officer taking passage to the garrison at Antigua and a Mrs Skinner, accompanied by her maid, on the last leg of her journey from England to join Major Skinner, Royal Marines, also at Antigua. The lady's cabin was directly below Lamb's feet and the sound of her voice as she berated her little maid came up clearly through the aft companionway. She was a large, forceful woman with a voice to match and Lamb wondered with what depths of joy the Major would welcome the other half of his flesh.

The quartermaster turned the glass and struck the bell.

'Hands to breakfast!' shouted Jamieson and the men melted

from the deck to the strident shrill of the boatswain's mate's whistle. Lamb gave a last look at Jamaica, a quick glance at the set of the topsail and went below, leaving the deck to Jamieson. He had leaned heavily on the young officer's experience of these waters while negotiating the channel out of Port Royal and had been pleased with the cheerful confidence which Jamieson had displayed. The youth had been on the *Heron* almost a year, ever since his leap from midshipman to lieutenant, and was well acquainted with everyone on board. They were all good men, he assured Lamb; one or two wags amongst them but no out-and-out villains if one discounted the cook, who was a law unto himself.

Sylvester was an efficient steward and Lamb's breakfast was on his table within one minute of his bellow.

'The lady's maid ain't none too well, sir,' he confided as he poured Lamb's coffee. 'Terrible sick she's been, all over the deck. The lady's none too happy with her, sir.'

'Yes, I can well imagine,' said Lamb, picturing the mess and stench in the tiny cabin as he hungrily cut into his bacon.

'I've had to swab out twice already and still it comes up. Like a regular pump she is, sir.'

Lamb paused in the act of buttering his bread. 'I hope you have washed your bloody hands well since,' he said sharply.

'O' course, sir,' said Sylvester cheerfully.

Lamb gave him a suspicious glance and bit into his bread. A thought struck him and he tapped the locked cupboard beside his table.

'What is in here, Sylvester?'

'Cap'n Pardoe's wine, sir. The key's on the ring – the little brass one, sir.'

The steward left the cabin before Lamb thought to ask him how he knew which key opened the wine cupboard and chewing busily he fished in his pocket for the key to the table drawer. The bunch of keys was large; there were locks to the spirit-room, bread store, mail-room, magazine, cable tier, purser's stores and arms chests, each of them requiring a large key, but hidden amongst them he found the little brass one and bent to open the cupboard. The bottles were stored upright in separate wooden racks to prevent them beating each other to pieces. He examined the labels, finding port, claret, Madeira, hock, gin and illicit brandy. Lamb scratched his chin, considering. He had been unable to afford to buy wine for himself and if he was ever called upon to entertain guests he would find himself acutely embarrassed if he could only offer them Admiralty issue. He could hardly steal from Pardoe's supply but if the man was at all reasonable he would not object to loaning a bottle or two for the sake of the good name of the ship. Lamb nodded, happy that he had solved a worrying problem; a note of hand in exchange for a bottle would take care of things if the need arose.

The cutter was heeling slightly under a moderate north-westerly breeze when Lamb emerged on deck. The air was warm and bright, the sun flashed and sparkled from a million points off the deep blue of the sea and the green, indented coastline of Jamaica, lush and dense to the water's edge, reared massively several miles to larboard. A seaman was coiling the log–line at the taffrail and the quartermaster, half-minute glass in hand, was reporting to Jamieson.

'Make it so,' Jamieson was saying to the quartermaster as Lamb approached.

'What did it give?' asked Lamb.

'Eight and a quarter, sir,' said Jamieson with a touch of pride in his voice.

Lamb nodded. It was a fair turn of speed with this wind but then the wind was on the larboard quarter, probably the cutter's best point of sailing. He would be interested in seeing how she sailed close-hauled, with the wind over the bow and the sheets hardened, and while he was considering whether or not to conduct a little trial for his own satisfaction his eye fell on the figure of Lieutenant Fox, leaning on the rail beside the larboard carronade and staring out at the distant mountain peaks. He turned, caught Lamb's gaze and smiled, courteously touching his hat in salute. Lamb strode forward and held out his hand.

'How d'you do? My name is Matthew Lamb. I am sorry I was too busy to greet you earlier.'

Fox shook his hand warmly and smiled again, showing perfect white teeth.

'Charles Fox. Delighted to make your acquaintance,

captain.' His voice was deep and melodious, imbued with years of quarterdeck authority.

'And I yours, sir. Most pleased to have you aboard. I understand you are to join Admiral Upton's staff?'

For all that Fox was well into middle age and was likely to climb no higher than his present rank, the man had a presence about him to which Lamb immediately warmed. His grey hair was still thick, handsomely curled, and his slight figure was as slim as a boy's. His face, although showing the lines of age, still displayed the good looks of his youth, with bright, penetrating grey eyes and a smile that was brilliant and sincere.

He has the look of a womanizer about him, thought Lamb as they talked, a charge he would have been more than happy to have levelled in his own direction.

The shrill, angry tones of Mrs Skinner burst into their quiet conversation.

'Mr Lamb! Commander, captain, whatever you are – I must speak with you, sir.'

Lamb swung round, a sharp frown of disapproval on his face. He might only be a lowly lieutenant but he was captain of this vessel and he was damned if he would allow the ignorant woman to speak to him as if he were a bloody cabman.

'Captain will serve very well, ma'am,' he said icily.

His tone was quite wasted on Mrs Skinner. She advanced on him with a determined look on her broad face, clutching her bonnet to her head.

'Have you seen the size of my room, sir, my cabin, that is? It is far too small, quite unsuitable for the two of us. There are not enough hooks for our clothes, the ceiling is extremely low and my maid will have to sleep on the floor next to the chamber pot. I was not at all happy with my accommodation on the *White Rose* but it was a mansion compared to that little cupboard downstairs. It just will not do, sir.'

Lamb caught the glint of amusement in Fox's eye and a broad grin on the face of Timms, the quartermaster, instantly replaced by a look of stone as Lamb shot him a glare over Mrs Skinner's shoulder.

'I am sorry you are not happy with your accommodation, ma'am,' he said, with deep insincerity. He gestured about the deck with a sweep of his arm. 'As you can see, this cannot compare with the *White Rose* – it is but a cutter, ma'am, a mail-packet, a very small ship. But there is a vacant cabin and if you wish, your maid shall have it.'

She drew in a deep breath, clearly amazed at his obtuseness. 'That will only add to my problems, young man. The wretched girl is prostrate with sickness and needs my constant attention – and if she were not, I would not dare let her out of my sight with all these sailors about. No, you must come up with something a little better than that, sir.'

Lamb struggled to conceal his anger. Had the lady's tone been less demanding he would have considered giving her his own cabin, painful as its loss would have been. Now, however, he was damned if he would.

'I am very sorry, ma'am, but I can help you no further in that regard. You must make the best of what space you have. I shall send the carpenter's mate to put up more hooks for you but there is nothing I can do about the height of your – your ceiling. And so far as your chamber pot is concerned you must make arrangements that suit you best. Now if you will excuse me, ma'am, I have more urgent duties to attend to.'

He gave a brief bow and strode aft, leaving Mrs Skinner's outraged 'Well!' hanging in the air. Stupid bloody woman, he raged, as he paced back and forth beside the tiller; does she imagine she is on a three-decker with state-rooms for the asking? Low ceiling indeed!

'Stand fast!' roared Lamb, the sound of the guns' thunder still echoing in his ears. The stench of gun smoke filled the deck and its dirty yellow haze danced over the bright, evening sea to leeward. 'Swab out! Secure the guns!'

He stood a little forward of the tiller watching the men and boys busy themselves about the guns. Their performance had pleased him; Pardoe had drilled them well, he thought. They were a trifle slow, perhaps, for his man-of-war standards but every man knew his duties and they had given a competent, workmanlike display. The *Heron*'s supply of gunpowder did not allow for its use in gun-drill and Lamb would have to account for every pound that he used but he had recklessly stretched a point to allow the gunners to fire a reduced charge at the final running-out of the guns. To his mind, the pantomime of silent exercise without the immensely satisfying crash and flame and smoke and smell of exploded powder was a dull affair unlikely to arouse the hands' enthusiasm for their work. He turned to Fox who had been regarding the proceedings with keen, professional interest.

'A credible performance, I thought, Mr Fox.'

'Indeed, sir. I was most impressed. It reflects favourably on their last commander – what was his name again?'

'Pardoe.'

'Pardoe, yes. It has never been my luck to serve on small ships and I think one tends, from the superior height of a man-o'-war's quarterdeck, to look down a trifle condescendingly on these little packets dashing about like energetic puppies on their little errands. And yet they are as regular Navy as the largest ship of the line, are they not? They have their own sharp teeth and are run on strict Navy lines in exactly the same way. Standing here, sir, and looking on, I did feel that a taut little vessel such as this is a delight to the eye and must equally be a delight to command.'

'I could not agree with you more, sir,' said Lamb.

He was gratified at the kind words but at the same time was aware of a tiny area of unease at the edge of his mind, an undefined suspicion which had arisen as Fox talked, as if an unknown sense had noticed something that had not consciously registered on ear or eye and thrown up a small burr, a doubt which he could not pin down.

'And you have a good set of men here, too, by the look of them,' continued Fox in his pleasant way. 'Apart from the boys, they all seem solid, mature hands, a credit to any ship. Any captain would give his eye-teeth for a few score men like these.'

'Yes, I am very pleased with what I have seen so far,' said Lamb.

Was it that Fox was a little too pleasant and agreeable, he wondered? His well modulated voice, frequent disarming smiles and air of warm, sincere interest might well be the natural attributes of a charming and congenial man; they could also be the carefully donned and practised trappings of a man

21

who bent too easily with the wind, who liked to be all things to all men. He gave a sideways glance at Fox's lined, intelligent face; the officer caught the look and his frank, grey eyes crinkled in such warm, friendly fashion that Lamb's vague misgivings instantly vanished.

'Perhaps you would care to sup with me this evening, Mr Fox? he suggested. 'I cannot vouch for the talents of the cook and the fare will mainly be with the compliments of the Admiralty but I would welcome your company.'

'I am at the mercy of the cook wherever I sup, sir,' smiled Fox. 'I have some fine claret in my cabin; perhaps you would be kind enough to give me your opinion of it at supper?'

'Consider my invitation doubled in strength, sir,' replied Lamb promptly and the two of them chuckled companionably together.

Fox went below and Lamb sent a man to the galley with instructions for the cook. He walked slowly along the weather side of the cutter and back by way of the lee, inspecting with a keen eye the lashings and wedges of the little guns, snubbed up tight against the sides. The sun was declining in red splendour astern, throwing long shadows over the quiet deck and the ship's bell sounded six times, the chimes loud and clear in the hushed, violet evening air. The boatswain appeared with his mate on the first stroke of the bell and stood expectantly, forward of the mainmast.

'Very well, Mr Snow,' called Lamb. 'Take in inner and outer jibs and reef the topsail.' It had always been Pardoe's custom, Jamieson had informed him, to shorten sail for the night and Lamb saw no reason to interfere with this sensible precaution.

The pipe shrilled and the watch scampered to their down-hauls and reef-points. Lamb paced back and forth along that section of the flush deck abaft the mainmast recognized as the quarterdeck and upon which no seaman would dream of trespassing unless in the course of his duties, watching with quiet pleasure the quick and practised motions of the men at their ropes. Within minutes their tasks were done and the *Heron* sailed on through the darkening water under reefed topsail, flying jib and mainsail alone. Lamb dismissed the watch below, leaving the deck to himself, the helmsman, quartermaster and the lookout at the masthead.

Lamb was very conscious that his command was small and that many of the privateers that prowled these waters were large, powerful and fast. The *Heron*'s main defence lay not in her guns but in her speed and manoeuvrability, aided by her ability to lie very close to the wind. The Caribbean was a huge sea and with luck the packet would sail across it unmolested, although from what Jamieson and the ship's log had told him the *Heron* had experienced several chases in the past year and at least one close shave, as testimony for which the taffrail bore evidence of cunningly replaced timbers. It had been Pardoe's practice to keep a lookout aloft for twenty-four hours a day and Lamb was only too happy to continue it. There was usually some visibility, even on the most moonless of nights, and Lamb was determined to sheer off at the merest suspicion of a sighting. Valour and aggression were all very well but for a mail-packet the safety of the King's mail must take precedence over all.

A burst of feminine-voiced vituperation came up from below, faint and unintelligible but unmistakable in source. Lamb smiled. By the sound of it the two women were preparing to settle down for the night and Mrs Skinner was not yet reconciled to the space of her quarters. He felt a twinge of guilt as he recalled his sharp words of the morning; taking care of her sea-sick maid in that cramped and close cabin could not be pleasant. Perhaps he had been a little less than considerate to the lady; he must make a point of being especially courteous and attentive to her tomorrow.

His stomach growled loudly, clamouring for sustenance. He felt quite empty and paced impatiently between taffrail and mainmast, eager for Jamieson to relieve him for his supper. It was uncommonly kind of Fox to suggest that he bring some wine with him, he thought; it may be that he had divined from the cracked shoes and a coat that was past its best that the captain's stores were unlikely to be well stocked. Lamb grinned into the darkness, determined not to allow the thought to embarrass him; he was not the first penniless lieutenant to find himself in this position nor, given the Admiralty's rates of pay, would he be the last.

He moved to the tiller and peered at the compass, dimly lit by the binnacle lantern. Satisfied that the helmsman was maintaining the same course as that marked on the slate, east -south-east, designed to keep the *Heron*'s course well south of the coast of Hispaniola – he took up his stance by the starboard rail and clasping his hands behind his back rocked to and fro on his heels, looking forward over the dark, shadowed deck of his command with a great deal of pride and pleasure, feeling perfectly content. Eight bells sounded, dim shapes moved about the deck and Jamieson loomed up before him.

The culinary talents of the cook might well have been of the highest but in the event, so far as Lamb's supper was concerned, they were not put to the test. Not even the most incompetent of cooks, blessed with half the patience and good humour of the villainous, one-eyed Harrison, could have ruined cold ham, cheese, fruit and bread baked only the day before in Port Royal. True, the butter was more than a trifle on the liquid side and was not improved by the introduction of Sylvester's thumb but these little blemishes apart, the meal gave Lamb no cause for shame and Fox was kindness itself in his appreciation. He had arrived bearing not one but two bottles of claret, a wine of which Lamb was particularly fond so long as it had not come from the Admiralty's suppliers, whose claret resembled that wine only in that it was red.

'A remarkably fine wine, this, Mr Fox,' said Lamb, lifting his glass to admire the clarity of its colour against the yellow light of the lantern.

'I am pleased you find it to your taste, sir.' Fox was immaculate in snowy shirt and well-brushed, well-fitting blue broadcloth. It was clear that he had honoured his host by shaving for the second time that day, making Lamb uneasily aware of his own incipient bristles and grateful that after some indecision he had donned a clean shirt for the evening.

'Good wine has always been a pleasure and a comfort to me,' Fox went on. 'Of the three major vices, I consider wine to be the least harmful and one of the many advantages in not having a wife to support is that I can afford to indulge myself. I would sooner have a quarter of a glass of this fine claret than a quart of

24

wardroom issue.'

'I am sure you are right, Mr Fox,' said Lamb, not at all convinced. 'What were the other two vices you had in mind?'

'Gambling and women; and of the two, women are by far the most dangerous, especially for unworldly naval officers, unused to their wiles.'

Lamb drained his glass; he could feel the wine beginning to take hold. 'Maybe so, maybe so. It strikes me you have suffered from their wiles, from your earnest tone. But as for being dangerous, surely danger is a spice to life, Mr Fox?'

Fox threw back his head and laughed.

'Indeed sir, and life would be very plain fare without a little spice to flavour it.' He reached for the bottle. 'I see your glass is empty again. The *Adriot* is on patrol in the Mona Passage, you say?' he asked as he poured. 'When is she due back at Port Royal?'

'In a month or so, I understand.'

'You will be sorry to leave this packet, I expect?'

'In some ways, yes, but as this is only a temporary command I am quite reconciled to losing it again. I was overjoyed to get it, of course, but there is no promotion in it and little hope of any prize money coming my way. No, I shall be happy enough to return to the *Adroit*.'

'Who is her captain now?'

'George Slade.'

'George Slade? George Slade . . .' Fox put a finger to his mouth, frowning. 'I know that name.' His face cleared and he smiled. 'Yes, of course. I knew him as a lieutenant many years ago. Would you care to hear a little story about George Slade?'

Lamb leaned back in his chair and cradled his glass. 'I would indeed. Tell on, sir.'

'It happened at Malta, some years before the French took it. You would not have known the *Excelsior*, I suppose? No, I thought not. She was a third-rate, lost some seven or eight years ago on the China station; but no matter. Slade was her second and I her third and we had put into Grand Harbour for a few days. Slade was a great one for swimming and took himself off to a secluded beach for the afternoon. I don't know what his temper is like now but in those days it was always on a very short fuse.'

'And it is still!'

'Yes. Well, he was not by any means a popular man and that may well have played some part in what happened, but it appears that when he came out of the water he found all his clothes had disappeared – completely vanished. You can imagine his predicament, of course; stark naked, a long walk back to the town and his ship in the middle of a crowded harbour. I never did find out how he managed it but he arrived at the harbour steps at dusk dressed in a petticoat with a shawl around his shoulders. And there, silently waiting, were the *Excelsior*'s midshipmen and a good few from the other ships. To give Slade his due, he stalked towards the steps as if he was dressed in his best, glared around him and growled: "Let me catch the faintest smirk!" Not a soul dared give the slightest twitch of a lip and he was rowed back to the ship in perfect silence. As to who stole his clothes, well, he might have had his suspicions – certainly all the middies were ashore that afternoon and not a one of them had cause to love him – but so far as I am aware he made no enquiries in that direction and as he found them all in a neat bundle in his cabin when he came back on board I imagine he preferred to let sleeping dogs lie.'

Lamb chuckled and shook his head. 'I would dearly have loved to see him rigged out in petticoat and shawl,' he said, an incongruous image of his stout, pompous captain in his mind.

'There is a little postscript to this affair that might amuse you,' continued Fox. 'We were in company with four or five other warships and the next morning every one of them was flying a shirt and a pair of breeches from the foremast shrouds.'

'God, how perfect!' Lamb slapped his leg and roared with laughter.

Fox chuckled and drew the cork from the second bottle. He recharged their glasses and began to talk of other officers he had known. His memory appeared to be phenomenal and his dry manner of delivery coupled with a good deal of claret soon had Lamb laughing helplessly in his chair. He told of the captain who, nodding over his table after a heavy meal and a glass or two too many, set alight his wig and subsequently rewarded his steward's quick presence of mind with a whipping for dousing him in greasy dish water; of the admiral who loved his dog above all and had a man permanently standing outside his quarters with cloth and bucket ready to respond to the great man's cry of 'Dog shit!'; of the captain whose love of the ladies was so strong that he could rarely bear to sail without one to embellish his cabin and, surprised by his first lieutenant in the middle of an intimate moment, cooly rebuked the officer for appearing before him with a button missing from his coat. He spoke of more serious matters, of the price of bread in England – 'Seventeen pence for a damned loaf, would you believe?' – of the high taxes, of the riots in London and the general war-weariness of the people.

Lamb listened and sipped his claret, aware that he was contributing little to the conversation but quite content to sit and smile and nod in response to Fox's elegant flow. Fox appeared to be quite unaffected by drink although he had matched Lamb glass for glass, but Lamb's head was swimming as Fox shared the last of the wine between them. He smiled as he saw Lamb stifling a furtive yawn.

'Forgive me, sir. I have talked too much and kept you from your cot.'

'No, no,' protested Lamb. 'Forgive my rudeness, Mr Fox. It is your excellent wine, not your conversation, which has got the better of me. I have enjoyed our evening tremendously.'

'And I, sir.' Fox pushed back his chair and brushed the crumbs from his lap. He glanced enquiringly at Lamb. 'I understand the carpenter stands the middle watch?'

'Yes. It is an arrangement of Pardoe's that I am happy to continue.'

'If it would assist you, I would be more than pleased to stand my watch. I find I am not cut out to be an idle passenger and would much prefer to earn my keep.'

It was on the tip of Lamb's tongue to take up the offer but, even half-drunk as he was, a tiny spark of caution glowed. Again, that vague, indeterminable doubt about the man arose in a far corner of his mind.

'That is very handsome of you, Mr Fox,' he said 'but I am reluctant to upset the present watch arrangements. I am, after

27

all, only a caretaker captain, as it were, and it would not do to make too many changes to established routine. Mr Mee might take it as a reflection on his competence were I to take him off watch.'

Fox accepted the refusal graciously. 'As you wish, sir,' he replied, smiling. 'I must keep you up no longer. Thank you for your kind hospitality, captain. I bid you goodnight.'

'Goodnight, Mr Fox, and thank you for your company. It has been a pleasant evening.'

Lamb leaned back in his chair and stretched out his long legs, free to indulge himself at last in an enormous, uncovered yawn. God, it had been a long day! His eye rested on his cot and for a moment the urge to throw himself onto it and sink his head onto the pillow was almost irresistable. He gave his head a violent shake in order to drive off the threatening, dizzy mists of sleep and scrubbed at his his face with his hands. No, first he must take a turn on deck, if only to acquaint young Jamieson with the watchful alertness of his new captain. The soft yellow light from the gimballed lantern suspended from the beam threw slowly shifting patterns across the table as the cutter rolled in the slight swell and in his wine glass the red heel-tap tilted minutely from side to side. The familiar groans and creaks of moving timbers suddenly receded and he slept, chin on chest, head rolling to and fro with the movement of the ship. He awoke with a start at the sound of the bell marking the passing of God knew what hour and made his way blindly to the cool, clean air of the dark deck, to find that Jamieson had long since gone below and the carpenter was standing wide-legged and watchful beside the tiller.

'All's well, Mr Mee?' he muttered as he peered in the binnacle with eyes that were scarcely functioning.

'Aye, sir, all's well,' replied the carpenter quietly.

Lamb stumbled below to his cot and throwing himself flat, prised off one shoe with the toe of the other. He fell asleep with the second shoe still firmly on his foot.

Chapter 3

Mr Snow was perhaps no more than three or four years older than Lamb and might have been considered by some to be a trifle young to hold his warrant as boatswain. There was no doubt about his competence, however, so far as Lamb was concerned, and watching from the quarterdeck as Snow supervised the hoisting of the inner and outer jibs with his silver whistle nestling in the black curls sprouting through the opening of his shirt and his silver-headed cane beneath his armpit, he was pleased to see that he had such an able, energetic officer in charge of the lower deck. Overhead, the night-time reefs were being shaken out of the little topsail and as the jibs rose one by one from the jib-boom and bowsprit, cracking and snapping in the fresh north-easterly, the *Heron* picked up her heels with a happy surge. The scrubbed deck gleamed damply beneath the early sun, drying patchily under the combined effects of wind and heat. Smoke puffed from the galley chimney and was snatched away to starboard, and Lamb rubbed a hand over his bristles and turned affectionate thoughts to coffee and breakfast.

'The quarter, sir,' growled the voice of Timms, the quarter-master, from behind him.

'Very well,' said Lamb. 'Mr Snow! Pipe to breakfast.'

The pipe shrilled and the hands vanished instantly below to their beer and burgoo. Lamb resumed his slow pacing, feeling the sun's pleasant warmth first on one cheek and then the other as he turned and turned again.

'Good morning, captain!'

It was Mrs Skinner, her head and shoulders protruding from the aft companionway, one hand clutching at the scarf bound round her head. Lamb strode quickly over to her, recalling his resolution of the evening before.

'Good morning, ma'am,' he cried cheerfully, stooping to offer her his hand. 'You are an early riser, I see.'

Mrs Skinner pulled herself on to the deck, her skirts buffeted by the wind and her scarf lifting to reveal a myriad little paper contrivances twisted into her hair.

'I was reared on a farm, captain. Rising early is bred into me. I never could abide to lie in bed when the sun is up – and when one's bedroom stinks of vomit I like it even less.' She took several long, deep breaths of the sparkling air.

'Your maid is still indisposed, then?'

'Oh, that girl!' She flapped her hand in disgust. 'I am almost convinced she brings it up on purpose to annoy me. No, I am being cruel – she was exactly the same the first few days out of England. She is feeling really wretched but she will be fine in a day or two. I have just spent ten minutes washing her and I thought I would have some fresh air while I left Sylvester to clean the cabin.' She gave Lamb a sharp, suspicious glance. 'He can be trusted, can he, that old man, alone with her?'

Lamb smiled reassuringly. 'I am sure of it, ma'am.' He was amused at the thought of the wizened little man trying his gap-toothed charms on the girl. 'You have not breakfasted yet, then?'

'Hardly, sir. When my cabin smells a little sweeter I shall see if I cannot persuade Brown to take something and perhaps take a bite myself.'

Lamb hesitated, took a breath, and steeled himself.

'I would be honoured, Mrs Skinner, if you would give me the pleasure of your company at my table this morning. I can promise no more than eggs, toast and coffee but . . .'

'Why, captain, how kind!' She was plainly delighted, her face transformed. 'I should like that immensely. Do you know, I never once ate with the captain on the *White Rose*, not once, although he had opportunity aplenty to invite me.' The ship's bell struck the end of the morning watch, men ran to and fro, Jamieson appeared on deck and Mrs Skinner raised her voice above the chimes of the bell. 'I must beg two minutes to make myself presentable.'

Lamb bowed. 'I shall give you fifteen, ma'am,' he said, shrewdly calculating that two minutes would scarcely be sufficient to de-paper her hair. 'I will send Sylvester to show you to my cabin.'

Lamb gave Sylvester his instructions while he shaved. 'Clean napkins, mind,' he warned, turning a half-lathered face to the steward, 'and give the silver an extra rub.' Lamb knew very little about ladies of Mrs Skinner's advanced years but it was his understanding they were very particular about clean linen and tableware.

'Aye aye, sir,' sighed Sylvester and went off to try his luck with the cook.

Lamb sighed too, as he scraped away at his bristles, wondering if he had not gone too far to mend his relations with the formidable Mrs Skinner; he dearly loved a solitary, peaceful breakfast.

The lady was pleasantness itself and as breakfast progressed Lamb found himself warming to her. It was clear that in spite of her previous sharp comments she was genuinely concerned about her maid's wretched sea-sickness, and Lamb suspected that beneath her bluff exterior lay a warm, maternal heart.

'Are you never sea-sick, ma'am?' he asked, watching her pour the coffee with a practised feminine hand.

She laughed at the notion. 'No, I am an old campaigner. I have followed my husband over a good deal of salt water in my time – though never in any ship quite as small as this. I have put up with mud and snow and storms and spiders and snakes over the years.'

'And cramped cabins too,' Lamb suggested wickedly.

'Now, now captain,' she chuckled, waving an admonishing finger. 'You must not tease a . . .'

'Sail ho!'

The lookout's hail filtered down through the companionway and the open cabin door. Lamb cocked an ear.

'Where away?' came Jamieson's bellow.

'Is something wrong, captain?' enquired Mrs Skinner, drowning the lookout's reply.

Lamb gave her a quick, reassuring smile. 'No, no, just the sighting of a distant sail.'

'A privateer, perhaps?' she asked shrewdly.

'Perhaps. More likely a harmless merchantman or a British man-o'-war. There are many ships in the Caribbean, ma'am.'

31

The sound of quick, bare feet on the companion steps was followed by a loud rap at the cabin door and the appearance of one of the ship's boys, a bright-eyed, carrot-haired youth who seemed to be quite unawed by the sight of his captain and guest at breakfast.

'Yes, lad?'

'Mr Jamieson sends his respects, sir, and there's a sail hull down on the larboard quarter.'

Lamb nodded. 'Tell Mr Jamieson I shall be up in a few minutes. What is your name, boy?'

'Spooner, sir,' said the lad with a cheerful grin. 'T'other boy's Lipton.'

'Very well, Spooner.'

The boy withdrew his head and skipped lightly up the companion steps. Had Lamb been breakfasting alone he would have followed hard on Spooner's heels but today such a precipitate action might have alarmed his guest and instead he leaned back in his chair and sipped his coffee, determined to give the impression of unconcerned ease.

'I make a habit of asking for names each time I speak to a fresh face,' he explained, by way of conversation. 'That way I get to know who is who very quickly. On a small vessel such as this it will not take long to get to know them all.'

Mrs Skinner looked puzzled. 'Have you a good many fresh faces on board, then, sir?'

Lamb laughed. 'Only mine, ma'am, only mine. Her captain fell ill and I took command at short notice just before you boarded.'

'But you are a proper captain, are you not?' she asked with a note of concern, as if fearful that her life had been entrusted to an imposter. 'I see you wear no epaulettes.'

Lamb debated whether he should attempt to explain the difference between a lieutenant in command, a commander and a post-captain but decided against it.

'I hold the same rank as the previous captain,' he contented himself with saying. 'Every officer in command of a warship, no matter how small his command, is always known as the captain.'

'Ah!' Mrs Skinner's face cleared. 'I understand, or I think I do. Royal Marine and Army ranks are so much more straight-forward. I can tell a lieutenant-colonel from a major at a glance but with you gentlemen, when a lieutenant can be a captain and a captain can be a commodore, it comes a mite confusing to my poor brain. I have a small folding chair in my baggage,' she went on without a pause, as if the one topic naturally led to the other. 'Would it be possible, captain, for you to find me a little spot upstairs out of the wind, preferably with a little shade, where I can take the air during the day?' She smiled brightly and cocked her head winsomely to one side.

Lamb smiled back, quite charmed by the look and thinking that for all her broad, red face she had a kindly eye.

'Of course, ma'am. It might be better, perhaps, if we wait a little while until we have identified that sail.' He pushed back his chair and reached for his hat. 'Now if you will excuse me, ma'am, I must go on deck. Please, do sit here and finish your coffee.'

Jamieson was aloft, perched on the jack at the masthead with his telescope trained over the larboard quarter. Lamb peered upwards and gave him a hail.

'What do you make of her, Mr Jamieson?'

'A brigantine, sir. French yards. T'gallant royal set and stuns'ls aloft and alow.'

'How's her head?'

'South-east, sir.'

Lamb grunted. So, a privateer, with canvas spread for a determined stern chase; from her heading, probably out of Port au Prince. 'Report on deck,' he called and walked aft. He glanced up at the trim of the topsail yard. The wind had fallen off somewhat in the past hour and shifted to the south-west, across the cutter's starboard quarter. The boatswain, his mate and the half dozen men on watch had heard every word of the brief exchange and were looking expectantly aft.

'Man the braces,' snapped Lamb, and as the men pattered aft: 'Larboard the helm. Steer south-east.'

Jamieson came up to him, his telescope clamped beneath his arm and a broad grin on his square, good-natured face.

'I've seen that Frenchman before. She was the one that kicked us up the arse.' He nodded at the taffrail, where the

33

repairs to the damaged timbers showed. 'Giving her a run for her money, are we?'

Lamb shot him a sharp glance, irritated by his cheerful, careless tone. He hesitated on the edge of a sarcastic retort but thought better of it; Jamieson might construe it as an attack of nerves.

'Yes.'

'Well, so long as the wind doesn't freshen we should show her a clean pair of heels again,' said Jamieson confidently, and raising his voice to an outraged bellow, shouted: 'Mr Snow! Who belayed that damned weather brace? See to it, if you please.'

Lamb now found Jamieson's confidence heartening, for he knew how the cutter would sail in these conditions far better than Lamb, who had never served in anything other than square-rigged ships, and nothing smaller than a frigate.

'Lend me your glass, Mr Jamieson,' he demanded, and thrusting the instrument through his belt walked forward and swung himself up into the mainmast shrouds. The lookout edged out on to the yard to make way for him as he came up and hooking an arm around the short topmast Lamb directed his glass astern over the upward-sloping gaff of the mainsail. Visibility in the cloudless, crystal air could not have been clearer and the brigantine's square-rigged foremast and fore-and-aft rigged mainmast sprang sharply to his eye. She was almost bows-on to the cutter and from that angle he could make out almost nothing of her gun ports; she would almost certainly be armed with carronades in addition to her long guns, he guessed.

He lowered his glass and turned to the lookout, a slim, leather-faced man with thinning, fair hair.

'What is your name, seaman?'

'Blackett, sir,' replied the man, looking shyly at the deck, uncomfortable at the close proximity of his new captain and the directness of his gaze.

'Well, Blackett, keep your eye on that Frenchman astern and when I sing out from below, let me know if she is gaining on us or otherwise.'

'Aye aye, sir'.

34

Lamb stepped off the jack onto the ratlines and made his way down to the deck. It was always difficult to judge the progress of a distant vessel when it was dead astern but he knew that an experienced seaman with a good eye could be as accurate and certainly quicker than an officer laboriously plotting angles.

The quartermaster and a seaman were preparing to cast the log under the watchful eyes of Jamieson when Lamb came aft. He returned Jamieson his telescope and took up his stance on the weather side of the quarterdeck, glancing down at the rush of water along the side as he played his private game of pitting his own estimation against the reading on the log-line, allowing himself a quarter of a knot either way, no more. It had been a little entertainment of his since he had been a midshipman and in those days, if he won, he would promise himself that he would have a lucky day. He had met with little luck in those days, even when he did win, but the habit had stayed with him.

Seven knots, he told himself firmly as he listened to the formal cries behind him.

'All clear!'

'Turn!'

'Stop!'

'Seven knots and a fathom, sir,' came the voice of the quartermaster.

'Very well, make it so,' said Jamieson.

Lamb smiled. A lucky day, a lucky day! sang the midshipman buried not too deeply within him; seven knots and a fathom, pondered the outer lieutenant. It was remarkably good, he thought, with the wind abeam as it was; if the brigantine was doing as well he would be surprised. If the wind freshened it would favour her, of course – in that case he would edge south and then south-west, to lie as close to the wind as possible. He would lose his easting but that would be a small price to pay to shake off the Frenchman. He stood rocking on his heels, waiting for the long minutes to pass. The cook emerged on deck, tipped a bucket of rubbish to leeward, cast an evil half-glare aft and disappeared below; a sweeper ran forward in response to Snow's shout and cleared some sweepings from beneath the larboard gun; the boatswain's mate scuttled aloft and busied himself at the topsail slablines. Lamb

35

cupped his hands to his mouth and hailed the lookout.

'What do you see, Blackett?'

'Can't be sure, sir, but she ain't gaining on us, at least.'

Jamieson caught Lamb's eye and grinned. 'We have the legs on that Frenchman, sir, I think. Another hour and we'll have lost her.'

'I hope you are right, Mr Jamieson,' said Lamb, a trifle distantly. Jamieson was a likeable enough young fellow but he felt it would not do to allow him to become too familiar. He gave an inward smile, suddenly amused; he was becoming as pompous in his new status as Captain Slade habitually was on the quarterdeck of the *Adroit*.

Another age of slow pacing went by; Blackett reported that the brigantine was certainly dropping back and Fox appeared from the aft companionway, the sun winking from his buttons and shoes and buckles. He touched his hat to Lamb and joined Jamieson on the other side of the quarterdeck.

'Good morning, Mr Fox,' said Lamb.

'Good morning, sir. I was given to understand from your lady passenger that we were about to be overwhelmed by a vast fleet of pirates and privateers.'

Lamb laughed. 'The lady exaggerated a trifle, I think. If you care to climb to the mast-head you might just catch a glimpse of our solitary Frenchman before we lose him.'

Fox glanced aloft and shook his head, smiling.

'I am not sure these old bones would carry me there, sir.'

'Nonsense, Mr Fox,' said Lamb genially. He nodded with a sly grin at Jamieson's squat, muscular body. 'Mr Jamieson would be happy to be as slim and supple, I am sure, and he is less than half your age, I'll warrant.'

'What? What? You do me an injustice, sir,' cried Jamieson, deeply hurt. He sucked in his stomach and patted it proudly. 'Look at that. As flat as a board – not a trace of fat at all.'

Fox and Lamb looked at one another and chuckled, amused at the indignation in the young man's voice. After a moment, infected by their laughter, Jamieson gave a reluctant grin.

'I knew, of course . . .' he began but was cut short by a hail from Blackett.

'Deck there! The Frenchman's wearing, sir – turning away –

36

heading north, sir.'

'Well, it appears you were right, Mr Jamieson,' said Lamb with a grin, happy to have shaken off the privateer. 'Keep her as she is for another ten minutes and then bring her on to our proper course. I shall be in my cabin.'

'Aye aye, sir,' said Jamieson, properly formal.

The ship's bell sounded as Lamb made his way below, the four strokes denoting the middle of the forenoon watch. He gave a bellow for Sylvester and ducked into his cabin, tossing his hat onto the spare chair. There was a great deal of paperwork outstanding from the *Heron*'s turn-round at Port Royal and he had decided it was time he got to grips with it. Nothing was issued to His Majesty's ships without exchanges of signatures, lists, authorizations, invoices and receipts and looking at the thick pile of papers thrust untidily into his table drawer he gave a muttered curse of disbelief, convinced that the Royal Navy employed more clerks than seamen.

'Yes, sir?'

Sylvester was at the door with a mop in one hand, a bucket in the other and a weary look of long-suffering harassment on his gnome-like face. Lamb glanced up from the papers he was shuffling together and frowned.

'It's a pot of coffee I was after, not a bloody swabbing-out.'

'Yes, sir. Sorry, sir. I'd just finished the lady's cabin when I heard your call, sir.'

'What, is that damned girl still throwing up?'

'No, she's a deal better this morning, sir. Up and about, she is. It would have been better had she stayed where she was 'cause she upset the bleedin' piss-pot, sir, beggin' your pardon. A bloody carry-on there was there too, sir. Mrs Skinner, she . . .'

'All right, Sylvester, spare me the details,' said Lamb hastily. 'Just make sure your scrub your hands before you make my coffee.'

'Aye aye, sir. Gettin' to be a habit, that, sir.'

'I'm glad to hear it.'

Lamb returned his attention to his paperwork and worked steadily for ten minutes, recklessly dashing off his signature where it was required and blindly taking on responsibility for

37

items he had not seen and was not likely to see unless he burrowed for them in the bowels and nooks and crannies of the ship; any self-respecting boatswain or purser would have wept tears of joy and avarice had they witnessed his simple trust.

Sylvester knocked, entered and placed Lamb's tray on the one corner of the little table not hidden by papers.

'Your coffee, sir.'

'Thank you, Sylvester,' murmured Lamb absently, wondering why the boatswain should need paint, yellow, lead, gallons, one, when there was not a square inch of yellow paint to be seen anywhere on the *Heron*. He shook his head and signed.

'The lady begs me to ask, sir, is it convenient for her to take the air now, sir?'

'What? Oh, yes, of course, I had forgotten. She has a folding chair somewhere. Find it and escort her to the quarterdeck. Put her up against the taffrail in a bit of shade – beside the larboard gun will keep her from underfoot, perhaps. Give my compliments to Mr Jamieson first, mind you.'

'Aye aye, sir.'

Lamb poured himself a cup of coffee and buried himself in his papers again, his coffee growing cold at his elbow. At last it was done. He closed the books and stacked his papers away with a short prayer of thanks. No doubt he would have much to answer for when he handed over to Pardoe or his successor, but that was some weeks off and he thrust his unease firmly into the back of his mind. He gulped the last of his now cold coffee, took up his hat and made his way up to the bright, fresh sunlight of the upper deck as a cry of 'Sail ho!' came ringing down from the masthead.

'Where away?' shouted Jamieson.

'Square on the starboard beam, sir.'

'Give me the loan of your glass, Mr Jamieson,' said Lamb, stretching out his hand. He strode to the weather shrouds and pulled himself up to join Blackett at the masthead.

'There she be, sir,' said Blackett, pointing directly abeam.

The stranger was a dancing white triangle far, far off to the south where the polished sea merged into the hard, blue sky. Lamb curled an arm around a topmast stay and levelled his telescope, the topsail beside him sighing and drumming in the faltering breeze. After careful, concentrated scrutiny he was able to make out a slim hull beneath a fore-and-aft rig carried on two masts, with a square topsail and topgallantsail on her foremast. She flew no colours but the cut of her narrow yards was unmistakable. Her present bearing, he judged, would take her across the *Heron*'s wake at a distance of some half dozen miles but if she was at all alert . . . He gave a quick, grim smile as on the thought he saw the shape of her sails alter.

He lowered his telescope and sucked thoughtfully at its brass rim; a topsail schooner would be fast, very fast, and moreover, she had the advantage of the weather gage. It was time for the *Heron* to pick up her skirts and run. Damn these light winds!

'Man the braces!' he roared as he scrambled down to the deck. 'Wear ship, Mr Jamieson.'

He ignored Fox's enquiring glance as he reached the quarterdeck and stood looking on until the bustle on the deck had finished and the cutter was heading north-east with the wind astern. Jamieson rejoined Fox, and Lamb crossed the deck and returned the telescope to its owner.

'A two-masted topsail schooner,' he informed the two men. 'It has distinctly unfriendly intentions, I feel.'

Fox smiled, as if the thought amused him. 'Goodbye to one Frenchman and how d'ye do to another – a somewhat crowded forenoon, sir. A topsail schooner, you say? She can probably make three knots to our two and in this t'gallant wind, perhaps more. May I offer my assistance at one of your guns, sir?'

'You may indeed, Mr Fox, and I shall be glad to have it,' said Lamb. 'Early days yet, though; it will be several hours or more before we need to think about manning the guns and many things could happen between then and now.' He caught sight of Mrs Skinner's face peering anxiously in his direction from beneath a large bonnet secured to her head with a scarf knotted beneath her chin. 'I must have a word with our other passenger – she looks a trifle concerned.'

Mrs Skinner was indeed concerned. She stared up at Lamb from the little chair on which she sat muffled against the wind with a disturbed frown on her large, homely face.

'Pray, Mr Lamb, is there something going on that I should know about? I see you rush up to the top of the mast and rush

39

down again roaring at the top of your voice; there are men running and pulling at ropes for all they are worth; I am nearly thrown off my chair as the deck tilts and the little piece of shade that I had has quite deserted me. And yet, when I look round, expecting to see a whole battalion of corsairs, I see nothing but empty sea.'

Lamb gave her a sympathetic smile and squatted beside her on the gun-carriage.

'I am sorry you were disconcerted, ma'am. There is, in fact, a corsair, a privateer, way off to the south. It is a schooner, a vessel something like this but with an extra mast, and larger and faster. It is my painful duty to have to tell you, ma'am, that it will almost certainly catch up with us this afternoon and if it does there will be some gunfire exchanged.'

'Gunfire, indeed! Well, I am no stranger to that. Just the one privateer, is there?'

'Yes, just the one, but she will have several times the number of men that we have and rather more in the way of guns. Though do not be overly concerned, ma'am; all the men are good, steady, well-trained fellows and you can be assured that we shall . . .'

Mrs Skinner gave a little laugh and patted his hand. 'But I am not at all concerned, captain. In truth, I am rather excited at the prospect and I have every confidence, every confidence in you and your brave men. If it comes to a fight, in what way can I best assist you? I can fire a pistol and load a musket, you know.'

Lamb stared at her, amazed at her coolness. She beamed back at him, blue eyes shining from her bluff, red face. For a moment he floundered, quite taken aback.

'I – well, I – you can best assist me, ma'am, by keeping to your cabin when the time comes. Your husband would never forgive me if you were hurt and in any case, things can get a trifle ugly on deck during battle. I shall be easier in my mind knowing that you and your maid are well out of harm's way.'

'The dead and wounded will not come strange to me, captain.' She gave his hand another maternal pat. 'But if it makes your task easier I shall stay in my cabin. I am touched by your concern, but I shall not be happy skulking downstairs, not

40

lifting a finger.'

Lamb fingered his chin and studied her honest face, contemplating a thought that had just entered his mind. The magazine was situated in the centre of the ship above the bilge, in the place least likely to be penetrated by enemy shot. If he could persuade Mrs Skinner and her maid to take themselves there, not only would they be in the safest part of the ship but they could also make themselves useful and perhaps release the gunner's mate for duty at the guns. He glanced at the embroidery work in her lap and the needles with their different coloured tails sprouting from her upper sleeve.

'It is clear you have nimble fingers, Mrs Skinner,' he said, smiling. 'How would you like to try your hand at making cartridges?'

Noon had come and gone. The quartermaster sounded four strokes on the ship's bell; it was two o'clock, midway through the afternoon watch.

The schooner had eaten up the distance between the two vessels, her shape growing clearer and larger by the hour and had now narrowed the gap to a little less than three miles. Lamb lifted his telescope to his eye, as he had done with increasing frequency in the past hour, and studied the privateer. She had not yet flown her colours but her nationality and purpose were beyond doubt; her narrow yards and black-painted masts and above all, her steady, ominous approach and the knots of men at her guns, told all. Her guns had been a matter for some discussion between the three officers but as the distance shortened they agreed that the six long guns were quite definitely six-pounders and her two carronades almost certainly eighteen-pounders – a broadside weight of metal some twice that of the *Heron*'s.

'An hour, would you say, Mr Fox?' murmured Lamb.

'Yes, sir, certainly no more.'

'If the wind holds,' said Jamieson.

'Yes,' said Lamb, frowning aloft at the topsail. The wind had become lazy in the past couple of hours, giving a fat, hard belly to the sails one minute and then allowing them to wrinkle and sag like old womens' breasts the next as it paused to catch its breath. Moody and unpredictable, it could well come back with renewed life and increased vigour at any second. There was no point in waiting any longer, he thought.

'Beat to quarters, Mr Jamieson,' he ordered.

There was no Marine drummer to beat a quick, blood-stirring rattle but Jamieson's roar and the boatswain's pipe served almost as well and the deck immediately became alive as men ran to their gun positions and began the task of preparing the cutter for battle. Fox strode energetically to his guns at the stern and Lamb turned to Jamieson with a slight smile.

'I must see how the gunner's new mates are coping with their duties. I shall not be a moment.'

Jamieson grinned. He had been vastly amused to hear that Mrs Skinner and Miss Brown were to assist Sedge, the acting-gunner, in the magazine. 'They may learn a few new expressions, if nothing else,' he had laughed.

Lamb made his way below, kicked off his shoes outside the magazine and pushed through the screens into the small, copper-lined room, lit by lanterns shining from the glass-fronted boxes built into the bulkheads. Mrs Skinner looked up as he entered and smiled and Sedge, sweat beading his bald, brown skull, glanced down at Lamb's feet to assure himself that no nailed shoes were trespassing on his fearnought-covered deck.

'Well, captain,' cried Mrs Skinner gaily, waving the copper scoop in her hand, 'you have not caught me slacking, you see.'

'Such a thought never occurred to me, ma'am,' said Lamb. 'Where have you hidden your maid?'

'Oh, the silly girl was quite useless – complaining of the heat, terrified she would blow herself up. I gave her a good slap and sent her packing. We are managing very well without her, are we not, Mr Sedge?'

'Yes, ma'am,' muttered the acting-gunner with a distinct lack of enthusiasm, shooting her a little sideways scowl. He had been aghast when Lamb had informed him that he was to have two ladies to assist him in his duties and while he had not actually dared to demur he had silently made his feelings plain, nevertheless. Sedge performed his work to an almost non-stop flow of foul language and foul wind, and the inhibitions imposed on both his outlets showed now in the frown of discomfort on his bony, bristled face.

'We should be in action very soon,' said Lamb. He glanced at the rows of filled cartridge bags on the racks and gave an approving nod. 'You have been busy, I see. What have we got there, Mr Sedge?'

'About three dozen of the pound-an'-'alf and 'alf as many of the three-pound, sir,' replied the gunner. 'We was just goin' to make a start on the one-pounders when you come in, sir.'

'Very good. I am pleased to see the pair of you coping so well.'

'I can 'andle the rest on my own, sir, if the lady is feelin' the 'eat a bit, like,' suggested Sedge, hopefully.

'Feeling the heat? Nonsense, Mr Sedge!' cried Mrs Skinner, shooting him an indignant glance. 'I am enjoying myself immensely. There is no need to concern yourself on my account.'

Lamb watched her as she poured powder from her brass scoop through the wooden former into the linen bag, her tongue nipped between her teeth as she concentrated on not giving the former a grain too much.

'There!' she exclaimed proudly as she closed the top of the cartridge and held it up for Lamb's inspection. 'You will not find much to complain about with my work, captain.'

'I am sure of that, ma'am. You make an excellent gunner's mate.'

She laughed, delighted at the notion. 'I must tell my husband that. He might not find it amusing.'

Lamb laughed with her and backed out of the airless, little cell. He donned his shoes and made his way up to the bright sunshine of the upper deck.

The schooner was now some two miles off the starboard quarter, her sharp bow and slim hull cutting effortlessly through the water, her tall, wide spread of sail catching the light of the sun and lending her the delicate lightness of a swooping gull. Lamb looked about the quiet deck. The loaded guns were snubbed up tight to the sides, awaiting the order for the ports to be raised and the guns to be run out. Around them stood their crews, still and silent, most of them bare to the

43

waist, with bright handkerchiefs around their foreheads. A number of the men were now familiar to him by name and voice and character: there was Sylvester at the starboard carronade, giving his awful grin as he saw Lamb's eye on him; the young giant Selby standing impassively with arms folded across his chest; the evil-looking cook, scratching his backside and twisting his head to give his eye a view of the schooner; Blackett, standing with head bowed; Snow and Mee, the two warrant officers, and Spooner and Lipton, the ship's boys, the one grinning and turning his red-topped head this way and that, the other pale and still. The deck was sanded, the coiled slow-matches glowed in their tubs and the water-buckets were full. The forward hatch, open to give access to the magazine, was screened against stray sparks by wet cloths and the boarding nets were draped loosely along the sides. Lamb glanced aloft, noting the chains securing the topsail yard and mainsail gaff. He nodded in quiet satisfaction; the *Heron* was as ready as she would ever be. What followed would rest largely on discipline, training, muscle, determination and luck and, to a lesser extent, on himself. He felt the old, familiar stirrings of nervousness in his stomach and took a deep breath; they would not last long, he knew.

'The first move shall be ours, I think, Mr Jamieson,' he murmured to the squat lieutenant beside him. 'Run up our colours, Mr Timms,' he snapped over his shoulder, and in a loud bellow along the deck: 'Open ports! Run out the guns!'

It was too soon yet to try and range but the gesture would serve to show the privateer that the cutter had teeth and was prepared to use them if she ventured closer. If those Frenchmen thought they had found an easy mark he would teach them otherwise, thought Lamb, his blood warming to the rumble of the gun-carriages on the planks.

The deck fell quiet, the men at the guns glancing at Lamb and the oncoming schooner. Lamb threw a quick glance over his shoulder at the approaching Frenchman and turned back to look along the deck, seeing the grave, unsmiling faces of his men; they were well aware they were outgunned and outmanned and Lamb was certain that many of them were experiencing the same tightness of chest and stomach that was plaguing

44

him. He tightened his jaw, angry at the fluttering treachery of his body. Should he speak to them, utter a few ringing words to stiffen their resolve? He struggled to find a stirring phrase or two but could think of nothing. He turned on his heel to look again at the schooner. Another five minutes and he would try his after gun, he thought, judging the range. Fox's glance met his; the elder lieutenant was hatless and in his shirt sleeves, his long, grey hair ruffled by the light wind, an expression of quiet amusement on his neat, tanned face. He smiled, a bright, confident grin that immediately warmed Lamb and he gave a smiling nod in return.

'They've hoisted the red flag, sir,' said Jamieson.

Lamb's eyes flashed to the schooner and to the splash of red at her mast-head. Shock and outrage flooded through him. The bastards! Fury welled up within him and he swung round to look along the length of his ship.

'Listen to me, men,' he cried angrily, the words tumbling up without conscious thought. 'Those bloody frogs are flying the red flag. You all know well what that means: if we are overwhelmed, no one, not even the ladies we have on board, can expect any mercy. Keep that thought well in your minds and let it add strength to your resolve. No doubt those bastards imagine they have found easy picking here. We must disabuse them of the notion. We shall show them that any one of us is worth three of them. So give of your best, my lads, and the day is ours!'

A thunderous cheer rose from the deck. Fists were raised in the air and defiant grins spread wide.

'Three on 'em, sir,' shouted Selby. 'I'll take any six on, and think naught on it!'

'Aye!'

'Aye!'

'And me, sir!' came Spooner's confident treble.

Lamb, his blood singing, flung out an arm and pointed to the schooner, now perhaps a mile off.

'See what your guns can do, Mr Fox!'

'Aye aye, sir,' snapped Fox enthusiastically. His starboard aft gun was trained hard round and ready, the quoin removed from beneath the breech to lift the muzzle as high as it would point. The stern rose to the slight swell, Fox's voice rang out and the gun spewed flame and smoke and thunder as it slammed backwards, the breechings taut and quivering as they halted the recoil. Lamb already had his glass to his eye but the range was extreme and he had little hope of seeing a strike. He was pleased, nevertheless, to have been the first to open the proceedings; it would demonstrate their determination to the Frenchmen and the taste of gun smoke would plunge his own men firmly into the spirit of battle.

The roundshot had been fired too high to skip and a brief plume of white water showed some two hundred yards short of the privateer.

'Well done that gun!' shouted Lamb, determined not to allow honesty to stand in the way of a little judicious priming of enthusiasm. 'Dead in line! Keep at 'em, Mr Fox. We'll teach the buggers not to come sniffing round our backside!'

Along the schooner's larboard side the gun-ports rose as one and the muzzles of her guns slid out to point over the water, the red-painted snouts trained forward at the *Heron*. Lamb pursed his lips, impressed in spite of himself by the smooth uniformity of the action; here was no indisciplined rabble of a crew but trained men acting together in prompt response to orders. A slight chill of unease touched him.

There was furious activity around Fox's gun as the crew wormed and swabbed and reloaded. Lamb kept his eye firmly on the schooner; on her present heading she could only usefully fire her bow-chaser and he watched and waited for the puff of gunsmoke that would signal her first ranging shot.

The smash of sound clapped at his ears as Fox's gun fired again. The four-pound ball fired from a warmer barrel travelled a little further, but was still half a cable short. The privateer's sails wrinkled and sagged, bellied half-heartedly then sagged again.

'Avast there, Mr Fox,' called Lamb as the *Heron*'s canvas whispered and shook and draped untidily in the dying wind.

A bright flash of flame showed from the schooner's bow as her gun fired, the smoke hanging low and listless in the nearly-still air. Lamb counted the seconds off in his head: one thousand, two thousand, three thousand, four thousand, fi . . .

the report of the gun reached his ears and a small disturbance marked the gently heaving water some two hundred yards astern. A little less than a mile, he told himself. If the wind had held for another five minutes it would have seen them both within effective range, banging away hammer and tongs, neither of them able to close or flee in the windless air. The breeze gave a last weary rally, barely lifting the canvas, and then died completely, leaving the *Heron* gliding on in silence as she gradually lost way. Lamb glanced at the sun; it was about half-past four, he judged.

The cutter rocked very gently on the slight swell. For long minutes the only sounds to be heard on the deck were the faint creaking of the mainmast and the quiet clearing of throats and shufflings of feet as the men stood silently at their guns staring out over the starboard quarter at the limp sails of the schooner. Lamb rocked to and fro on his heels, gazing at the privateer, glancing up at the topsail, quietly praying for the wind to pick up again. The sun's heat struck warmly through the shoulders of his coat as he stared aft, his shadow stretching before him as the sun crept down towards the western edge of the sea. He became aware of the quiet murmurings of the hands as the tension of imminent battle drained from them and, shaking himself free of his near dreamlike state, he spun round and hailed the boatswain.

'Hands to supper, Mr Snow. Ten minutes, no more. And tell the cook to break out some cheese and raisins.'

The pipe shrilled, the cook threw an angry glare aft as he hurried from his place at the forward gun and dived muttering below. Lamb saw the look of fury on the man's hideous face and gave an amused smile; Harrison might well be outraged at his captain's free-handedness with the ship's stores but Lamb felt that the usual beer and biscuit alone would not stand a man's stomach in good stead for what could well be a long stint at the guns if the wind should revive. He suddenly remembered Mrs Skinner, toiling manfully away in the sweatbox of the magazine and felt a sharp stab of guilt.

'Mr Jamieson,' he called, lifting his finger as he walked towards him. 'Would you be so good as to rescue Mrs Skinner from the magazine? Get Sylvester to muster some refreshment

47

for her and Miss Brown – and a word or two of my appreciation would not come amiss, I think.'

She would be craving for tea, no doubt, he thought, but she would be out of luck; the galley fire had long been damped.

'Of course, sir,' said Jamieson. 'If you can spare me, would you like me to entertain the ladies? I have some Rhenish and the remains of a passable cake in my cabin.'

'What an excellent fellow you are!' said Lamb, clapping the lieutenant on the shoulder. 'There is a fair chance that you may yet grow up to be a gentleman.'

'I shall not let it come between us if I do, sir,' promised Jamieson and hastily put some distance and the upper deck between him and his captain.

Lamb stared broodingly at the motionless schooner for several minutes and then wandered aimlessly forward with his hands clasped behind his back and stood beneath the lifeless inner jib looking out over the smooth, metallic-looking sea. Calms were not infrequent in this area, he knew, and some of them could last an infuriatingly long time. If this spell continued into the dark hours or longer it would put the privateer at a decided advantage; she would certainly be carrying sweeps and have sufficient crew to man them – and it did not require much thought to guess her master's next move if the calm persisted.

The boatswain began to roar his threats as he made his way aft, the men tumbling up still chewing and clutching a handful of raisins or a hunk of cheese, the yeasty smell of the beer on their breaths strong in the warm, still air. Fox raised an eyebrow as Lamb approached and jerked his head at the distant vessel.

'Come dark and she'll be putting out her sweeps.'

'Yes,' said Lamb abstractedly, noting with mild envy the fine cut and delicate needlework of Fox's shirt. 'Yes,' he said again, 'I have already given some thought to that. I think if I was her master, I would narrow the distance during the night, lay off until just before dawn and then make a dash for us. He will not chance a night action, I fancy.'

'My thoughts exactly, sir. He would be a fool to try and board in the dark, with no moon to assist him.'

'Quite. Nevertheless, we must keep a good watch throughout

the night. The hands can sleep at their guns with their boarding weapons in their hands. It may well be a long night, Mr Fox; may I suggest that you take your supper now, while things are quiet?'

'Excellent notion, sir,' smiled Fox and walked with his quick, light step to the companionway.

Lamb stared pensively at the schooner for a moment and then went below to his cabin to fetch his keys.

'Mr Snow,' he called when he emerged on deck. He brandished the bunch of keys. 'Break out the boarding weapons, if you please. I doubt if they will be needed tonight,' he added as the boatswain trotted up to him, 'but it is as well to be prepared.'

He watched Snow supervise the issue of the weapons, calling the men by name to the arms-chest. The boatswain was clearly familiar with each man's preference, judging by the way the men grinned and hefted a cutlass or axe or half-pike as they were handed them. The several pistols and musketoons were given to a favoured few; Mr Mee, he noticed, took one of each, tucking the pistol into his belt and the short, heavy, massively-damaging musketoon beneath his arm. He did not envy the carpenter his choice – the musketoon fired a huge ball weighing nearly half a pound and to use it was like being kicked by a horse.

Lamb debated whether he should buckle on his sword but on reflection decided that the heavier cutlass would be more useful at repelling boarders and allowed Snow to select for him the best weapon from those few remaining. He gripped the black japanned hilt in its basket guard and swung the yard of steel in a few practice cuts and thrusts. The edge had been recently ground and the blade lightly greased; it was a good deal heavier than his own slim blade but it could deliver a cutting blow sufficient to sever a man's arm, and for all its weight it felt comfortable in his hand.

The boatswain grinned at Lamb's swings and lunges.

'You're at home with that, sir, I can see. Captain Pardoe, he was the same, sir, always took a cutlass. Said his own sword was too good to use on hard French heads, sir, too precious, like.'

Lamb gained the impression that the boatswain had in some

49

way paid him a compliment. He grinned back at him.

'It feels very much as if it belongs, Mr Snow. I fancy if you stood quite still I could give you a good, close shave.'

The boatswain took a discreet pace backwards.

'Very kind of you, sir, but I'll stick to my razor if its all the same to you, sir.'

Fox was leaning his arms on the taffrail and he turned his head as Lamb approached.

'You have supped, Mr Fox?' asked Lamb.

'Yes, sir, such as it was. I am grateful I was not hungry.' He nodded at the schooner. 'I can see little point in their flying the red flag. It can serve them no useful purpose – quite the opposite, in fact. It is bound to make any opponent fight the harder.' He glanced up at Lamb with a smile. 'That was a very stirring little speech you made earlier, sir, most admirable. You struck just the right note, I thought.'

'Much good it did,' grunted Lamb. He gestured at the guns and the men squatting idly beside them. 'I could have saved my breath. Damn the wind.'

Chapter 4

The last of the thin, orange glow clinging to the hard, black line of the western horizon blinked and vanished. Lamb sat with his head thrown back, his eyes filled with the cold light of ten thousand stars undimmed by the smallest vestige of a moon, his mind occupied with the pressing question of what to do with his last beef sandwich. Liberally flavoured with mustard, it lay on a plate on his lap, the sole survivor of a set of four brought to the quarterdeck with Sylvester's unspoken compliments and accompanied by Mrs Skinner's little folding chair, sent up for him with her very best wishes. Lamb could not, with any degree of honesty, be accused of owning a delicate appetite and the first three sandwiches had been despatched with his usual enthusiasm, washed down with half a pint of wine and water; deep in thought throughout his meal, he had lost count of what he had eaten, gulped down the last of his watered wine and settled back in his chair. Ten minutes later he had been astonished when his hand fell upon yet another sandwich. His wine was finished and his belly felt full; he certainly could not eat another mustard-smeared sandwich but it went sorely against the grain to leave the perfectly wholesome thing untouched. He mulled over the problem for a few minutes and arrived at a happy compromise; he took a large bite from its centre and tossed the remainder overboard with an easy conscience.

The deck was dark and hushed and still. The men were stretched out by the indistinct bulks of the guns and, if Lamb knew anything at all about seamen, sound asleep already in spite of the hard, unyielding planks on which they lay. To his left loomed the square, sturdy shape of Jamieson, blotting out the light from several thousand stars. Almost all of the ship's company were on the upper deck; only Fox, the two women and the two ship's boys were below – the younger boy, Lipton, sent

51

to the comfort of his hammock by Lamb out of compassion for his years and the other, Spooner, sent along with him to keep him company. At the taffrail, mast-head and forepeak were the lookouts, very much awake, Lamb hoped, yawning in his chair; he must make a round of the deck and visit each of them presently.

He yawned again and stretched dangerously in the little chair, feeling the ache of the long day in his legs and spine, and crossing his ankles, folded his arms and settled his chin onto his chest. There was absolutely no fear of his falling asleep, he knew. His mind was clear and sharp in spite of his weary bones and muscles, busy with thoughts of the coming struggle, of defence and attack. He would give his limbs a few minutes' well-deserved rest and then make his round of the night-watchmen. He remembered, too, that he had not yet collected his pistols from his cabin; they would need to be cleaned, primed and loaded – why had he not thought of them earlier?

Lamb opened his eyes with a start, the ringing laughter of a teasing, naked Mrs Mainwaring still loud in his ears, suddenly aware that he had been dreaming and uncomfortably conscious of a proud erection. His sleep had not lasted for more than ten or fifteen minutes, he thought, seeing Jamieson's dim bulk in the same position and still humming the same monotonous melody. Scrubbing at his face with his hands, Lamb levered himself from the chair.

'All quiet, Mr Jamieson?' he asked softly.

'As the grave, sir,' murmured the youth.

'Good. I shall have a word with the lookouts.'

Lamb stared over the black sea astern but he could see no light nor the faintest shadow of the privateer and turned and made his way forward. The lookouts were wide-eyed and alert. Lamb made his way down the dark companionway to his cabin, trying to remember when he had last cleaned his pistols. Fox was still awake, he noticed, glimpsing the dim sliver of light beneath the lieutenant's door, and turned to his right to enter his cabin. A low chuckle stopped him short. He turned back, stared at Fox's door and gave a wry shake of his head. That damned Fox! Making free with the delightful little Miss Brown! He felt a certain admiration for the man's initiative, mixed with a degree of envy; she was a pretty thing, albeit a little vacant. He wondered how Fox had managed to steal her away from the watchful Mrs Skinner. Well, good luck to you both, he thought, and turned back to his cabin door. The muted laughter came again – two voices this time – and he swung round with a frown of suspicion on his face and an ugly thought blossoming in his mind. He walked quietly to Fox's cabin door and stood close, listening to the low murmuring within, his suspicion suddenly a sickening certainty. Rage and disgust flooded through him. Fumbling at the handle, he flung open the door, meeting Fox's startled gaze as the man's head jerked round, seeing the arm around Spooner's naked shoulder and the hand on the boy's trousered hip. The two of them sprang apart and for a long moment there was shocked silence. The boy, his eyes wide with fear, shuffled backwards until his legs came up against the edge of the cot.

'What have we here, Mr Fox?' asked Lamb in a low, cold voice.

The lieutenant's face was ashen, quite drained of colour.

'How dare you burst in here!' he breathed, his voice scarcely audible. 'Get out, damn you!'

Lamb took a pace into the cabin. 'Did you hear me, sir?' he demanded. 'Do you want me to question the boy instead?'

Fox did not answer but stared back at Lamb as if transfixed. His mouth moved soundlessly, tongue dabbing at pale lips.

'Get out, Spooner,' snapped Lamb. 'Go on deck. I shall speak with you later.'

The boy sidled between the two men, his head downcast, and the sound of his bare, pattering feet disappeared forward. His going seemed to shake Fox out of his shocked trance. He turned away from Lamb, sat himself on the cot and crossed one leg comfortably over the other. His gaze was level and direct, his voice composed.

'It is not what it seems, captain, believe me. I can understand your suspicions, your very natural suspicions, and no doubt had I been in your shoes I would have the same misgivings.' He gave a low chuckle and a rueful shake of the head. 'I must confess to feeling more than a little foolish now. On reflection, I can see it was not very wise to speak to the boy in my cabin, but

53

it was all quite innocent, sir, quite innocent. You have my word on that.'

Lamb gazed coldly at him, saying nothing, recalling his previous amorphous doubts about the man, crystallized now into hard certainty. His disgust gave way to growing anger at the easy, unconvincing lies rolling smoothly from Fox's tongue.

'It might be better if I explained,' Fox went on, glancing up at Lamb with a companionable smile. 'The boy came into my cabin yesterday on an errand and expressed an interest in the books on my shelf there. I was surprised to discover he could read, after a fashion, and was pleased to offer him the loan of a book. I mentioned that I would be happy to help him with any words that proved difficult and that is how he happened to be in my cabin this evening. What you interrupted was a little lesson in reading, sir – nothing more. Look, here is the very book beside me.'

He held it up for Lamb to see. It was ignored.

'A reading lesson?' repeated Lamb. 'At this time of night, behind a closed door, with your arms around him? And in spite of the regulations forbidding. . . ?'

Fox sprang to his feet, his face set hard with anger.

'I have told you exactly what happened, sir, and I resent these ugly insinuations. I have given you my word on it and let that be an end to the matter.'

'I shall see what the boy has to say,' said Lamb tightly and turned to the door.

Fox gripped him by the arm and spun him round.

'That boy is the dregs of the lower deck,' he grated. 'He would probably lie on principle. Would you take his word in preference to mine? What you saw . . .'

'Do not tell me what I saw,' snapped Lamb, his anger boiling over. 'I know what I saw and it was not very pretty. I saw you within a whisker of breaching Article Twenty-Nine, I know that much. Now take your bloody hand off me unless you want to be clapped in irons.'

Fox dropped his hand and stepped back a pace, his eyes very black in his white face.

'That is an ugly accusation, sir. You will withdraw it or by God I shall give you cause to regret it!'

'I withdraw nothing. I am not blind nor am I a fool. You can count yourself fortunate I did not come in five minutes later. As it is, what you had in mind is between you, me and the boy. If he keeps his mouth shut you are safe – not that I care much either way. I have more important problems on my mind tonight.'

'No, by God!' Fox burst out. 'It cannot end there. You have made disgusting accusations, sir, and thrown my word back in my face. You will apologize now, or give me satisfaction as soon as we reach Antigua – unless you intend to shelter behind your temporary rank?'

Fox added these last words with such sneering emphasis that Lamb very nearly struck him. He clenched his fists as he fought to control his fury.

'You shall have your chance, for what good it may do you,' he retorted. 'Until then, you will do me the kindness of keeping out of my bloody way.'

He stepped back out of the cabin, and with enormous control managed to shut the door without slamming it, cutting off the sight of Fox's white, wild-eyed face. His own was probably as white, he thought, conscious of the turmoil in his chest and the trembling of his hands. The bastard sodomite! The fucking bum-lover! The dirty, lying, devious turd! Playing the part of outraged honour when we both knew full well what his bloody game was!

He found himself on the upper deck, pacing furiously up and down between the guns and the sprawled, sleeping men, his mind a whirl of disgust and rage. His temper gradually cooled but his disgust and sense of flouted trust, of deceit and betrayal, remained. He crossed to the side and stared blindly out over the dark, still sea as he waited for his blood to cool, the snores and grunts of the sleeping men loud in the quiet, windless air. Forget the bastard, he told himself firmly; there are more pressing things to occupy your mind tonight. He turned away from the side and made his way aft, almost cannoning into the boatswain.

'Beg pardon, sir,' said Snow, side-stepping.

'Send the boy Spooner to me, Mr Snow, if you please,' murmured Lamb. 'He is on the deck somewhere.'

It was the one loose end he must tie up before he could put

55

the affair to one side. Spooner was clearly very frightened but he had sense enough to say very little. What was he doing in Fox's cabin? The officer had stopped him as he went below and asked him to stop by at his cabin, sir. For what reason? The officer didn't say, sir – could have been anything. He had to do all sorts of tasks for the officers, sir: clean their shoes, fetch them water, things like that, sir. Could he read? Read, sir? No, sir. He could put an 'x' for his name, sir, that's all.

Lamb did not press him further; the fact that his story, such as it was, differed widely from Fox's account, was enough. It was clear that Spooner was no wide-eyed young innocent, green and unknowing; he had been at sea long enough to know about the unnatural lusts of certain men – aye, and to profit from them, very likely.

'You know what Article Twenty-Nine deals with, Spooner?' he asked, keeping his voice low. 'You have heard it read out, on Sundays?'

'Yes, sir,' muttered the boy.

'And you know the punishment if you are found guilty of breaching it?'

'Yes, sir.'

Lamb said nothing for a few moments, allowing the significance of what he had said to sink in. The boy stood with his head downcast, staring at his feet.

'I shall say no more on this matter,' said Lamb. 'And you would be well advised to keep a still tongue in your head, for your own sake. Do you understand me?'

'Yes, sir.'

'Off you go.'

Lamb walked slowly back to the quarterdeck, feeling bone-weary, drained of strength. Bloody Fox, he thought savagely, as he settled himself into his little chair; why had he picked tonight for his bloody games, of all times? He closed his eyes, his mind buzzing. His first thought when Jamieson roused him at midnight was of his forgotten pistols.

It was that fleeting moment when the first tentative advance of day and the reluctant retreat of night are still undecided, the moment when it is not yet possible to determine the features of a man's face a bare stride away but his bulk is suddenly visible against a sky that is no longer black. It was that low time when men who are abruptly wrenched from sleep feel neither gladness that the long night is over nor joy at the promise of an untouched day but fix their frowsty minds in sullen contemplation of the torpid moment, hugging their numb misery and cosseting tempers as brittle as frosted puddles. The crew of the *Heron* exhibited all these little tendernesses to some degree as they unfolded themselves from the hard, damp deck, silently willing their loud and cheerful commander to stow his bloody noise. Lamb's own temper was rarely less than edgy at this time of day, particularly when his tongue was still awaiting its early unction of coffee, but this morning he fairly exuded good humour as he strode about the deck exhorting his men to rouse themselves, to shake a leg, to stand to.

It had been a long night for Lamb, a night of silent hours wrapped in sombre thoughts, of slow pacing of the quarterdeck, of hourly visits to the mast-head and the lookouts forward and aft, of deep envy of the death-like sleep of the men at the guns. An hour before dawn he had shaken Jamieson into life from where he sprawled wedged into Mrs Skinner's chair and descended to his cabin. He had shaved in cold water, changed his linen and brought the log up to date. Sylvester had appeared unbidden, placed a glass of steaming lemon grog on the table and vanished without a word. Lamb did not enquire how this miracle had been achieved in the absence of a galley fire or what rum was doing outside of an Admiralty keg at that time of the day but downed it gratefully and went up to the dark deck with its warming influence spreading cheerfully through his veins, feeling clean, alert and refreshed.

As his men quietly cursed and hawked and muttered and stood to he jumped up into the shrouds and climbed the ratlines to the topmast.

'Good morning, Jackson,' he said brightly as he set his feet on the jack.

'Morning, sir,' murmured the lookout with the touch of a tarry finger to his forehead as he gave way to his captain and edged out along the yard. Suddenly, greatly daring, he muttered: 'I ain't Jackson, sir, beggin' your pardon. I'm

57

Johnson, sir. Jackson is on for'ard lookout.'

Lamb was peering intently over the misty darkness of the sea to starboard.

'Yes, of course,' he murmured absently. 'Well, I was pretty close, pretty close.'

He was waiting for that moment when the slow roll of the earth would bring the light of the sun to the eastern horizon and the length of his vision would leap from a dozen yards to a hundred, to five hundred, to a mile.

'Keep your eyes skinned now, Jackson,' he muttered. 'The instant you see that Frenchman, sing out.'

'Aye aye, sir,' said Johnson sadly as he gazed to larboard.

A whisper of wind, no more than a sigh, kissed Lamb's right cheek. The limp topsail stirred, the mainmast creaked and the cutter curtseyed very slightly. The breath died and almost immediately returned, stronger now, lifting the canvas of the topsail beside Lamb and bringing the *Heron* to life. Suddenly the schooner was visible, three hundred yards off the larboard quarter, foresail and mainsail brailed in, her sweeps showing as a white thrash of water along her side. Johnson's arm was thrust out, pointing.

'There she is, sir!'

'Stand by the larboard guns!' roared Lamb. 'Open ports! Run out the guns!'

His feet hit the deck as the guns trundled their muzzles out over the black water. The mainsail filled and bellied as the new-born wind came over the larboard quarter and Lamb suddenly knew what he must do.

'Luff up! Luff up!' he shouted urgently. 'Mainsheet haul! Smartly now!'

'Luff up it is, sir,' sang out the helmsman, pushing at the tiller as Snow and his sail-handlers ran to the sheets and braces.

The *Heron* swung rocking and heeling on to the larboard tack and ran down towards the schooner's bow. The light was growing stronger by the second and Lamb could see furious activity aboard her as the sweeps were hurriedly hauled inboard and men ran to loose the sails. The cutter crossed the privateer's bow and his heart lifted in a great, soundless shout of joy when he saw the closed gun-ports along her larboard side

58

and men swarming across the deck – too late! – from her starboard guns. He shot a quick glance about his own deck, at the gun-captains bent over their flintlocks and blowing gently on to the glowing ends of their slow-matches in order to have a bright ember ready should their flints fail them; at the after guns – and Fox – and quickly on, to Sylvester's ragged grin at the carronade, an elf amongst his mates; at the forward guns and the scowling cook with a rammer in his hand and a cleaver through his belt, and the two ship's boys – Spooner sullen and hangdog, avoiding everyone's eyes – and the solid, dependable figure of Jamieson standing wide-legged with a huge grin on his face at the French flat-footedness.

The Frenchmen were quick. The schooner's larboard ports were raised and her guns were thrusting out as the *Heron*'s jib-boom came level with her foremast with barely fifty yards of water between them.

'Fire!' yelled Lamb.

Scarlet tongues of flame flared from the muzzles, lighting up the dark sea. The deck of the privateer, thick with men, was swept by a murderous hail of lead and iron. Long shards of timber, torn from the low bulwark, whirred through the air and ripped at sails and ropes and men.

'Load! Load! Stir yourselves!' Jamieson's urgent shout came hard on the heels of the gun's roar, while the thick, gritty smoke was still swirling about the deck.

'Down helm!' snapped Lamb. 'Hard over!'

'Down helm. Hard over it is, sir,' called the stolid, imperturbable helmsman, and the *Heron* turned sharply into the wind.

Fire on the uproll, Lamb told himself, punching his hand in excitement; killing Frenchmen was all very well, but it made better sense to endeavour to cripple her spars.

'Midships the helm!'

'Midships the helm it is, sir.'

The Frenchman was already turning to meet her as its lacerated sails were sheeted home, hampered by the severed rigging, but it was slow – much too slow.

'Fire as you bear!' bellowed Lamb as the bow crossed the schooner's stern at pistol shot range.

59

The forward gun banged, sending its double load of grapeshot and roundshot tearing through the canvas and rigging of the mainsail. The other guns fired in quick succession and a wild cheer rang out as the privateer's main topmast lurched sideways in a tangle of hanging gaff topsail and staysail. The stern gun of the schooner flashed flame and a six-pound ball screamed low over the *Heron*'s deck and out to sea, touching nothing but shaving so close past the helmsman that he staggered, shooting an indignant glare at the Frenchman. Muskets, too, were popping by the dozen from the schooner's rail and tops, the little balls whistling about the cutter's deck and thudding into the timbers. For a brief instant Lamb hesitated, his blood hot and racing with excitement, his tongue trembling on the verge of ordering the helmsman to complete the turn, to put the *Heron* on the schooner's starboard side. Caution and sense stayed him – the cutter was a mail-packet, not a man-of-war, and his first responsibility was to the King's mail. Instead he ordered the helmsman to keep her steady.

The *Heron* headed away from the privateer with the wind almost directly astern. The French broadside, able to bear at last, sped her on her way as she pointed her nose at the orange light beginning to flood the eastern horizon. The last shot of the brief engagement struck the *Heron* high on the larboard quarter, sending splinters flying and bringing Fox to his knees with a foot-long shard driven through his hand.

He was the *Heron*'s only casualty; Lamb threw him an unsympathetic glance as he was helped below and returned his attention to the schooner, reflecting with a degree of grim satisfaction that of all men he could not have chosen one more fitting to stand in the splinter's path. The schooner was making no attempt to chase; she had been stung too badly. Lifting his telescope, Lamb studied her mauled spars and rigging, seeing men working at her drunken main topmast. He gave a triumphant grin as he saw her nod round and head northwards in the direction of distant Hispaniola. Goodbye and good riddance, he thought, closing his telescope with a decisive snap.

'Swab out,' he ordered. 'Secure the guns. Close ports.'

The men were noisily cheerful, laughing and chattering amongst themselves as they worked at the guns, happy and relieved to have escaped the privateer so lightly and so quickly. Lamb watched them at their work for a few minutes, unwilling to let the moment pass unmarked. What they had done this morning could hardly be called a victory – more a case of tip and run – but nevertheless they had hit hard and acquitted themselves well.

'You did well today, men,' he called at last, somewhat shyly. 'I thank you all.'

His little speech was stirring enough to cause one or two heads to lift and grin but most of the men, with thoughts more immediately concerned with breakfast and their morning beer, gave not the slightest whit of attention and he raised his telescope again and pretended to interest himself in the schooner, thinking ruefully that he could well have saved his breath.

The carpenter and his mate began to hack and chisel and curse at the damaged bulwark and smoke began to puff cheerfully from the galley chimney as the *Heron* slipped easily eastwards, heading straight for the red brow of the sun peering angrily over the edge of the sea. Thoughts of steaming coffee and hot bacon were beginning to insinuate themselves into the warm glow of satisfaction enveloping Lamb's mind when Jamieson appeared at his elbow, his white breeches smeared with blood.

'Fox's hand is in a bad way, sir,' he said. 'Have I your leave to borrow Mr Mee and his saw for a few minutes?'

Lamb raised his eyebrows. 'Lord, as bad as that, is it?'

'No, no,' Jamieson grinned, 'although it may well come to that. We are having trouble removing the splinter. If Mr Mee can cut it through close to the flesh, we should be able to pull it out. It's a nasty mess, very nasty, but Fox is being damned stoical about it all – not a whimper from him, so far.'

'Really? Yes, borrow Mr Mee and his saw, by all means. Mr Snow! Pipe to breakfast, if you please.'

The wind dropped right away shortly after noon, picked up listlessly for a few hours' in the evening and died away again until the early morning. The next twenty-four hours followed much the same pattern and two days after the brush with the privateer the *Heron* was sitting on a glassy sea a bare sixty miles further east, with the cook's galley rubbish clinging obstinately to the ship's side at the waterline. It was Sunday morning, the day set aside by the Admiralty for the captain's inspection of his ship and the uplifting of the men's hearts and minds by the reading of the Articles of War or a reading from the Scriptures.

Lamb emerged on deck at five bells in the morning watch. The sun was well up and the prospect of another hot, still day was promised by the early heat and cloudless sky. The hands were lined up ready for inspection, their faces shining and close-shaven, their pigtails stiff and neat. Lamb walked quickly along the lines, glancing at familiar faces to which he could now put names and running his eye over clean shirts and trousers or petticoat-breeches.

'Very good, Mr Jamieson,' he said as he walked away from the last man and with Jamieson, Snow and Mee in tow descended into the bowels of the ship by way of the forward hatch. He commenced his inspection in the hold, poking at ribs and knees and futtocks and peering at the state of the carpenter's chain pump. He looked in at the magazine and the cable tiers, inspected rather more closely the canvas in the sail-locker, glanced about the spartan cleanliness of the men's quarters, opened up the bread-room and spirit-room and carefully locked them again and led his retinue into the galley. Harrison stood and watched, his evil eye glaring as Lamb sniffed at the bags boiling in the huge kettle and ran his fingers around the inside of the copper pans and ladles. Lamb glanced at the scrubbed deck and the neatly hung utensils and gave Harrison a satisfied nod.

'Very good, Harrison,' he said pleasantly and was alarmed to see the cook's unscarred cheek and the corner of his mouth lift in what he took to be a hideous snarl of demonic rage and then realized was Harrison's attempt at a smile.

'Very good, Mr Jamieson,' said Lamb as the party left the galley, the ship's inspection over. 'I am very pleased with the condition of the ship.'

'Thank you, sir,' said Jamieson, with a touch of his hat. He nodded behind him in the direction of the cabins. 'Do you wish to look in on Mr Fox while you are here, sir? He is not too well, I am afraid. His wound is badly inflamed and he is in a fever.'

'No, I think not,' replied Lamb and led the way up to the brilliance of the upper deck. He made his way to the quarterdeck as the hands were called aft and turned the pages of Pardoe's Bible while he waited for the hands to settle themselves before him, squatting on the deck or standing as their preference took them. He read the parable of the Good Samaritan, knowing well how seamen detested sermons but loved a story, no matter how familiar.

'We will join in prayer,' he said as he closed the Bible. The men rose to their feet, clasped their hands and looked at the deck.

'Our Father, which art in Heaven . . .'

The crew's deep rumble swelled up into the still air as they murmured the old phrases. Looking over their bowed heads as he led them in prayer, Lamb felt deeply moved, partly by the sound of the familiar, comforting words learned in childhood but also by the feeling that he was privilege to a certain shared closeness, almost a brotherhood, with these men. The prayer ended, the men raised their heads, Sylvester bared his several stumps in an ugly grin and the cook turned his scarred head to level his good eye at Lamb in a villainous glare; Lamb's sense of empathy gave way to his usual cynical forebearance.

'Dismiss the hands, if you please, Mr Jamieson,' he ordered and strolled over to the side to join Mrs Skinner and her maid.

'Good morning to you, ma'am,' he said. 'Good morning, Miss Brown.'

'Good morning, captain,' said Mrs Skinner. 'What an enjoyable little service that was; a little short, I thought, but a great comfort, nevertheless.'

'I am pleased you enjoyed it,' smiled Lamb, casting a sly eye at the demure and pretty Miss Brown and thinking what a delightful little morsel she was. The girl shot him a quick glance from beneath her lashes and looked shyly at the deck with a hint of a smile on her innocent cheek. 'Would you care to join me for a cup of tea, Mrs Skinner? And Miss Brown, of course. We can take it on the deck here, if you would prefer. It will not take the bosun a moment to rig up an awning.'

'Why, how kind you are,' beamed Mrs Skinner. 'I should

love a cup of tea. Perhaps Sylvester could bring up my folding chair and a cushion for Brown to sit on.'

The chair and the cushion were brought up and Snow fashioned an awning from an odd length of number five canvas slung between the rail and the mainmast back-stay; the tea arrived shortly afterwards accompanied by three cups, but Lamb, taking pity on Jamieson's duty-stiff back and thoughtfully-pursed lips, invited the youth to join the party by way of a jerk of the head after catching his eye with no great difficulty. Jamieson hurried over with a wide grin of pleasure and took up a position from where he could leer at the unresponsive Miss Brown without being seen by her employer or his captain. She squatted daintily on her cushion beside her mistress's chair with her ankles decently beneath her and her eyes fixed demurely on the deck, only occasionally raising them to look thoughtfully at the brown, half-naked bodies of the younger seamen sprawled at their ease at the other end of the deck.

Mrs Skinner demonstrated the happy, feminine knack of being able to manage several tasks simultaneously with comfortable ease, plying her embroidery needles, sipping tea, fanning herself, keeping a gaoler's eye on Miss Brown and entertaining the two officers with a stream of bright, cheerful chatter.

'Yes, the elder, James, has settled into a very nice living at a village called Shillington in Hertfordshire – or is it Bedfordshire? – well, one or the other, I have his letter in my box. A small parish, he tells me, and with a child on the way he may find things a little hard later on, I suspect, but as I tell him, he cannot expect to become a bishop overnight. (What do you find so interesting along there, Brown? I have told you before, it is very rude to stare.) And the youngest, Ralph, has followed his father into the Marines. Such a lively boy, quite unlike his brother. You would both take to him immediately, I am sure. He is at Chatham now, at the barracks there. I know the town well; Major Skinner and I were married there – he was not a major then, of course. Let me fill your cup, Captain Lamb. And you, Mr Jamieson? Tea is so refreshing in the heat, is it not? Here you are, Brown, try not to spill it, for once. And how is Mr Fox today, gentlemen?'

64

'He is in a poor way, ma'am,' said Jamieson. 'His hand has turned quite black. I fear it is poisoned. I think he may well have to lose it when we reach Antigua.'

'The poor man,' said Mrs Skinner with a frown of concern. 'It is black, you say? Does it smell? Have you sniffed at it?'

'It – um – it comes over pretty strong, ma'am,' said Jamieson uncomfortably, not at all sure that it was proper to discuss strong smells in mixed company.

'Gangrene, a pound to a penny. Once you have smelled that you never forget it. I must take a look at it.' Mrs Skinner drained her cup and stuffing her embroidery into her work-bag, lifted her arm to Lamb who hauled her to her feet. 'Thank you, captain. I shall not be a moment, Brown. Just stay where you are and keep your eyes to this end of the ship. Come along, Mr Jamieson.'

Jamieson cast an appealing glance at Lamb.

'I am not sure, ma'am, if I . . .'

'Cut along,' said Lamb with a jerk of his head.

They were not gone many minutes. When they returned to the quarterdeck Mrs Skinner's face showed a look of grave concern.

'How many more days before we reach Antigua, captain?' she demanded abruptly.

'With a good following wind, three days,' replied Lamb. 'Otherwise' – he spread his hands – 'it could be a week, perhaps longer.'

'Then it must come off, the sooner the better,' she said firmly.

'Come off, ma'am?'

She gave a tut of impatience. 'His hand, of course, before the mortification spreads to his arm and he loses that, too. He has a fever as it is.'

Lamb studied her determined face in silence for a few moments.

'I shall take a look at him,' he said and strode away.

Fox's cabin door was open to catch any breath of air that might pass through the ship. Lamb stood in the doorway and looked at Fox lying with closed eyes on his cot. His face was flushed and damp with sweat and the wounded left hand, wrapped in linen, rested on his chest.

'Are you awake, Mr Fox?' asked Lamb loudly, stepping into the cabin.

Fox opened his eyes. 'What do you want?' His voice was weak but his rasp of dislike was clear.

'I must take a look at your hand.'

'I can do without your help,' Fox said shortly and closed his eyes.

'Take off that bandage, sir,' snapped Lamb, stepping close. 'Or do you want me to do it?'

Fox shot him a vicious glance out of sunken, red-rimmed eyes and tore savagely at his dressing.

'There!' he snarled, thrusting his hand up at Lamb's face. 'Take a good look. Pretty, don't you think?'

Lamb gripped Fox's wrist and held the hand steady. The wound was large and ugly, the ragged lips extending from beneath the ring-finger almost to the ball of the thumb. The back of the hand was torn badly around the area of the exit wound and Lamb guessed that there would be at least one broken bone, probably more. The flesh of the hand was swollen, sodden-looking and very dark, almost black, the pink, healthy flesh of the wrist clearly demarcated. Lamb bent his head and gingerly sniffed; he quickly straightened, disgusted by the smell of the septic inflammation. He gently prodded the flesh with a tentative finger.

'Careful, damn you!' cried Fox.

Lamb released the wrist. He put his hands in his pockets and stared coldly down at Fox's hot, fevered face.

'It will have to come off, you know, and very soon unless you want to lose your arm. It is entirely up to you, of course.'

Fox closed his eyes and turned his head to the bulkhead. 'Do as you damn well like,' he muttered weakly.

Lamb cleared his lungs of the fetid atmosphere of Fox's cabin by means of several deep breaths of the hot, forenoon air and stepping to the side, raised a beckoning finger to Jamieson.

'There are no two ways about it, from what I can see. Mrs Skinner is right; his hand will have to come off – and pretty damned quick, by the look of it.'

Jamieson nodded soberly. 'My thoughts exactly, sir. It didn't need a surgeon's eye to see that. Will you do it, sir?'

'Me?' Lamb shook his head. 'Not if I can avoid it. It's more of a job for the carpenter, I should have thought – unless you have a mind to volunteer?'

'What, chop off a man's hand in cold blood?' Jamieson gave a frown of distaste. 'I've no stomach for a surgeon's work, sir. I'd like as not close my eyes and cut off something I shouldn't. I'll pass the word for Mr Mee, shall I, sir?'

The carpenter took a hasty step backwards when the proposition was put to him, as if to distance himself from the notion. 'Gawd, sir, no, sir, begging your pardon, sir. I ain't no surgeon, sir, nor never wanted to be. 'Sides, sir, what happens when he dies, which he's bound to, after? He ain't no common seaman, sir – he's a passenger and an officer. It wouldn't look too good, him cutting his painter, like, at the hands of the carpenter. Wouldn't look good at all that, sir, would it?' He leaned closer and lowered his voice. 'If you ask me, sir, 'tis best to leave him as he is. There won't be no awkward questions then, like. Just give him a day or two and let him die natural. If you want my opinion, sir . . .'

'I do not, Mr Mee, thank you all the same,' said Lamb coldly. 'You have given me too many already. Perhaps you could find me a sharp hand-axe and some hot pitch, if that would not be too much trouble.'

'Why, bless your heart, sir, it'll be no trouble, no trouble at all,' cried the old man, blithely unaware of Lamb's sarcasm. 'I'll get the pitch pot a-heating this very minute and I'll find you a axe so sharp you could shave yourself with it, if you had a mind to.'

Lamb gave the ancient officer a hard look as he stumped away on his stiff-jointed legs.

'He's got more tongue than enough, that one,' he remarked. 'A pity he has not the backbone to match.'

Jamieson coloured slightly. 'Well, he's an old man, sir,' he said lamely.

Lamb grunted. 'I can't see what difference that makes. Still, it's true I daresay. If Fox dies, Mr Mee might well have a finger pointed at him. I shall have to take the damned thing off myself.'

'It would seem best, sir,' said Jamieson, more cheerful as the prospect of his involvement vanished. 'You will need a hand, of course.' He slapped his thigh and cackled. 'Need a hand! Heh, heh, heh!'

Lamb gave him a cold, unamused stare. 'Since you find the thing so entertaining, you can act as surgeon's mate.' Jamieson's grin abruptly disappeared. 'If you have any clothes older than those you are wearing, which I can scarcely believe, you had better change into them. I shall be in my cabin.'

As he reached the companion ladder, Lamb paused at the hatchway, trying to call to mind what little he knew of surgery. A swift chop with an axe and an application of pitch to the stump had the advantage of quickness but little else to commend it. If the man did not die he was left in great pain for weeks and an ugly, puckered stump that often took an age to heal. A few minutes patient work with a knife, however, could produce a stump neatly covered with healthy flesh, leading to a quicker, surer recovery. Lamb pressed his finger to his lip and pondered. The axe was tempting; it was quick and if Fox should die, what did it matter? The answer was plain: much as he detested the man, he would be failing in his duty if he did not do his best for him – and in any case, the knowledge that he had shirked the better course because it was the more difficult would never rest easily in his mind. He made his decision and descended to his cabin.

Pardoe had evidently not been much of a reader. The row of books on his shelf was short and was mostly concerned with mathematics, gunnery and horticulture, but Lamb's eye fell on one slim volume with a title that vaguely suggested medicine and he plucked it out and leafed through it. Mr William Salmon's *The English Herbal* might have proved very useful if Lamb had been interested in easing the discomfort of gout or the pains of childbirth and the cutter had been surrounded by English meadows and country gardens but it was quite useless in the way of advice for amputations and Lamb thrust it back amongst its fellows with a snort of disgust.

There came a tap at his door and Sylvester sidled in with some of Lamb's laundered linen folded over his arm. 'I'll just put this away, sir.'

'Very good,' said Lamb absently.

'The pitch is a-bubbling on the stove, sir, and Mr Mee is making the sparks fly from the stone with his axe. You'll be doing the chopping, sir, I hear.'

Lamb frowned at the little man. 'You talk too much. Put that linen away and remove yourself.'

'Aye aye, sir,' said the steward cheerfully. 'I just wondered if you needed a hand, that's all, sir. I'm only too willing.'

'No thank you, Sylvester. No, wait. Have we any men on board who were once loblolly boys, do you know?'

Sylvester stuck out his lip and pulled an ugly grimace. 'No, sir, can't say as we have,' he said at last, his face returning to its normal elfin puckishness. 'Course, there's the cook. He was a porter in an orspital when he was a lad, he told me.'

Lamb shook his head. 'Never mind. Off you go.'

He sat at his table, foraged for a scrap of paper and prepared to make a list of what he thought he would need, dredging up hazy memories of the swift butchery he had witnessed in dark, crowded cockpits after battle. He recalled the deft work of the surgeons and their mates with knife and saw, the quick stitching with threaded needle plucked from the surgeon's lapel with a bloodied hand, the casual tossing of the severed part into a barrel – but little else. He knew that flaps were cut to fold over the bone in order to produce a neat stump; he had heard Andrews, the surgeon on the *Adroit*, talk enthusiastically of the new circular cut and of drawing the skin up so as to 'cut long'. What did that mean? He shook his head; flaps seemed much more straightforward for his inexperienced hand. But what of the blood vessels? How was it possible to cut through these without draining a man dry? He placed his finger over his radial artery and felt the steady beat of his pulse. The answer came to him: the blood must be made to stop flowing before the first cut was made. A knotted circle of cloth, wrapped around the crook of the elbow and tightened by the turning of a short spike should serve. Each blood vessel could then be tied off as it was severed, without too much loss of blood. He gave a short, dry laugh, certain that things would not be that simple – they never were, in practice. Jamieson could do the tying up, he decided, while he did the cutting and sawing. Another pair of hands would be needed to hold Fox steady – Snow, perhaps; a

69

little blood would be nothing to him. Now the flaps – how would he make those? He drew a little sketch on his paper. Yes, that should serve. He must find a keen-edged knife to make his cuts; and a fine-toothed saw from the carpenter for the bone; and needle, thread and scissors; yes, and a wick to drain off any puss that might collect behind the flaps. He dipped his pen and began to make his list.

The blocking of the light from the open door brought his head up. Mrs Skinner smiled in at him.

'No, please do not get up,' she said as Lamb pushed back his chair. 'I would not have you crack your head on these low beams for me. May I come in?'

She advanced into the cabin and seated herself at the table.

'I hear from Mr Jamieson that you are going to deal with Mr Fox very shortly.'

'Yes. You were quite right, ma'am – it cannot be delayed. We shall take it off this morning. I have just been making a list of what we shall need.'

'Indeed? Well, from what I hear of your intentions, I hope a good aim is high on your list.'

Lamb smiled and shook his head. 'It will not be necessary, ma'am. I know little of the surgeon's art but I have decided it is called for, in Mr Fox's case. Whether or not I am successful will depend on a little luck and a good deal of prayer, I think.'

'You are going to cut, then, like a regular surgeon?'

'Such is my intention, ma'am. Mr Fox will have to excuse my inexperienced hand, particularly in the way of stitches, but I am sure . . .'

'Do not worry yourself about stitches, captain!' she cried, beaming. 'They lie rather more in my province than yours, I think, and I am a very fair needlewoman.'

'No, no, ma'am.' Lamb leaned back in his chair, aghast at the notion. 'It is quite out of the question. Thank you kindly, but I hardly think such a . . .'

'Nonsense, captain! That is why I came down here, to offer my services. The sight of blood is not new to me, you know. I am not a green girl, all a-tremble and smelling salts at the thought of a thorn prick. Leave the stitching to me; I fancy I shall make a neater finish to it.' She rose from her chair with the air of one who has said her final word and would brook no further argument. 'I shall change out of this dress. I would rather not have blood over my new taffeta.'

Lamb sighed at her departing back and bellowed for his steward.

'Take this list to Mr Jamieson with my compliments. Tell him that I particularly asked for the knife and saw to be sharp and clean.'

'Sharp and clean, aye aye, sir.'

Fox stared up at Lamb from eyes sunk deep into his flushed, shrunken face. Lamb looked down at him without the slightest twinge of pity, his dislike as strong as ever.

'This is going to hurt you, Mr Fox. It might be better if we strapped you down.'

'I need no straps,' Fox whispered, holding out his hand. He closed his eyes. 'Do whatever you have to do.'

Lamb tied the knotted handkerchief around Fox's elbow, slipped a spike through the loop and turned it round and round until the cloth was biting deeply into the flesh. He glanced at his two assistants.

'Are we ready?'

Jamieson gave him a solemn nod and Mrs Skinner flashed a reassuring little smile. Lamb tested the sharpness of the knife with his thumb; the carpenter had put an edge on it that would have put his razor to shame.

'If you would care to stand back a trifle, Mrs Skinner. Clap a firm hold on that arm now, Mr Jamieson.'

He put a finger to Fox's pulse; the beat of blood in the wrist was undetectable. Clenching his teeth, he took a firm grip on the knife and drew the blade slowly across the pink flesh of the wrist. The scratch oozed a little blood. Damn! He was being too lily-livered; he had barely broken the skin. He cut again, pressing firmly down, and this time the flesh opened like pale lips. There was a sudden run of blood; Mrs Skinner reached forward and wiped it away with her cloth. Two more quick, deep cuts and the three sides of the first flap were complete. Sliding his blade beneath, he sliced the flap free of the underlying tissue and turned it back with his knife. Fox gave a

71

deep, tortured groan and turned his face to the bulkhead. Lamb was surprised at his own coolness; he had imagined that he would be nervous and squeamish but he felt little more emotion than if he had been carving a ham. The severed ends of the smaller blood vessels and the great radial artery trickled redly and steadily, spreading blood over the wrist and dripping onto the scrap of old sail spread beneath Fox. In a few moments there was a large pool of it collecting in a hollow in the canvas and Lamb was suddenly aghast, his coolness gone. There was far too much blood, surely? For a brief instant blind panic welled up and he stared at what he had done, helpless and horrified.

Mrs Skinner, calmness itself, dabbed and patted and wiped. With her deft embroiderer's fingers she slipped a loop of thread around the artery and pulled it tight, twisted the thread round again and tied a neat knot. Her little scissors flashed and snipped it close. A bright bead of blood hung suspended from the end of the artery.

'That was prettily done, ma'am,' breathed Lamb, relief flooding through him. She made no answer, busy with her loops of thread and scissors, frowning in concentration. He gave Jamieson a nod. 'Pass the word for that hot knife, Mr Jamieson.'

'Aye aye, sir,' said the lieutenant and putting his head round the door, gave the lurking Sylvester a call. 'Knife!'

The suggestion of cauterization had come from Jamieson. He had not been very sure of its purpose or its usefulness and neither had Lamb, but they had agreed it could help to staunch the bleeding and a long-handled knife had been thrust into the glowing coals of Harrison's galley stove.

'I have done my best there, I think,' said Mrs Skinner, stepping back and wiping her red fingers on her apron as Sylvester appeared at the door holding out the knife with its handle wrapped in a cloth.

'Hold him firm now,' said Lamb as he took the knife, wincing at the heat from its blade. At the first, hissing touch of the metal Fox gave a great, choking grunt and jerked wildly, his arm flailing in Lamb's grip.

'Hold him still, damn you!' cried Lamb, struggling to hold

the hot steel in place. Jamieson gave him a reproachful look and pressed his bulk down harder onto Fox's chest and shoulders. Fox suddenly slumped still, his face bone white.

'He's fainted, sir,' said Jamieson, his face very nearly as colourless as Fox's.

'Thank God for that,' grunted Lamb. He handed Jamieson the cautery and took up his sharp knife again.

Cutting the second flap, on the outer surface of the wrist, proved easier; there were fewer blood vessels and less blood, and it was with a sense of relief that Lamb reached for the saw.

'Stand by,' he muttered to Jamieson. 'Clap a firm grip on him.' He dashed his sleeve over his forehead, wiping away the sweat that threatened to blind him. 'It might be best, Mrs Skinner, if you stepped outside for a moment. This will not be a pretty sight.'

'No, Mr Lamb! Saw away; I have seen worse sights in childbirth.'

Lamb took a tight grip with his left hand on Fox's wrist and lined up his saw blade close to the turned-back flaps. Fox lay limp and still.

'Is he still breathing?' asked Lamb in sudden alarm.

Jamieson bent low over the cot.

'Yes, sir, still breathing.'

Lamb's initial stroke with the saw skidded on the smooth, shining bone. He set his jaw and tried again, pressing the blade against his thumb in the manner of a regular carpenter and using short, delicate strokes in order to make the first initial notch. The fine, sharp teeth bit through the first bone in a moment and he set the edge against the second. Jamieson gave a groan and collapsed in a limp heap across Fox's chest, wrenching the saw from Lamb's grasp before sliding to the deck and hitting his head with a crash that rattled the planks.

'Christ All-bloody-mighty!' shouted Lamb in fright and rage, startled. He shot a guilty look at Mrs Skinner, bending over Jamieson's sprawled body. 'I beg pardon, ma'am.'

Sylvester appeared at the doorway and saw the problem at a glance.

'I'll get rid of him, sir,' he said and darted in. 'Gawd,' he breathed as he squeezed past Lamb and caught sight of the bloody wrist in his grip. He and Mrs Skinner dragged Jamieson's heavy bulk to the doorway.

'That will do,' said Lamb, taking up his saw again. 'Leave him there, the damned milksop.'

'No, no, do not be so hard on him, captain,' protested Mrs Skinner, taking Jamieson's place at Lamb's side. 'He is only a boy.' She added her grip to Fox's arm. 'Saw away,' she said firmly.

The blackened hand fell heavily to the deck and Lamb kicked it from under his feet. It slid along the deck and nestled lovingly against Jamieson's cheek.

'Now the flaps,' muttered Lamb, feeling his stomach beginning to churn as he stared at the pink bone ends and the bloody, dripping stump, certain that he had killed Fox with his blundering butchery.

'We must not forget the wick,' said Mrs Skinner as he bent over the stump. She removed the length of cord from where it lay coiled at the bottom of a glass in two inches of Pardoe's gin, shook it dry and tucked it beneath the first flap of skin as Lamb folded it over the stump, leaving a short length protruding. He folded the second flap over, held the two firm and cut away as much of the excess skin as he dared.

'Ply your needle, ma'am.'

She plucked a threaded needle from the bosom of her dress and kneeling beside the cot deftly stitched the edges of the flaps together, pulling each stitch tight with careful little jerks of her needle, bringing to Lamb's mind distant, half-forgotten memories of his mother kneeling before him as she replaced a button on his child's smock.

'There!' exclaimed Mrs Skinner as she passed her needle through the loop of the last stitch and gently tugged it tight. She cut the thread with her scissors and dabbed the stump with her cloth.

'Excellent, ma'am. Very well done indeed. Shall we see if it leaks?'

Lamb cautiously slackened off the tourniquet. They bent, their heads close, and peered anxiously at the stump. A little blood oozed from the fleshy join.

'Not too much to worry about there, I think,' said Mrs

74

Skinner confidently, and dipping a cloth into her bowl of water she began to wash the stump free of blood.

Lamb looked down on Fox's white, lined face, thinking that he had taken on the look of an old, old man. His grey hair was clinging wetly to his forehead and his sunken cheeks showed the white bristles that had grown in the past few days. He was breathing in quick, shallow, panting gasps, much like a dog after a run. Lamb shook his head, feeling at last a spasm of pity for the man and guilt at the butchery he had inflicted on him. Suddenly, desperately, he wanted Fox to live, to survive the awful thing he had done to him. He took a clean scrap of old petticoat Mrs Skinner had supplied and wiped the sweat from the pinched, bloodless face.

'I fancy he looks better already,' said Mrs Skinner, busily swathing the stump in a yard or so of white linen. 'Do you know, captain, I bought this cambric in France, many years ago. It is excellent quality, really excellent, and has lasted these many years without a sign of yellowing. I never thought when I bought it that it would end up on the stump of a man's arm. What a strange world we live in! Put your finger on that knot, my dear – captain, I mean. There, does that not look better, all clean and white and neatly wrapped? I must say, captain, that I think you did splendidly and I am quite certain Mr Fox will be eternally grateful to you.'

'Any gratitude that he has must go to you, ma'am, above all. I am filled with admiration at your steadiness.'

'But, sir! I did nothing, nothing at all.' She put her hand on his arm with a look of concern on her honest, homely face. 'Why, captain, you look almost as pale as Mr Fox. I hope you are not going to join Mr Jamieson on the floor?'

'No, ma'am, I am fine.'

Jamieson groaned and stirred, opened his eyes, stared blankly at the clawed, bloody, blackened hand an inch from his nose and rolled away with a little shriek of fright.

'Stow that noise, Mr Jamieson,' growled Lamb. 'A damn fine loblolly boy you turned out to be. Kindly take yourself up to the deck and dispose of that thing over the side.'

'Yes, sir. Sorry, sir.'

Jamieson pulled himself to his feet, swayed, clutched at the back of his head and stared at Fox's white-swathed stump.

'It's all done then, sir?'

'Yes, Mrs Skinner and I finished if off while you were sleeping.'

Jamieson slowly shook his head, mystified at his lost moments. He picked up the severed hand by its little finger and holding it gingerly at a safe distance, staggered off.

Mrs Skinner straightened Fox's sheets with a few practised twitches, lifted his head to plump his pillow and bent to collect the bloody swabs from the deck. Lamb stayed her with a hand on her shoulder.

'Leave all that, ma'am. You have done more than enough today. What do you say to sharing a pot of tea with me?'

'What a delightful idea.' She beamed and patted Lamb's hand. 'Give me ten minutes to wash and put myself to rights. I shall send Brown in to sit with Mr Fox; even she could manage that, I dare say.'

Lamb put his head round the side of the door.

'Sylvester! A pot of tea in my cabin, if you please, and then be so good as to clean up in here.'

The charms of the diminutive Miss Brown were no less apparent to the *Heron*'s crew than they were to her officers and Sylvester's wicked old eyes lit up when he entered Fox's cabin with his bucket and swabs and saw the girl sitting demurely on a chair beside the cot.

'Don't mind me, miss,' he leered. 'Just sit where you are. You won't be in my way.'

She made no answer, sitting with bowed head looking at her hands folded in her lap as he busied himself about the cabin and sweetened the air with the fumes of his midday rum, glancing at her from time to time and baring his surviving teeth in a beguiling smile. She might have been made of stone for all the effect his ensnaring magic had on her and stayed unmoved without so much as a flicker of her eyes even when a sly elbow brushed against her calf as he swabbed with undue diligence around the area of her chair. The glass in which the wick had been soaking caught his eye as he raised himself from his ancient knees and taking it to the bucket he was on the point of tipping the liquid into it when his experienced nose detected the smell of gin and he tipped it down a grateful throat instead. Smacking his lips he finished his little chores, and with his courage warmed by rum and gin and his lust inflamed by the girl's nearness, he placed himself squarely in front of her and resting his hands on his knees, bent to bring his face on a level with her's and rolled his eyes enticingly.

'What ho, my dear,' he whispered hoarsely, drenching her in aromatic fumes.

Fox whimpered and stirred, the maid turned her head to the cot and Lamb's muted bellow of 'Sylvester!' came from aft. The steward scowled, tossed his head and departed muttering from the cabin, convinced that certain bliss had been snatched from him. He was despatched to convey the captain's compliments to Mr Jamieson with the request that the noise on deck be kept to an absolute minimum; Mrs Skinner had averred that silence was an invaluable aid to recovery and with his new-found concern for the invalid, Lamb was determined that no shouts, running feet or boatswain's pipes should endanger him.

For the next few hours the boatswain gave his orders in a husky growl and the hands, seizing gleefully at the chance to irritate him without fear of reprisal, tip-toed in exaggerated fashion about the deck until, in the hushed, violet light of the evening, the wind whispered its way up from the south-west. By midnight the whisper had developed into a roar accompanied by near-solid rain, driving the *Heron* eastwards under a minimum of sail with the deck canted over at a sharp angle and the lee scuppers in the sea. The weather kept Lamb on deck throughout the night but Sylvester brought up occasional reports of Fox's condition.

'His stump's weeping a bit, sir.'

'He's awake, sir, but he don't look good. I wouldn't be surprised if he cut his painter afore long, sir.'

The rain abruptly ceased, the wind eased and the clouds rolled away to the north-east. The damp deck began to dry rapidly from the heat of the new sun and Lamb stretched, yawned, ordered the mainsail to be loosed and the reefs shaken out of the topsail, and went below for his breakfast.

'The lady said to tell you she thinks Mr Fox is a little improved, sir,' said Sylvester when he brought in the coffee.

'She's changed his bandage and she's says his stump's stopped weeping, sir.'

'I'm glad to hear it,' said Lamb, and turned into his cot with his coffee scarcely tasted.

Three hours later, with a fresh pot of coffee on the table, Lamb buttoned his shirt and listened to Sylvester's latest report.

'Mr Fox is sitting up, sir, and the lady is feeding him a little soup. She said to tell you his fever's down considerable and she's asked me to give him a shave, sir.'

'Good, good,' said Lamb.

He felt an extraordinary uplifting of his spirits at the news, a mixture of pride in his workmanship and relief that he had not, after all, killed the man – a feeling somewhat at odds with his basic, unchanged dislike and contempt for him. It was, he wryly recognized, decidedly strange to find himself so pleased about the recovery of a man who was set on killing him; a man, indeed, whose death he could accept without the slightest twinge of regret – but not yet, not until he knew for certain that he was not to die from the crude surgery. Lamb was thankful that it had been the left hand which he had removed; he had no wish to be accused of having an unfair advantage if and when he ever faced Fox over the barrel of a duelling pistol.

The day was very hot and Lamb took the noon observation in his shirt sleeves, his foot braced against the carriage of the aftermost gun and his sextant to his eye, waiting for that moment when the sun's centre passed the meridian of the ship, the moment of apparent noon which astronomers termed the sun's culmination and the navy knew as twelve o'clock.

'Captain, might I have a word?' called Mrs Skinner from behind him, cheerfully unaware of the sanctity of the moment and of the shocked frown of disapproval on the quartermaster's face.

'Just give me a second, ma'am,' muttered Lamb. 'Make it twelve!' he cried, lowering his instrument and scribbling the reading on his shirt cuff.

'Strike eight bells!' roared the quartermaster.

The empty glass was turned, the first stroke of the bell sounded, and Timm's voice shivered the air again. 'Pipe to

78

dinner!'

The waiting seamen, who had been hovering with sharp appetites, dry tongues and ears cocked for the magic call, melted below almost before Snow had licked his whistle, leaving the deck to the helmsman, the quartermaster, Lamb and Mrs Skinner.

'My, they don't need calling twice, do they?' murmured the lady in admiration, gazing in wonder at the suddenly empty deck.

'Food and rum are ever uppermost in a seaman's mind, ma'am,' said Lamb, carefully omitting the other major consideration.

'It would certainly seem so and they need it, I dare say, with all the fresh air they have. I do like to see a man eat hearty. I have come to give you news of Mr Fox, captain. His fever is almost gone and his colour is back in his cheeks. He has twice taken nourishment and when I left him just now he was sitting up in bed, quite cheerful, still weak, but as charming as ever. Will you not go downstairs to call on him? He would be so pleased to see you, I know.'

'I am certain he would, ma'am, but at the moment I am afraid my duties keep me on the deck. Perhaps this afternoon, if I find the time. How is his arm?'

'His stump is hot and the wick is still draining a little pus but the rest of his arm is cool to the touch. It is very encouraging, I think, and although his stump is very tender I am sure he is over the worst now. Poor man! It is a terrible thing to lose a hand, I am sure, but it should not put an end to his life in the Navy, should it? I have seen a number of officers similarly marked – why, Admiral Nelson has but one eye and one arm, has he not? And Mr Fox has both his eyes in his favour. He is such a pleasant, likeable man, don't you think, captain? He is courtesy itself to me and never a word of his pain. Perhaps when the ship is a little steadier we could bring him on deck to take the air? It would do him the world of good.'

'I will bear it in mind, ma'am, certainly. I am very pleased to hear he is doing well.'

Lamb's pleasure was weighted considerably more to the success of his surgery than to Fox's well-being and it was with

79

some reluctance that he later made his way to Fox's cabin. The patient was asleep, his bandaged stump resting on his chest, and Lamb turned away from the open door thankful to have postponed the awkward moment. He would have been happy not to have another meeting with Fox at all, but the suspicion that he was being cowardly over the matter troubled him. He decided to take the bull firmly by the horns and when Jamieson relieved him at the start of the forenoon watch the next morning he went directly to Fox's cabin.

The lieutenant was propped up against a couple of pillows, a bowl of oatmeal on his lap and an open book resting in the crook of his shortened arm. He glanced up as Lamb blocked the light from the door, looked down at his book and carefully spooned some porridge into his mouth, his face expressionless.

'Good morning,' said Lamb curtly, advancing into the cabin. 'You are looking rather better than when I last saw you.'

Fox laid his spoon in the bowl and dabbed at his lips with his napkin. His face gleamed from the closeness of a recent shave and his grey hair had been brushed and tied back in a neat queue.

'To what do I owe the honour of this visit?' he asked, his voice almost back to its previous rich resonance. 'To apologize, perhaps?'

'Apologize? For what? For taking your hand off?'

'No, not that. We both know for what.'

Lamb's lips tightened. 'Yes, and we both know you deserve no apology,' he snapped, his anger swelling.

Fox nodded, as if the reply was not unexpected. 'In that case our arrangement still stands,' he said in a level voice. He picked up his spoon and turned his attention to his book. 'Good day to you, sir.'

Chapter 5

The round, rocky head of the little island of Redonda thrusting a thousand feet into the air was sighted off the starboard beam at first light and shortly after midday the *Heron* was threading her way past the low cliffs that led to the entrance to English Harbour.

'Eleven guns!' shouted Lamb as the cutter turned towards the near-land-locked inner harbour and he picked out the rear-admiral's flag flying lazily in the warm air above the two-decker moored at its western end.

The rolling bark of the *Heron*'s guns rattled off Monk's Hill and Shirley Heights, the grumbling echoes fading amidst the steep, volcanic hills to the west and briefly swelling again to the deeper sound of the flagship's reply. The best bower raised a small explosion of white water beside the starboard bow and the *Heron* sat rocking gently on the blue surface of the harbour. Mrs Skinner and Miss Brown stood at the side as they had for the past hour, with their eyes fixed firmly on the sprawl of buildings ashore. Behind them were piled their bags, boxes and trunks, brought up on deck at Mrs Skinner's insistence several hours before and which she had not counted more than three or four times an hour since. A red-uniformed figure detached itself from the small crowd of watchers ashore and moved towards the jetty steps with a slow, solemn wave at the cutter. Mrs Skinner waved wildly back, fairly dancing with excitement as she saw the Marine clamber down into a boat. She turned towards Lamb with a tiny square of lacy cambric pressed to her large nose.

'He is here, captain.' She dabbed at her eyes. 'Oh, you must excuse me. I cannot help it. What a silly woman I am, being so tearful at my age.'

Lamb smiled, touched by her tears. 'Not at all, ma'am. It is a very happy day for you. Look, his boat is shoving off now.'

He had developed a warm affection for Mrs Skinner since their first, frosty meeting and her many-faceted nature – by turns hectoring, warm, garrulous, caring, demanding and infuriating – had been a daily source of surprise, exasperation and amusement for him. Her gallant husband, he thought, might have had a wearing life with her but it could scarcely have been dull.

'You will call on us before you leave?' she asked. 'You and Mr Jamieson?'

'I insist on doing so, ma'am,' said Lamb. He gave a roguish smile. 'I have much to tell Major Skinner about the activities of a certain lady acquaintance of mine.' She laughed at this, delighted.

The boat from the Harbour Captain's office hooked onto the chains, the boat carrying Major Skinner came alongside and Lamb and Jamieson busied themselves in surpervising the transfer of the mail-bags as the major clambered aboard and took his wife in his arms. Jamieson followed the mail down into the boat and was pulled towards the shore. Lamb was introduced to the major, a heavy, bluff, laughing man so much like his wife in appearance that they might have shared the same parents.

'I am happy to make your acquaintance, captain,' said the major, crushing Lamb's hand in his massive paw.

'And I yours, sir.' Lamb caught sight of Fox emerging from the aft companionway supported by Sylvester, his left arm strapped across his chest. 'I must not keep the admiral waiting for his mail but I hope to see you and Mrs Skinner again before I sail. Perhaps you would be kind enough to find room in your boat for Mr Fox there?'

'Of course, of course,' cried Mrs Skinner, answering for her husband.

Lamb bowed. 'I will say goodbye, then, ma'am. Major. Miss Brown.'

'Goodbye, Mr Lamb. We will see you again soon, do not forget,' said Mrs Skinner, clinging to her husband's arm.

'I am pleased to have met you, sir,' smiled the major.

Miss Brown said nothing but lifted her head long enough to give Lamb a flash of her bright, blue eyes. Lamb thought that it had been a great error on his part not to have insisted that the delightful Miss Brown have a cabin to herself. Another of life's lost opportunities, he sighed.

Timms was waiting at the side standing guard over the leather pouches containing the admiral's official mail. Fox, standing near him, kept his gaze firmly to his front as Lamb passed him.

'Right, down you go, quartermaster,' said Lamb.

The quartermaster descended nimbly into the boat, where he was transformed instantly into the captain's coxswain, and held up his hand for the pouches. Lamb swung his leg over the side. For a brief, cold moment he found himself looking into Fox's eyes and then Fox had turned his head away and Lamb was lowering himself into the boat.

'Shove off,' ordered Lamb. 'Give way together.'

The boat pulled away from the side. Lamb lifted the pouches from the bottom of the boat and draped them over his knee.

'The flagship's signalling, sir,' growled Timms. 'Our number, sir.'

Lamb glanced at the flagship's bare masts. He had seen the same signal often enough to know it immediately.

'Captain to repair aboard, sir,' translated Timms.

'Thank you, Timms,' said Lamb. 'Don't bother to acknowledge,' he added, raising a smile from the quartermaster's weatherbeaten face, while wondering uneasily for what reason a lowly packet commander would be summoned to the flagship.

Had Lamb been a captain in the proper sense of the word, sporting at least one epaulette on his shoulder, he would have stepped onto the deck of the *Hengist* to the stamp and clash of Marine feet and muskets, the wail of the boatswain's pipe and the respectful attendance of white-gloved side-boys. As a mere penny-a-dozen lieutenant, and a rather shabby one at that, he expected to be greeted by no one grander than the duty officer and was a little alarmed to be met not only by that officer but also by the captain of the flagship himself, a tall, imposing individual with an epaulette on each shoulder.

Lamb touched his hat to the quarterdeck, touched it again for the benefit of the captain and brought his hand down to

83

shake the proffered hand.

'How d'ye do? My name is Mortimer. This is Lieutenant Ironfellow.'

'Lamb, sir. I am pleased to meet you, sir. And you, Mr Ironfellow.'

'Take care of the mail, Mr Ironfellow,' said Mortimer. The lieutenant, an officer dressed to such perfection that Lamb blushed to stand beside him, gave a pleasant smile and relieved Lamb of his pouches. Mortimer turned towards the quarter-deck and Lamb fell into step alongside.

'I was rather expecting to see Pardoe,' said the captain as they paced along the vast, white deck, so perfectly scrubbed that the tiniest spot of tar fallen from aloft would have shrieked its trespass to the heavens.

'He is in hospital at Port Royal, sir, I am sorry to say.'

'Indeed? The admiral has asked for a word with you. I believe he has a small favour to beg. Did you have a quiet trip?'

'Fair to middling, sir. We had one slight brush with a French privateer, a topsail schooner.'

'Oh, yes?' murmured Mortimer with a complete lack of interest. 'I would appreciate a quiet word when the admiral has finished with you, if you would be so kind.'

'Of course, sir,' said Lamb, his unease giving way to sudden alarm.

They mounted the wide companion ladder to the quarter-deck, crossed the immaculate planks in silence and halted at the door beneath the poop-deck, flanked on one side by a Marine sentry stiff with pipe clay, crossed belts and discipline and on the other by a lieutenant who flashed a well-practised smile at Lamb and a nervous glance at Mortimer.

'Lieutenant Lamb, Lieutenant Bowers,' said Mortimer, gesturing from one to the other by way of introduction. 'Mr Bowers is the admiral's flag lieutenant.'

Bowers was a round, plump young man with a round, plump young face. He shot out his hand. 'Delighted to make your acquaintance. Were you not with the *Adroit* and Captain Slade?'

'Yes,' said Lamb. 'I still am, officially. The packet is a very temporary command.'

'Then you must be the fellow who stormed the fort on San Paulo. I recollect . . .'

'Mr Bowers will take you in to the admiral,' cut in Mortimer briskly. 'You can manage that, can you, Mr Bowers, without getting lost or falling down?'

'I will do my best, sir,' said Bowers, giving Lamb a slightly desperate grin.

Lamb gathered from this little exchange that the flag lieutenant did not bask in the warmth of Mortimer's unreserved admiration and he stepped quickly into the breach in order to forestall any further attack on the poor fellow's feelings.

'You are very kind, Mr Bowers.'

Mortimer gave a cynical grunt and strode off, leaving Lamb to follow the flag lieutenant and to arrive, quite without mishap, at the door of the admiral's great aft cabin.

'Lieutenant Lamb, sir, of the packet *Heron*,' announced Bowers.

'Lamb? Lamb?' cried the admiral from behind his enormous table. 'Come in, sir, come in. What have you done with Pardoe?'

Lamb tucked his hat beneath his arm and advanced into the wide cabin, bathed in the strong light streaming in from the great windows at the admiral's back.

'I regret to say that he was taken ill, sir. He is in hospital at Port Royal.'

Rear-Admiral Sir Sydney Upton removed his shapeless, yellowing wig, tossed it on to his cluttered table and vigorously scratched his hairless skull.

'Sit yourself down, Mr Lamb, there's a good fellow. I shall damage my neck looking up at you. Now, you have mail for Barbados, I take it?'

'Yes, sir.'

'And from there you head back to Port Royal?'

'Yes, sir.'

'Yes.' Upton drummed his fingers and stared thoughtfully at Lamb for a few seconds. Lamb sat upright on his chair with his hat on his lap and fixed his eyes at the corner of the cabin, thinking that if it was only a small favour the admiral had to ask, he was being damned long-winded about it. His sense of

85

nervousness increased. Upton cleared his throat.

'I have a small favour to beg of you, Mr Lamb. A domestic matter. Some twelve months ago my nephew, Commander Brett, was drowned off Tortuga. His widow has remained on Antigua since his death and now I am desirous that she should be returned – she should return to her family in England and to that end I would be grateful if you would give her passage to Kingston from where she can take the next convoy home.'

'I shall be happy to, sir,' said Lamb, wondering why the lady's departure was thought to be so urgent that she could not wait for the next homeward-bound ship from Antigua.

'I have no wish to burden you with my family problems, Mr Lamb,' continued Upton, picking up his pen and studying it with great interest. 'It will be sufficient for me to say, I think, that it would be better all round if Mrs Brett leaves Antigua without delay and if that means she has to travel home by way of Jamaica, so be it.'

'I see, sir,' murmured Lamb.

Upton shot him a sharp glance. 'I doubt that you do, but we will leave it at that. Now unfortunately I must delay your departure until Thursday. His Excellency is giving a ball at Clarence House on Wednesday evening to celebrate his niece's engagement and Mrs Brett has set her heart on attending. She is quite adamant, in fact, that she will not leave Antigua until after Wednesday and I had to give way on that point. I hope you can accommodate me on the matter, Mr Lamb.'

'Of course, sir,' said Lamb, whose option on the matter was nil.

'You are very kind. I will make sure that you and your first lieutenant receive invitations for Wednesday evening. It may give you a chance to make your acquaintance with the lady. Bowers can take you along; he knows everyone on the island.'

'You are most kind, sir.'

'I hope so, Mr Lamb, I hope so.' Upton sighed and shook his ancient head. 'God save us simple seamen from the unfathomable minds and moods of women. Good day to you, Mr Lamb.'

Mortimer was standing at the quarterdeck rail as Lamb left the admiral's quarters and he raised a beckoning finger.

'The admiral has asked his favour?' he enquired as Lamb

touched his hat.

'Yes, sir. I am to give passage to a Mrs Brett as far as Kingston.'

'Yes, I know. Did he give you any reason for her departure?'

Lamb hesitated, not sure if it was proper to discuss the admiral's private affairs with his flag captain.

'I have particular reasons for asking,' said Mortimer. 'I am well acquainted with the lady, as it happens.'

A certain earnestness in his tone and look came through to Lamb and with it the probable reason for Mrs Brett's hasty return to England. Oh ho! So that's the way of it, he thought.

'Admiral Upton gave no reason, sir,' he said firmly. 'I understand it is a family matter of his, that is all.'

Mortimer smiled. 'I see.' He took Lamb by the elbow and steered him towards the quarterdeck ladder. 'You will not be sailing until Thursday, I gather?'

'No, sir. Apparently Mrs Brett has set her heart on attending the Governor's ball.'

'Well, a day here or there makes no difference to you fellows,' said Mortimer genially. 'I had charge of a cutter once, many years ago. They were happy days! I lost it in the Gulf of Lions – run down one night by a first-rate.'

They halted at the entry port and Mortimer nodded downwards. 'I took the liberty of sending your boat away but my gig will take you back to the *Heron*. Good day to you, captain.'

Mortimer strode away over his faultless planking leaving Lamb to stare after him with an indignant glare. Sending his boat away, indeed! Embarrassed to have it alongside his damned perfection of a ship, no doubt. Presumptious bastard! He climbed down into the gig and took his seat in the stern. The gig was manned by a crew brilliantly and uniformly rigged out in red and white stripes and the boat itself was a model of scrubbed timber and fresh, gleaming, unmarked paintwork. Lamb was rowed back to the cutter feeling like a shabby intruder.

The gig arrived at the *Heron*'s side just ahead of the cutter's own boat returning from the shore with Jamieson on board and Lamb noticed with a keen sense of shame the superior,

87

deprecatory glances of the *Hengist*'s men at the ill-matched, stained and patched clothing sported by his own men. As he reached the deck of the *Heron* and the red and white stripes pulled away, he heard a low, indistinct voice from among them call out something to the cutter's boat in an insulting tone and the loud, clear voice of Blackett in scornful reply: 'Fuckin' barber's poles!'

Lamb grinned and walked aft with his heart lightened.

The Navy Office proved to be astonishingly accommodating and Lamb returned to the *Heron* with a month's pay jingling endearingly in his pocket. Sylvester was despatched ashore with a long list and most of Lamb's money and the pair of them were checking the purchases against the list and going over the steward's unconventional arithmetic for the third or fourth time when Jamieson appeared at the door with Bowers's beaming face behind him.

'Good afternoon, Mr Bowers,' cried Lamb over Sylvester's shoulder. 'To what do I owe the pleasure of this visit?'

'I come as postman, sir,' said Bowers, holding two envelopes in the air. 'One for you and one for Jamieson here.'

'Well, that deserves a glass or two of wine, at least. Step in, sir, and take a seat. You, too, Mr Jamieson – sit yourself on my cot. Just move my new stockings along first. If you tore them I would never forgive you. You would never believe what they cost me – according to Sylvester here, that is.'

Sylvester dredged up an expression of deep hurt and sidled his way out of the cabin while Lamb brushed wisps of straw from a bottle and pulled the cork.

'Here you are, sir,' said Bowers, dropping the envelopes onto the table. 'Invitations to the ball. There is no need to reply; I took the liberty of doing that for you when I collected them. Not that it would have mattered, in any case, because these affairs are pretty informal, as a rule. The admiral has asked me to accompany you and I shall be happy to do so, if you have no objections.'

'None at all,' said Lamb as he poured the wine. 'You are most kind. Perhaps there will be an opportunity for Mr Jamieson and me to meet our new passenger, Mrs Brett.'

88

'Ah, the lovely Charlotte.' Bowers took a gulp from his glass and smacked his lips appreciatively. 'Delightful, sir. Your very good health. Yes, I heard that you were taking the lady from us. There will be a great many hopes and ambitions dashed when she leaves – and a good deal of relief in the mind of one particular person of my acquaintance.'

'Admiral Upton, d'you mean?'

Bowers drained his glass and placed it on the table next to the bottle. 'Yes, perhaps, but he was not the one I had in mind. I must not say too much, of course, but without mentioning any names – ah, thank you, a delightful wine, this – yes, without mentioning any names I can say that a certain senior officer's marriage and career prospects will not be damaged by Charlotte's departure.'

'And why would that be?' demanded Jamieson bluntly.

'Why? Well, when you have the widow – the young widow – of a commander who has been dead for little more than a year, and that commander was the nephew of the admiral, and the widow causes tongues to wag over her relationship with a senior officer on the admiral's staff, and the officer's own wife is in a certain delicate condition and is apparently unaware of the gossip, why, there you have all the ingredients of a situation that can only cause grief. I think that Admiral Upton has taken the only move he could to defuse the thing before it explodes.'

Lamb collected the glasses and refilled them with the last of the wine in the bottle. He reached for another from its straw packing in the case.

'And is there any truth in these rumours?' he asked.

Bowers smiled and spread his hands. 'Who knows? There's no smoke without fire, they say. Charlotte is a very attractive woman and any man, married or not, who did not take his chance if it was offered . . . Well, need I say more?'

'I look forward to meeting this siren,' grinned Lamb.

'No, I would not describe her as a siren,' said Bowers seriously. 'As a matter of fact, I put out a tentative feeler in her direction myself one time but was slapped down in no uncertain fashion. She is a delight to the eye, there is no doubt about that, but by God, she has a sharp tongue on occasion.'

'Show me a woman who has not,' said Lamb. 'Is that an

empty glass in your hand I see?'

'Why, what remarkably keen vision you have, sir,' exclaimed Bowers thrusting forward his glass.

'I would not have said so,' said Jamieson, looking mournfully at his own empty glass.

Lamb laughed, feeling very happy. 'Hand it here, Mr Jamieson, and do me the goodness of opening another bottle.' It was really extremely good wine; he could not remember when he had enjoyed a wine so much.

'Sylvester!' shouted Lamb as he ducked into his cabin and threw his hat onto the cot. He removed his coat, tossed it after his hat and slumped wearily into his chair.

'Sir?'

'Bring me a pot of coffee, there's a good fellow. No, tea, make it tea.'

'One pot of tea it is, sir.'

Major and Mrs Skinner had been lavish in their hospitality but Lamb was now of the opinion that topping up an enormous luncheon with half a bottle of port taken during the hottest hours of the day was a pastime he would in future avoid. His tongue was dry and sticky, the residue of the headache he had earned the afternoon before obstinately refused to leave his skull and he felt quite limp with sweat. He stripped off his shirt and splashed gratefully at his wash basin for a few minutes.

'One pot of tea, sir.'

'Good man.'

'Look, sir, here's the letter you was brought yesterday, under the table, all dirty.' Sylvester crouched and retrieved the envelope, wiping it on his sleeve. 'Look, sir, not even opened yet. From Government House it is.'

'I know it is. Just leave it there.' Lamb towelled his damp hair. 'Find me a clean shirt, would you?'

'That dozen of wine took a fair pasting yesterday, didn't it, sir?' remarked Sylvester as he cast a gloomy eye at Lamb's clean shirt. 'Five of'em gone already. That's – that's nearly half of it gone in one day. You would have done better to spend your money on a new shirt, if you ask me, sir.'

'Stop your bloody blethering, man, and take that dirty shirt away with you. I shall want it back tomorrow looking better than new.'

'I can but try, sir. Any other little miracles you want doing while I'm at it, sir?'

'Yes, a civil tongue from you, for a start.'

Cold water, a clean shirt and a pint of tea left Lamb feeling considerably more comfortable and he leaned back in his chair and opened the crested envelope with a sense of cool well-being. As he was admiring the elegant loops and whirls of the script on the card, he felt a slight bump against the side of the cutter and his chair tilted a fraction as the deck heeled to the weight of someone climbing aboard. He sat up and hurriedly squared off his books and papers; the harbour captain had yesterday intimated that he might find time to pay the *Heron* a visit and Lamb had no wish to receive him across an untidy table; the cutter's replenishment of supplies and victuals could well suffer over such trifles. He had slipped the tea-tray out of sight beneath his cot and was buttoning his coat when knuckles rapped at his door and the quartermaster put his square, brown face around the edge of it.

'Beg pardon, sir. There's a Marine lieutenant on deck asking if he can have a word with you, sir. Shitwell, he said his name was, sir.'

Lamb paused in the act of buttoning.

'What name did you say?'

'Shitwell, sir.' The quartermaster's face was stonily expressionless.

'Right, Timms, show Mr – show him down.'

The Marine was very large and very bulky, almost filling the doorway as he ducked his head to enter.

'Come and sit yourself down, sir,' said Lamb, fearful of a nasty encounter between the giant's skull and the low beams.

'You are very kind,' grunted the lieutenant with relief as he lowered his massive buttocks onto the chair. He extended a slab of a hand across the table. 'Charles Sitwell, sir.'

Lamb noted with inward amusement that his visitor spoke with a marked lisp. 'Matthew Lamb. I am pleased to meet you, Mr Sitwell. What can I do for you?'

'I must tell you at the outset that this is no courtesy visit, sir,' said Sitwell. His hair was cropped unfashionably short, giving him a slightly villainous appearance and making his large head seem even larger. Sweat ran from every pore, collecting on the points of nose and chin and dripping onto his scarlet coat. 'I call on you on behalf of Lieutenant Fox, a recent passenger of yours.'

Lamb leaned back in his chair. 'I have been expecting a visit from one of his friends. But you look a trifle warm, sir. Will you not take some refreshment – a glass of wine, or some tea, perhaps?'

'Thank you, sir, but no. I shall not take up many moments of your time.' He extracted a handkerchief from the tight confines of a pocket and mopped his face and neck. 'This is not a task in which I find any pleasure. I can assure you, sir, that I and others have done our damnedest to try to persuade Fox to drop the thing. He is quite fixed on the matter, quite fixed – considers it to be a point of honour and will not be moved at all. I do not know the cause of the – um – disagreement between you, other than his claim that you besmirched his name, and as a consequence, so far as trying to bring the matter to an amicable conclusion is concerned, my hands are tied some-what. Fox says he will accept an apology from you and that is the only other option open to me. I must ask you, sir: are you willing to apologize?'

'No.'

Sitwell nodded. 'Have you any thoughts on the matter at all that you wish to communicate to me, sir?'

'None at all, except that I consider the whole thing to be a bloody nonsense. But if Fox is adamant then I have no choice but to go along with it.'

'Quite, sir.' Sitwell looked far from happy. 'In that case, I must ask you for the name of your second.'

Lamb had given this question some thought over the past few days; he had considered asking Jamieson to be his friend and no doubt the youth would have eagerly acquiesed, if only out of loyalty. A little thought, however, had persuaded Lamb that it would not be proper for his first officer to act for him. In addition, there was always the very real chance of either himself or Fox being killed, and while a duel itself was not unlawful, if it resulted in a death then the seconds on both sides were liable to be charged with conspiracy to murder. Jamieson was barely eighteen years old and Lamb, with his superiority of several years, did not consider it to be fair for the young lieutenant to be put at such risk on his behalf. He had no such qualms about Lieutenant Bowers; not only was the flag lieutenant of much the same age as Lamb and unconnected with the *Heron*, he was also, in Lamb's opinion, a person one could easily grow to dislike with the very shortest of acquaintance.

'I had thought of asking Lieutenant Bowers, the admiral's flag lieutenant,' he said. 'Are you acquainted with him?'

'Oh, yes. He is a very suitable choice. I am sure he would agree. He has acted as second on at least one other occasion, to my knowledge.'

'I will have a word with him this afternoon. You will be discussing details with him, I take it, if he is agreeable?'

'I will, indeed, sir. Perhaps you could ask him to call on me at the garrison later today? The sooner the matter is finished the better for all concerned; if it reaches the ears of the authorities they will certainly do their best to stop it. Would first light tomorrow suit you?'

'It will have to,' said Lamb. 'I sail for Barbados the morning after.'

'And I sincerely hope you do, sir, with all my heart.' The Marine shifted uneasily in his chair and examined his furry knuckles. 'There is one avenue which has been suggested to me as worth exploring.' He glanced at Lamb with a hesitant smile on his broad face. 'You will not take offence if I mention it?'

'I am sure you would not be deliberately offensive, Mr Sitwell. Speak on.'

'It is a legal point, a somewhat obscure one, perhaps, but one that you might care to reflect on. It has been pointed out to me that although Mr Fox was a passenger on your vessel, he also served at the guns during your skirmish with a privateer. He thus, temporarily at least, became an officer serving under your command, and for him to challenge his captain would, of course, be quite illegal. It is a point worth considering, sir, and one that you could take up with no loss of honour.'

Lamb shook his head. 'I think not. It is a moot point and as you say, an obscure one. I will certainly not hide behind such fine niceties. So far as I am concerned, Mr Fox was a passenger and is an officer of equal rank. If you have nothing more to say, Mr Sitwell, then I will bid you good-day.'

Sitwell nodded. 'Very well, sir. I did not think for one moment that you would give it serious consideration but I would have been failing in my duty had I not brought it up. I will see you at first light tomorrow, sir.'

He rose from his chair and drove his skull on to one of the deck beams with a force that shook the cabin and set the lantern swinging. Lamb sprang from his chair and gripped Sitwell by the arm as he staggered blindly with eyes shut tight and both hands pressed tightly to his scalp.

'Have you damaged yourself, Mr Sitwell?' enquired Lamb solicitously, doing his utmost to control the wide grin that threatened to overcome his clenched cheek muscles. He had cracked his own head often enough in the past and knew of the intense agony it gave; it was always the occasion for vast hilarity for everyone but the poor sufferer.

'No, no, it was nothing, the merest touch,' said Sitwell bravely. He gave a ghastly grin, tears of pain glistening on his eyelashes. 'Truly, I scarcely felt it.'

'I am relieved to hear it,' said Lamb, guiding his visitor to the foot of the companionway. 'You were fortunate, sir. I have known such encounters to be quite painful.'

'Give way together,' ordered Lamb quietly, and settled back against the transom with his hand on the boat's tiller. It was still quite dark; to the west and overhead, the stars shone coldly and brilliantly in the black, cloudless sky but to the east their sharp radiance was already dimming under the influence of the approaching day.

Half an hour to dawn, thought Lamb, perhaps the last sunrise he would ever see, and although the air was warm, he felt suddenly chilled. He pressed his breast pocket wherein was the letter he had written to his father and wondered whether he would have the sweet pleasure of tearing it into shreds before the morning was an hour older. The sound of a sentry's challenge rang out through the hushed air from the towering

94

Shirley Heights and was followed by the faint clash of nailed shoes and musket butts on the stone flags of the fort as the guard was changed. Lamb burrowed his chin deeper into his collar, feeling the rasp of his hastily shaven jaw against the cloth. He had slept badly, long periods of wakefulness interspersed with fitful dozing and dreaming, and had at last fallen into a deep sleep only minutes, it had seemed, before the night watchman had called him. The cold water and the vigorous splashing and towelling had driven the sleep from his brain. While he was dressing, Sylvester – blessed man! – had silently entered the cabin and placed a steaming mug of coffee on the table; the hot, invigorating essence had been like nectar. He had said nothing of his appointment this morning, not even to Jamieson, but he was quite certain that there was not a man on board the *Heron* who was not aware of what was in the wind; their grave, set faces, the complete absence of laughter and Sylvester's unsolicited mug of coffee delivered without a word told all. Lamb was not surprised; he had long known that seamen had the ability to extract information from a ship's very timbers.

The night lantern above the head of the slow-pacing sentry at the powder magazine was lined up with the bow and Lamb shifted the tiller slightly, aiming to land a little to the west, away from any curious eyes that might already be awake at the capstan house or the malt and canvas stores.

'In oars,' he murmured as the pale line of narrow beach loomed ahead. The boat dug her nose gently into the gritty shallows and Lamb picked his way between the oarsmen and stepped into the few inches of warm, black water.

'Back to the ship, Timms,' he ordered. 'Pick me up at the steps at six bells.'

'Aye aye, sir,' came the quartermaster's low growl. 'Good luck, sir,' he added quietly as Lamb turned away. Lamb made no answer and plunged into the low scrub edging the beach, heading for the narrow, twisting road that led up to the heights overlooking the harbour.

It was a steep, leg-wracking climb and he pushed himself hard, worried by the slipping minutes. He was warm and panting when he breasted the heights and saw the lone figure of Bowers silhouetted against the paling sky, his cloak wrapped tightly around him.

'Lamb?' called Bowers anxiously.

'The very same.'

'Thank God! I was beginning to think that you were not coming.'

Lamb gave a dry laugh. 'It is my going that you should be more concerned about.' He tugged his watch from his waistcoat pocket and thumbing it open, tilted it towards the pink and lime sky to the east. 'Twenty minutes past. We are in good time.'

'There is the path,' said Bowers, pointing. 'We just have to follow it.'

They struck out over the rough, hilly ground to the west, away from the squat, brooding massiveness of the fort, following the narrow path that meandered through the low bush and sparse grass. Seven or eight minutes of silent walking brought them above a small area of level ground, a short, blind valley between low, volcanic hills, cut off by steeply rising ground at one end and giving a glimpse of the sea at the other. The darkness had softened, thinned and given way to the pink light that filled the eastern sky during their walk and Bowers halted and gestured below him.

'There,' he said, somewhat breathless. 'Just the place, is it not? Very quiet, nicely out of the way and the hills muffle the sound of the pistols.'

'Yes, excellent,' muttered Lamb, quite without enthusiasm.

'The others are there waiting, look,' said Bowers. 'Come, let us step out. It would not do to be late.'

A figure separated from the small group below as Lamb and Bowers descended and walked towards them with a cheerful wave of his arm.

'This is Harry Winterton, your other second,' said Bowers.

'How d'you do?' said Lamb, extending his hand. 'It is very good of you to come along.'

Winterton beamed and vigorously pumped Lamb's hand. 'Not at all, my dear sir. A pleasure, an absolute pleasure. I jumped at the chance when Bowers asked me.' His round, youthful face shone with pleasurable anticipation. 'We have walked up and down kicking all the loose rocks to one side.

There is no fear of either of you stumbling; you could play billiards on it, almost.'

'Thank you. I am vastly comforted,' said Lamb dryly. He glanced across at the other men. Fox had his back to him, a black sling supporting his left arm, his right hand resting on a stout cane. The bulky figure of Sitwell towered over him, a large, flat box tucked beneath his arm; he was engaged in earnest conversation with another Marine – Fox's other second, Lamb surmised. A little to one side a fat man in dirty stockings and shapeless green coat sat on a convenient rock thoughtfully puffing at a pipe. He had the look of a surgeon or surgeon's mate written large all over him.

Sitwell finished his discussion and strode towards them.

'Good morning, gentlemen,' he boomed. 'Mr Lamb, my principal informs me that he is willing, even at this late stage, to accept an apology from you, sir.'

'I have no doubt he is, but I must disappoint him,' said Lamb. The sun winked redly above the edge of the distant sea, flooding the hills with warm light and deep pockets of black shadow. Lamb began to remove his coat, suddenly impatient to have the business over. 'Let us get on with the damned thing – it is what we are here for, is it not?'

'Very well, sir.' Sitwell jerked at the hem of his jacket and walked away with his head up, huge and dignified.

Lamb dropped his coat and waistcoat in an untidy heap at his feet. 'There is a letter for my father in my coat pocket, Mr Bowers. If the need arises, would you be kind enough to send it off at the earliest opportunity?'

'Of course. Are you quite ready?'

Lamb nodded and they set off to where Sitwell stood like a massive outcrop of red rock. They waited in silence for Fox to join them; he and his other second were having some difficulty in removing his coat and the surgeon stepped over from his boulder and assisted them in the awkward business of easing the sleeve over the thickly bandaged stump. Ready at last, with his arm settled again into its sling, Fox took up his stick and picked his way across the uneven ground.

'I am sorry to have kept you waiting, gentlemen,' he said cheerfully as he drew near. He nodded politely to Bowers, his

97

grey eyes rested briefly on Lamb's face, and he tossed his cane to one side. 'I am at your disposal, Mr Sitwell.'

The Marine removed the box from beneath his arm and turned back the lid, balancing the case on one broad hand.

'Primed and loaded with one-ounce ball but not cocked, as you can see. They have hair-triggers, gentlemen; they need but the very slightest pull.' He proffered the case to Lamb. 'It is your privilege to have the first choice, sir.'

Lamb took the nearest pistol from its velvet nest and hefted its weight in his hand. It was a beautiful weapon, superbly balanced, with chased silver overlay around the breech and inlaid with silver and ivory on the butt. Just one of the pair would have cost him a year's pay, he thought.

'Stand back to back, gentlemen, if you please,' said Bowers, pompously coming into his own. 'Be so good as to point your weapons at the sky. I shall count to ten. At the count of one, you will commence your pacing. At the count of ten, you will turn and fire at will. Cock your weapons.'

Lamb thumbed back the hammer, keeping his eyes on the distant, wrinkled sea, feeling faintly surprised at his calmness. He felt no fear, no anger, not a trace of nervousness, but idiotically, only a sense of regret that he had smudged the ink on the hastily sealed letter to his father. He should have taken the trouble to use a fresh envelope, he thought; it would not have taken a moment.

'One!'

Lamb walked slowly forward, keeping his eyes on the sea, taking his pace from Bower's counting. The low, red sun, still only a quarter above the horizon, was full in his face and he looked a little to one side, anxious not to lose the sharpness of his vision. The thought flashed through his mind that he would have the advantage of having the sun at his back when he turned.

'Five!'

Until this moment he had not known what he would do when he turned to face Fox but suddenly, without further thought, the decision was made, clear and hard. He would let Fox fire first. If he was hit and could still stand he would aim to kill. If Fox should miss, then he would aim wide.

'Ten!'

Lamb spun on his heel, his mind cold, his arm outstretched and his eye along the barrel aimed squarely at Fox's chest. He saw Fox stagger as he aimed his pistol, perhaps still weak on his legs as he turned or unbalanced because of his slung arm. For a moment Lamb thought he would fall as his pistol waved wildly, and Sitwell took a pace towards him, reaching out with his arm.

'Stand back!' snapped Fox, recovering himself. 'Leave me alone.'

Lamb waited, his arm and pistol absolutely steady. He could have killed him then, he thought, felled him as he stood. Fox levelled his weapon again and for a long, timeless instant Lamb stared at its blind, black, evil little eye. His hand is none too steady, he reflected, and with the thought, Fox fired. The breath of the bullet's passage close to his ear and the stunning bang of the pistol froze his mind for a second; he was certain that he had been hit. Fox lowered his weapon and stared at him with bitter disappointment, anguish written on every line of his face. Then a wave of relief and exultation swept through Lamb as he realized he was unharmed and with slow, grim determination he brought down his pistol until it was aimed unmistakably at Fox's groin. A loud hiss of indrawn breath sounded from one of the watching men. Fox held Lamb's gaze, his eyes wide, his mouth slightly agape. For a long, stretched moment it was so quiet that Lamb could hear the rushing of the blood in his ears.

Fox hurled his pistol at him. 'Damn you!' he cried. 'Shoot! Shoot!'

Lamb moved his arm widely to one side and pulled the trigger. The ball kicked up a puff of dust twenty yards away. He turned and strode back to his clothes, tossing the pistol to Winterton as he passed, the young lieutenant staring after him open-mouthed. Bowers came hurrying over, stretching out his hand and wearing an enormous grin.

'Well done, well done, my dear fellow! Give me your hand. What coolness you showed! How sick that fellow Fox must be feeling!' He peered up at Lamb's left ear. 'I saw you start and thought you had been hit hard, but it is almost nothing, the merest nick, more blood than anything.' He groped for Lamb's hand again and pumped it. 'It was quite the coolest thing I've seen. God, how humiliated Fox must feel!'

Lamb craned his head round and peered at his shoulder, startled to see bright blood staining his shirt. He put his hand to his ear and winced as his fingers felt wet, torn flesh, the pain not great but insistently smarting. Fox had been too bloody close there, he thought; another inch to the right and he would have been a dead man.

'Hold hard, sir!' It was the surgeon, picking his way across the rough ground, his pipe sticking jauntily from his mouth. 'Let me take a look at that wound before you don your coat.'

He had lost a tiny part of his earlobe, the surgeon informed him, hardly a wound at all, not worth the expense of a dressing. It was nothing for him to be concerned over, it would not affect his hearing and he would be as attractive to the ladies as ever – perhaps even more so, the man added, with a wheezy, tobacco-rich chuckle.

Lamb glanced covertly at Fox as the surgeon's pipe bubbled busily beside his ear. The lieutenant was seated on a large boulder staring grim-faced into the distance as his second struggled to get his sleeve over his arm. Sitwell stood over him, talking very earnestly and shaking one of his pistols beneath Fox's nose; from the expression on the Marine's face, he was not pleased at the cavalier way Fox had treated his pistol.

The surgeon gave Lamb's ear a final dab and tossed the bloody swab to the ground. 'There, sir, I can do no more for you.' He chuckled. 'If you should ever wish to sport an earring, your choice of ear is now limited to one. Good day to you, sir.'

Lamb shrugged into his coat and carefully placed his hat on his head at a rakish angle to keep it clear of his torn ear. He grinned at Bowers and Winterton. 'I thank you both, gentlemen, for your kindness this morning. There is nothing to keep us here now, I think. Shall we go?'

Chapter 6

Bowers was waiting for them at the steps and he and Lamb and Jamieson made the long climb up the hill in the soft, warm, dark air, the plump flag lieutenant begging them to halt from time to time, complaining that the damned hill would kill him one of these days. The veranda and windows of both floors of Clarence House were ablaze with lights and as they approached they could hear the sound of music from within, violins, violoncellos and flutes. Several Marine officers, splendid in scarlet, lounged on the steps, clutching glasses and roaring with laughter. The veranda was thronged with colour, scarlet uniforms glowing amidst the plain blue and white of the Navy and the severer black and white of the civilians but here and there, outshining even the Marines, gleaming stones, soft white shoulders and upthrust bosoms overflowed from dresses of the palest blue and green and gold and pink.

'Hold hard, wait a second, you fellows,' panted Bowers as they neared the steps. 'I am gushing sweat from every pore, damn it.' He plucked his handkerchief from his cuff and mopped his streaming face and neck. Lamb and Jamieson grinned slyly at each other, amused. 'That's better. Damn that bloody hill!'

They ascended the steps, eased their way through the crush on the veranda and dropped their cards on to the silver tray held by the ancient black footman.

'A word of advice,' said Bowers as they walked towards the open doors of the ballroom. 'Steer clear of the sherry. It is quite abominable. I always stick to the punch at His Excellency's affairs. It is very drinkable but be warned – it is more potent than it tastes.'

They entered the large, brightly-lit room where couples pranced and swirled beneath the high domed ceiling and music swelled from a small dais at the far end. It was already crowded; people sat and stood at the small tables ranged along the sides of the room and wandered between them. The room hummed with voices attempting to be heard over the sound of the music, and loud laughter and the noise of dancing, drumming feet swelled to the ceiling. Bowers paused in the doorway and carefully scanned the room.

'My beloved captain is here already,' he said, nodding towards one end of the room. 'We shall keep our distance, if you have no objection. The punch-bowl is this way, fortunately.'

The sharp astringency of lime, lemon and alcohol was delicious. Lamb sipped appreciatively from his glass as Bowers pointed out various notables to him and Jamieson and introduced them both to passing acquaintances. It soon became clear to Lamb that he was the object of a great deal of interest. Strangers came up to him, introduced themselves, shook his hand, peered at his ear and left smiling. Ladies gave him curious glances as they passed by, turning their heads to look again, whispering behind their fans. The business of the morning's exchange of shots with Fox was never once mentioned, not even obliquely, but it was quite apparent that the affair and Lamb's part in it were widely known. He wondered uneasily whether he was regarded as hero, villain or fool and he was grateful for the company of the loquacious Bowers and the silent, beaming, steadily-imbibing Jamieson; had he been on his own with all this attention levelled at him he might have broken and run.

Sitwell came up to him, huge, sweating, much the worse for drink, his lisp more pronounced than ever.

'Ha-ha! Here he is, the cool dog!' His booming laugh rang out above the music, causing heads to turn and stare. 'Give me your hand, sir – you left before I had the chance to shake it this morning.' He crushed Lamb's fingers in his enormous spade of a hand and leaned close, lowering his voice to a confidential shout. 'That fellow Fox bloody near shit himself this morning, ha! ha! ha! And serve him right, the bloody toad. Damned near ruined my pistol, the bugger!' He gave Lamb a friendly, bruising slap on the arm and moved off through the crowd, threading his way delicately through the maze of little tables and leaving behind him a trail of spilled glasses and indignant stares and curses.

'Look,' said Bowers, giving Lamb a nudge. 'There is the Governor's niece, the dwarfish girl in pink, betrothed to the poor fool dancing all over her feet. Did you ever see such an ill-matched pair? The only thing they have in common is money: she has it and he wants it.'

Jamieson, well into his fourth or fifth glass, giggled as he drank, and choked and coughed, soaking his shirt front with punch.

'Oh, very good, very good.' he spluttered.

Bowers slapped him on the back to restore his wind and whispered something into his ear, bringing on another shout of laughter. Lamb turned away from them a little in order to distance himself from their juvenile behaviour and gazed at the swirl of colour and warm flesh in the centre of the room, entranced by the sight of so many flushed, excited female faces and the delightful spectacle of dozens of half-exposed, bobbing breasts parading past his appreciative eye. He bent his head towards the inanely chuckling officers beside him.

'Bowers, which of these lovelies is Mrs Brett?' he asked.

Bowers raised himself on his toes and surveyed the dancers. 'I'm damned if I can see her. You will not mistake her once you lay eyes on her for she's by far the best-looking woman on the island. I expect she's surrounded by a horde of . . . Ah, there she is. At the far end, talking to Mrs Mortimer. She has her back to you.'

'Which, the dark one in blue?'

'Yes. I do like Mrs Mortimer. But she is such a sweet innocent. She has no idea . . .' Bowers stopped short, glanced up at Lamb and laughed, shaking his head. 'Never mind. I was on the verge of being indiscreet, there.'

'Oh, yes?' murmured Lamb absently, intent on studying the cause of so much concern to Admiral Upton and danger to Captain Mortimer's career.

She was of middling height, slim and, from what Lamb could see of her profile, quite lovely. She was standing beside the chair of Mrs Mortimer, a pretty woman some ten years older and quite obviously pregnant. Lamb silently willed Mrs Brett to turn her head so that he could see her face but her attention was held by the animated conversation of Mrs Mortimer. Captain Mortimer was close by, with Admiral Upton and the Governor and his lady. As Lamb watched they were joined by another lady and a man who, from his uniform and rank, Lamb guessed to be the garrison commander. The men and their wives formed a little group of higher beings surrounded by an area of clear space, its margins undefined but scrupulously observed by the passing strollers and the whirling dancers. Lamb's eye was idly resting on the Governor, a grey, imposing man with a weary smile, when he saw Mortimer raise an arm and crook a finger, and he realized with a start of surprise that the captain was signalling to him. He lifted his hand in acknowledgement and turned to break into Bowers's whispered conversation with Jamieson.

'Excuse me for a moment, you two,' he said. 'Captain Mortimer has just beckoned me.'

'Has he, by God?' exclaimed Bowers, giving him a horrified look. 'Ten to one your affair with Fox has reached his ear. Christ, I hope he doesn't know that I was involved; he will make my life hell. We do not get on too well, you know.'

'Courage, my friend,' laughed Lamb, his spirits uplifted by a pint or so of strong punch. He patted Bowers comfortingly on the shoulder. 'If he should ask to see you, I shall tell him you are too drunk to walk.'

'What? What?'

Lamb escaped Bowers's clutching hand and made his way through the press of people, chairs and tables. He paused for a moment with a radiant Mrs Skinner and her husband and broke through into the Governor's little area of uncluttered floor space.

'Ah, good evening, captain,' said Mortimer, tall and splendid, advancing to meet him. 'It was good of you to come over. I thought you might care to meet your passenger, Mrs Brett.' He put a friendly hand on Lamb's shoulder and guided him forward. 'You may find her a trifle edgy,' he murmured quietly. 'You'll forgive her, I'm sure. The prospect of leaving her friends has made her a little – er – triste.'

'Of course, sir,' said Lamb understandingly.

He bent over Mrs Mortimer's hand, received an impression

of a soft, Welsh voice and smiling brown eyes, and was moved on by Mortimer to meet a pair of unsmiling blue eyes set in a stern, beautiful face.

He bowed. 'I am delighted to make your acquaintance, Mrs Brett. I understand you are sailing with me tomorrow.'

'That is my understanding, too, sir,' she said coldly, with a bitter sideways glance at Admiral Upton. That individual, engaged in quiet dialogue with the garrison commander, glanced round as he caught her biting tone, gave her an unrepentant smile, nodded pleasantly to Lamb and resumed his discussion.

'We weigh at eight o'clock, ma'am,' said Lamb. In spite of her chill manner, he found the clear, precise symmetry of her features so entrancing that he was in danger of staring. He smiled down at her. 'You may find things a little cramped but we shall do our best to make you comfortable.'

'Pray, sir, do not put yourself out unnecessarily on my account,' she said. 'I am well used to shipboard life; it holds no terrors or surprises for me.'

'Indeed, that's true, Mr Lamb,' said Mrs Mortimer, giving her a fond smile. 'When her husband was alive they spent many weeks at sea together. I only wish I were as brave.'

Mrs Brett seated herself beside Mrs Mortimer and smoothed the skirt of her dress. 'What is the name of the packet?' she asked, glancing up at Lamb.

'The *Heron*, ma'am.'

She nodded, her eyes travelling slowly from his raw, ragged ear to his worn, hard-brushed coat and his cracked, hard-polished shoes. He found his cheeks beginning to grow warm.

She gave a small smile. 'And you are the captain?' she enquired, in a tone which suggested that this was scarcely possible.

The insult could not have been more clear. Hot blood rushed to Lamb's cheeks.

'I have that honour, ma'am,' he said coldly, seething with humiliation. His entrancement was suddenly gone. The insolent bitch!

Mortimer moved hastily to smooth the ripples. 'Can I get you a glass of something, captain? I do not recommend the sherry but . . .'

'Thank you, sir, but no,' said Lamb. 'I must get back to my friends. If you will excuse me, sir?'

'Oh, captain,' purred Mrs Brett, smiling up at him, suddenly all honey, 'would you be a dear man and fetch me a glass of lime juice? I am dying for want of something cool.'

'Yes, you do look a trifle shiny, ma'am,' said Lamb, rage still boiling within him. 'I shall send one over to you.' He bowed. 'Your servant, ma'am.'

He bowed to Mrs Mortimer and strode off, easing himself into the crowd and working his way back to the punch-bowl.

Bowers gave him a wary look. 'You look none too happy, all of a sudden. Have you had words?'

Lamb forced a reassuring grin and shook his head. 'No, not at all. And not a word about this morning's affair, either. He simply wanted me to meet my new passenger, Mrs Brett.'

'Ah, the lovely Charlotte! A peach, isn't she?'

'Yes, quite charming.' Lamb frowned at Jamieson, slowly swaying backwards and fowards while he beamed happily over his glass at the passing women. 'Can you walk without falling down, Mr Jamieson?'

'Walk, sir? Oh, indeed yes, I can still walk. But give me time, give me time.' Jamieson chuckled inordinately at his wit.

'Well, be so good as to find yourself a glass of lime juice and take it to Mrs Brett with my compliments. And if you can avoid being sick over His Excellency and the Admiral I shall be vastly grateful.'

Lamb poured himself a glass of punch and listened with half an ear to some nonsense from Bowers while he brooded, smarting from his encounter with Mrs Brett. Bloody impudent woman! He ran a critical eye over his uniform and shoes and gave a rueful sigh. He was distinctly shabby, there were no two ways about it. Damn this poverty!

Jamieson returned with his tipsy grin wider than ever, conveying Mrs Brett's grateful thanks and asserting that she was a vision, an absolute vision. Such eyes, such a smile – he was in love, he was sure of it! The supper bell put an end to his ecstatic exclamations and like grains of sand in an hour glass the people in the room began to flow towards the door from all

106

sides, carrying the three lieutenants along with them.

'Smartly, now,' advised Bowers over his shoulder as he insinuated himself firmly into the vortex. 'The hungry wretches will have eaten all the lobster if we don't make haste.'

The hungry wretches had not eaten all the lobster and the inroads they had already made into the cold supper were being quickly made good by the line of bewigged, white-gloved attendants standing behind the long line of tables crowded with sufficient food to convince any midshipman that he had reached Heaven. There were no midshipmen at the Governor's residence tonight but their superiors' appetites almost made up for their absence and the three officers retired to a quiet corner of the supper room with their plates piled high.

A portly man, eyes swimming with drink, lurched up to Lamb and laid a heavy hand on his arm.

'Your pardon, sir, but would your name be Lamb, by any chance?'

'It would, sir,' said Lamb through a mouthful of lobster, drawing his head back from the man's odious breath.

'I am Plumm, sir, garrison physician. Your passenger Lieutenant Fox is under my care. I want to tell you that you did a damned fine piece of knife-work on his arm. Not overly neat, mind you, but in the circus – circum – circumstances, bearing in mind the – er . . . er – circumstances, in the absence of a surgeon, that is, well, in those circumstances . . .' He gave a puzzled frown. 'I keep saying that damned word. Now where was I? I've lost myself somewhere.'

'In the circumstances?' prompted Lamb, giving the grinning Jamieson a sharp look.

'Exactly, sir. Couldn't have put it better.' Plumm beamed, happy to have got his point across. He leaned closer, his breath almost solid on Lamb's face, and tapping him solemnly on the shoulder with his forefinger, whispered: 'I heard of that little affair between the two of you this morning. It would have been a waste of your good surgery had you killed him. Eh? Ha, ha, ha!'

He patted Lamb companionably on the shoulder and staggered off, moving largely crabwise and with his supper in danger of sliding from his plate. Captain Mortimer, crossing the floor with a plate in each hand, stepped smartly out of the way as Plumm blundered past him with a hair's breadth to spare.

'Drunken oaf,' muttered the captain as he shepherded his wife to Lamb's corner. 'Hello, again, Mr Lamb. Do you mind if we join you with our plates?'

'Delighted, sir.'

'Good evening, Bowers. Don't edge away, man, I shan't bite you.' Mortimer settled his wife into a chair and placed her plate on her lap before her overhang. 'Come and talk to Mrs Mortimer, Bowers. Entertain her with some of your vast store of gossip.'

'Take no notice of his bark, Mr Bowers,' said the lady, admonishing her husband's arm with her fan. 'But come and talk with me, anyway. I get precious little in the way of human conversation from him.'

Mortimer stepped close to Lamb. 'I am sorry Mrs Brett was so damned unpleasant to you just now,' he murmured. 'It was quite inexcusable.'

'Not at all, sir,' said Lamb. 'You did warn me she was feeling a little low.'

'Yes,' said Mortimer slowly. He gave his wife a quick, sideways glance. 'In a way, that is partly my fault, and so I must take some of the blame for her rudeness. Between ourselves, Mr Lamb, she is very close to tears tonight, and without burdening you with explanations . . .'

'Ah, here's Charlotte!' cried Mrs Mortimer. 'Harold, help her with her plate and fetch her here, there's a dear.'

Lamb nibbled at his cold chicken and watched Mortimer take Charlotte's arm and lead her to the supper table. They moved slowly along its length, he smiling and talking a great deal and she grave-faced and saying little, her eyes fixed on his face. They reached the end of the table with very little on her plate and as they turned away Lamb saw their hands touch and quickly grip and fall away. He glanced at Mrs Mortimer but she was giggling with her hand over her mouth at something Bowers had said. In spite of the mortification that still rankled within him, the beauty and bearing of Charlotte as she walked towards him almost took Lamb's breath away. She was, without a doubt, the most attractive woman he had ever seen. What a pity, he thought, that her tongue was so sharp.

'My God, what a bosom!' breathed Jamieson into his ear.

'Steady, now!' growled Lamb warningly.

Charlotte sat herself next to Mrs Mortimer without a word and began to nibble daintily at her tiny supper, frequently dabbing at her lips with her napkin. Lamb studied her covertly as he ate, admiring the perfect line of her profile, the generous breadth of forehead, the slim column of her neck brushed by the long, coiled springs of dark hair and the deep, shadowed divide of the breasts swelling from the pale blue of her dress.

'You have made a pretty little mess of your ear,' remarked Mortimer beside him. 'How did you come to do that?'

'A trifling accident, sir,' said Lamb. 'It looks worse than it feels.'

The captain gave a cynical grin. 'I will spare you having to invent some improbable story, Lamb. I am well aware of how you came by that ear and I tell you now, if I had got wind of this morning's affair in time, I would certainly have put a stop to it. You were both damned lucky that neither of you suffered any real injury because Admiral Upton would have had no mercy. He is not in favour of duels and neither am I. They are a bloody foolish waste of good men, usually.'

'Yes, sir,' said Lamb, contriving to inject some contriteness into his voice. The two ladies, he saw, were now deep in murmured conversation with each other and Bowers was standing beside them looking lost, shut out from their discussion but not anxious to rejoin Lamb and Jamieson while the flag captain stood between them.

Mortimer put down his plate and briskly rubbed his hands together. 'You gentlemen are all too damned solemn. What you need is a little alcohol. Bowers, exercise your initiative and conjure up full glasses all round, there's a good fellow.'

'Yes, sir. What should I fetch, sir?'

'How the devil should I know? Anything except that bloody awful sherry.'

Bowers duly exercised his initiative, so much to everyone's satisfaction that he was very quickly despatched to exercise it again. Mortimer grew loud and cheerful and joined a nearby

109

group of cronies, from where his jovial laugh boomed out from time to time. The two ladies talked quietly together over their coffee while the lieutenants drank more punch and puffed at Bowers's cigars. Presently Jamieson became very white and unsteady and was led out to the garden by the grinning Bowers. Lamb stood alone, listening to the soft murmur of Mrs Mortimer's voice discoursing on curtains and cots and christening gowns, and casting sly glances at Mrs Brett's perfect profile and the tantalizing lift and fall of her bosom. This entertainment threatened to make him a public disgrace and he hastily dragged his eyes away and tugged discreetly at his breeches. He lifted his glass to his mouth and found himself looking at Fox, staring at him from the doorway leading to the garden. Without conscious thought, Lamb walked towards him, aware from his floating step that he was more than a trifle drunk.

He extended his hand and smiled. 'Good evening, Mr Fox. Will you not shake hands and put the past behind us?'

Fox made no reply, leaving Lamb with his hand foolishly outstretched. Lamb dropped his hand and removed his smile.

'Damn you, then,' he said, and turned away.

'Wait,' said Fox.

Lamb turned back. 'Yes?'

Fox's voice was low and intense. 'I give you fair warning: the quarrel between us is not settled. You made me look a fool this morning. You hadn't the stomach to shoot me when you had the chance and chose instead to humiliate me. One day you'll regret that. I hear you are sailing tomorrow. Well, I can wait. It may be months or years but we shall meet again, have no fear of that. And by God, I'll make you pay for today.'

He turned and vanished into the darkness of the garden. Lamb stared after him for a moment, taken aback by the virulence of his last words. He shook his head in sorrow, feeling a sense of pity rather than anger. The poor fool, he thought; he's crippled in more ways than one.

Mrs Brett glanced up at him as he walked slowly back and picked up his glass. 'Would that have been Lieutenant Fox I saw at the door?'

'Yes, ma'am. Are you acquainted with him?'

110

'No.' She gave a slight smile. 'I heard of his name for the first time today, as it happens. We were told he was something of a crack shot, were we not, Molly? Rather better than some, we were led to understand.'

'Now then, Charlotte,' said Mrs Mortimer, tapping Mrs Brett's knee with her fan. She smiled up at Lamb. 'Take no account of her teasing, Mr Lamb. From what we heard, you came out best by far.'

The music began to swell again from the next room and Captain Mortimer strode towards them with both hands outstretched.

'Now which of you two ladies is going to dance the minuet with me?' he asked, smiling from one to the other.

Charlotte began to rise eagerly from her chair but Mrs Mortimer put a quick hand on her shoulder.

'No, no, my dear, never dance with a man who cannot tell the difference between a minuet and a gavotte,' she said firmly. 'He does the same steps to both, in any case.' She held out her hand. 'Come along, Harold, if you are to tread on anyone's feet, they had best be mine.'

Mortimer laughed. 'I doubt if I can get near enough to you to do that,' he said, and received a buffeting from her fan as they walked away.

The evening's drinking was begining to affect Lamb's balance; after one or two hasty shifts of his feet to keep himself erect on the gently heaving floor, he enquired warily if Mrs Brett had any objection to his sitting beside her.

'Not at all, sir,' she said, smiling and mellifluous, the very essence of sweetness. 'I think it might be better if you did.'

Lamb folded himself into Mrs Mortimer's chair, from where he had the advantage of being able to study Charlotte's ear and cheek and nose and chin while she gazed at the dancers whirling past the wide doorway. It also gave him a new angle from which to dwell on the rise and fall of her breasts and after a moment or two he found that the dislike for her which their first meeting had engendered had vanished completely; in its place was a tender feeling of growing lust. His perfidious flesh began to stir itself again.

'Captain Mortimer has told me that I was somehow uncivil

to you when we met earlier,' said Charlotte, turning her head towards him and causing him to shift his line of sight quickly upwards. 'If I was, it was quite unintentional and I apologize for it. If I am to spend some time on your little ship it is best that we start off on good terms, don't you think? And now, if you are quite certain that my bosom passes your scrutiny, you may take me through and partner me in what is left of this gavotte.'

She gave a tiny smile and rose from her chair. Lamb scrambled quickly upright, blushing at her words and feeling mortified by her offer. The waltz he could manage, after a fashion; the polka was lively enough to mask his untutored steps; but the slow and stately gavotte was quite beyond him.

'I am desolate, ma'am,' he said, feeling very warm. 'The gavotte is something I have never been able to master. I would probably do your shoes fearful damage.'

'Then, sir, what are you good at, may I ask?' she said lightly, and walked away towards the noise and movement of the next room.

Lamb swore, softly and horribly, and strode out through the other door in search of Jamieson, determined not to spend another minute in a place where he had been twice humiliated in one evening. He found the officer in the steadying clutch of a giggling Bowers with very little to choose between them in the way of drunkenness. Jamieson greeted Lamb with a joyful cry as for a long-lost brother and was hurt and astonished when he was savagely ordered to wipe that disgusting fucking mess from his waistcoat and remove himself to the *Heron* forthwith; he was not fit to be bloody-well seen in decent society.

The two men made their way down the dark hill to the harbour, Lamb striding as furiously as the steep descent would allow and Jamieson trailing behind in miserable, wounded silence, occasionally breaking into a trot for fear he should be left boatless at the steps.

Chapter 7

Mrs Brett arrived on board the *Heron* twenty minutes before
eight o'clock, accompanied by a good deal in the way of bags
and boxes and assisted to the deck by Admiral Upton. The
sighting of the admiral's gig caused much last-minute activity
on the cutter and considerable alarm in the suffering brain of
Lieutenant Jamieson, whose recall of his behaviour at Clarence
House was far from complete. When the boatswain's pipe had
finished its frantic shrilling and the admiral had completed the
usual pleasantries, he enquired of the whereabouts of Mrs
Brett's cabin and turned to escort her below. She was standing
by the side with the fresh wind teasing her dress and her hand
on her bonnet, staring intently at the flagship. Lamb and
Upton followed her gaze; Captain Mortimer stood at his
quarterdeck rail with his telescope to his eye. Mrs Brett raised a
farewell arm and he immediately lowered his glass and turned
away.

'Come, my dear,' said Upton, taking her by the elbow. 'Let
me see you settled into your cabin before I leave.'

He ushered her down the aft companionway. Lamb caught a
glimpse of her face as she disappeared from view; it was very
pale and it seemed to him that she was on the verge of tears.

It was ten minutes before Upton returned to the upper deck
and he stood absently scratching his chin for a few moments,
idly watching Mrs Brett's luggage being carried below, before
strolling the few paces to Lamb standing stiffly erect with his
hat beneath his arm.

'I don't like her mood, Mr Lamb. I don't like it at all. She is not
her normal self – far from it. I tell you straight, captain, she is not
happy – do you follow me? I would be obliged if a close eye is kept
on her whenever she is on deck. You understand me?'

'Yes, sir,' replied Lamb soberly.

'I commend her to your care, then, captain. Good day to you, sir.'

The pipe sounded its mournful notes, the admiral carefully lowered his ancient bones into his gig and Lamb replaced his hat on his head.

'Stand by to weigh anchor,' he called. 'Man the tops'l gaskets.'

The anchor cable dripped water across the deck and the *Heron* was suddenly skittish in the lively wind.

'Let fall!' shouted Lamb. 'Helm a-lee! Take her out, quartermaster.'

The morning was dull and grey with an easterly wind that laid the cutter over at a moderate angle and threw up a short sea which had every spar and timber groaning in protest. Lamb stood with his arm curled round a back-stay until the volcanic heights of Boggy Peak began to blur into the haze of distance and then, with his head clear of its earlier alcoholic ache, went down to enjoy a late breakfast, happy to have cast loose the problems of the shore again.

Hot toast made with fresh English Harbour bread and prepared by the cook with such delicacy of touch that most of it was quite free of charcoal, two chops almost warm, a handful of little Antiguan bananas scarcely larger than his finger and a pot of strong coffee brewed from fresh beans left Lamb feeling very content, and he leaned back in his chair and gave a satisfied belch.

'Pardon me,' he murmured politely to himself, and braced a long leg against the bulkhead as his chair began to shift on the sloping deck.

'Steer small, blast your eyes!'

The angry snap from Jamieson came down from the deck through Lamb's open door and he gave an amused grin. Jamieson's head and stomach would be paying the price now for their owner's blithe indulgence of the night before and the unfortunate helmsman, steering small or not, must also be expected to suffer. Lamb fell to mulling over what the admiral had said to him on deck; Upton was being a trifle over-anxious he thought, if his oblique warning really suggested the possibility of suicide. Surely no young woman, however

114

despairing, could ever contemplate such a dreadful step simply because of a broken love affair? He knew very little of the workings of the female mind but such a course was unthinkable to him, and although he was unacquainted with the intangibles of love and infatuation, he could never see them acting upon him in that way. Nevertheless, women being the strange, moody, unpredictable creatures that they were, he thought it best that he take the admiral's warning to heart. He would have a discreet word with Jamieson later – that would ensure that whenever Mrs Brett ventured on deck at least one pair of watchful eyes would always be on her.

'Sylvester!' he roared.

The pattering of feet sounded on the deck and the steward's hideous grin showed itself at the door.

'All finished, sir? Clear away, shall I?'

'Yes. Is our passenger comfortable? Have you made yourself known to her yet?'

'Comfortable, sir? No telling, I ain't seen her yet. I intrydooced meself through the door, like, that's all, sir, see if she wanted anything, like. She said she'd let me know if she did. Course, it could be that the lady ain't none too well, sir, in this bit of sea.'

The cutter lurched to a sudden, heavy swell and Sylvester steadied himself with a braced arm against the door post as Lamb neatly caught the coffee-pot. The little man grinned evilly.

'Could be a lot worse, too, in a while. Let me take that coffee-pot off you, sir.'

Lamb made his way up the pitching companionway to the upper deck. The sky had darkened considerably since he had descended for his breakfast and the wind had shifted to the south-east. He glanced at the sea, a dreary, grey-green waste of long, white-topped waves; they were in for a blow, he thought.

'Wind's picking up a bit, sir,' said Jamieson as Lamb reached him.

'Yes. Roust out Mr Snow and make sure all is snug and fast on deck, if you please.'

He did not want to lose the advantage of this splendid wind yet – he would shorten sail when he judged it to be still safe to do so but it was as well to make sure that everything on deck was secure in the meantime; he knew only too well how a sudden sea could lay a ship over on her beam ends. He clung to the mainmast back-stay, watching with a critical eye as Jamieson, Snow and a couple of hands made their careful way around the deck, doubling the breechings of the guns and adding extra lashings to the ship's boat and the main hatch-cover. He stood there throughout the morning as the wind came round to the south and the bow rose and fell with increasing height and motion; an extra helmsman was put on the tiller, the outer and flying jibs were lowered and the topsail was reefed and reefed again. Noon came and went with no more chance of determining the sun's altitude than if it had been midnight. Lamb took his meal of cheese and ship's biscuit with one arm hooked around the thrumming, jerking backstay, watching the bowsprit bury itself in green water, and white water tumble over the deck.

Jamieson came back on watch and the two officers stood side by side at the weather rail. Standing watch and watch about as they normally did, Lamb had not had a real opportunity to converse with the young lieutenant other than on the business of the day to day running of the ship, and he and Jamieson spent many of the dreary hours of the afternoon with their heads close together and their voices raised against the noise of wind and sea and canvas. He was surprised to find that Jamieson had an intelligence and humour belied by his squat, muscular body and youthful, prize-fighter's face, and after a while Lamb found that he had put aside the cloak of distant authority which he had worn since his first day on the *Heron* and the two men talked and laughed together in easy companionship as the long afternoon wore wearily on. Lamb learned that Jamieson came from Devon, was the son of a naval surgeon and had been to sea since he was eleven years old.

'I did not like it one little bit,' said Jamieson with a chuckle. 'I had dreamed of going to sea since I was a scrap of a thing standing at my father's knee. He would tell me of the wonderful times he'd had and the places he had visited and the sights he had seen, so, of course, I could not wait to join. He still had friends in the navy and he arranged for me to be taken on by a captain of his acquaintance. He took me down to Plymouth, saw me aboard, gave me a Bible and two guineas, shook my hand and left. I was taken down to the cockpit blubbing like a baby and was immediately given a thrashing by the senior middy. I went straight up on deck, saw a boat about to leave the ship's side and climbed down into it. Nobody challenged me and I got ashore but was picked up half an hour later trying to book a seat on the London coach. They hauled me back to the ship, gave me a stern lecture and another drubbing and tied me to my sea-chest until we sailed. I often wonder what would have happened to me had I caught that coach to London.'

'Yes, you might have been another Dick Wittington and made your fortune,' grinned Lamb, 'or had your throat slit for the sake of your coat and breeches.'

'There were times in those first few weeks when I thought I might be better dead, I remember,' said Jamieson with a wry smile. 'I was only a little 'un then and for my pains I was put in charge of the cockpit glim and the snuffers. Time and again I was beaten for falling asleep and failing to trim the candle and there were not many nights when I did not crawl into my hammock with my arse smarting. Things improved when I began to stand my watch and they became much better when I learned to stand up for myself. By the time the ship reached Bermuda I found I was thoroughly enjoying myself. Now, the thought of any life but this quite depresses me. May Boney live and fight for many a year yet, say I.'

'I echo that,' said Lamb, and tightened his hold as the *Heron* almost buried her lee rail under the buffet of a sudden heavy wave. He threw a quick glance aloft and ordered the helm a point nearer the wind. The angle of the deck eased and he turned back to Jamieson. 'Yes, when I think of my midshipman days it is the perpetual hunger and weariness that comes most strongly to mind – particularly the hunger. I seemed to spend most of my days thinking of food and my nights dreaming of it. I remember a wardroom pig was killed one time and the first lieutenant had promised to send half a leg and as much crackling as we could eat to the cockpit. Well, for some reason or other the senior middy fell out of favour with him and as a consequence we got nothing. We were all absolutely desolate

117

– quite heartbroken. Vengeance was vowed on the wardroom and all kinds of horrible notions were put forward, but in the end we decided to put the wardroom pigs in mourning out of respect for their comrade, of whom we had not tasted so much as a bristle. A black handkerchief was cut into strips and when the wardroom officers were at their breakfast the next morning – eating fresh rashers of pork, no doubt – we boarded the pig-sty and after a great deal of struggling and squealing we managed to place a black arm band on each of the porkers' forelegs – and a fair amount of pig-shit on ourselves, I remember. There was a shout from the quarterdeck, a great panic from us as we attempted to leave the sty unseen and an almighty squealing and snorting as the damned pigs escaped onto the maindeck, just as the officers returned to the deck from their breakfast. Absolute pandemonium reigned for some ten or fifteen minutes with the captain and first lieutenant roaring from the quarter-deck, the pigs grunting and squealing as they charged about the deck displaying their black arm bands, and the hands laughing fit to burst as they chased them from beneath the guns and the boats and out of the galley.'

'Dear Lord,' said Jamieson, laughing, 'that is something I would love to have seen. What was the outcome; were you all keel-hauled or flogged round the fleet?'

'No, nothing so drastic. We all had to toe the line for a tremendous scolding and then the whole party of us were sent aloft to hang out to dry for the day. Some of us were perched on the topgallant yardarms, some on the topmast crosstrees and I, being very small, dangled at the jib-boom end balanced by another little person abaft at the end of the gaff. And there we stayed, with not so much as a crumb of biscuit, until it was dark. But when we crept down to the cockpit, cold, stiff and famished, we found a bucket full to the brim with cold crackling, compliments of the first lieutenant. Lord, how we fell on that!'

The weather worsened as the hours passed and by the end of the afternoon the wind was coming almost solid over the bow, buffeting Lamb and Jamieson as they clung to the aft rigging, glancing off the rock-like figure of Snow at the mainmast shrouds and lifting the pigtails of the helmsmen lashed to the tiller. The *Heron* pitched and rolled with a wild, twisting motion, the masts and spars and blocks groaning and rattling their protest and the sheets cracking like whips. The bow climbed and plunged, staggering over waves beaten ragged by the wind and dropping into the troughs with an explosion of white water that brought sea sweeping along the deck. Shortly before the dim murk of the afternoon gave way to the marginally greater darkness of the evening, the mainsail, its canvas stretched and thinned by the long days of hot sun and salt winds of the Caribbean, blew itself to streaming tatters with a report that made the men on deck start as if they had been shot. Nothing could be done about it in that weather; the imperturbable Snow barely gave the slapping remnants a glance as he made his slow, steady way aft to lend his weight to the men at the tiller and the cutter fought her way into the wind and the wild night under reefed topsail and inner jib alone.

At the end of the first dog-watch or thereabouts Lamb arranged for the helmsman to be relieved and sent Jamieson below – there being little point in both officers exhausting themselves on deck. Snow also went below but was back at the tiller within minutes, fortified by rum and a hasty supper. Lamb was pleased to see his solid, reassuring presence close by. The boatswain was a quiet man, except in the way of giving orders; a self-contained man – short, square and very strong, he kept himself to himself, mixing with neither the lower deck nor the officers, a man apart. Like most boatswains, he was something of a bully (but not as bad as some of the brutal tyrants Lamb had known) and carried with him an air of confident, quiet authority and a clear contempt for most of the men under him. Snow was typical of his kind: sea-wise, strong, utterly dependable in all possible conditions of war and weather; he was the iron link between forecastle and quarter-deck, the linchpin upon which a captain could always rely. It was, thought Lamb, musing in the wild darkness, part of the navy's strength that it was able to constantly throw up such men whenever they were needed – an indication, perhaps, of the rich seam from which they came and which made Britain's navy what it was.

Sylvester appeared from below and made a dash across the

wet, heaving deck to present Lamb with a couple of beef sandwiches wrapped in a napkin.

'I thought you might want the use of Cap'n Pardoe's tarp'lin jacket, sir,' he bellowed. 'It'll be a mite small, I expect, but it'll keep your shoulders dry, at least.'

It was more than a mite small – Pardoe must have been a very little man indeed because the cuffs ended just below Lamb's elbows – but he was thankful for its tight warmth nevertheless and he bit into his sandwich with hungry enthusiasm.

'How is Mrs Brett bearing up?' he asked, busily chewing. 'Have you seen her at all?'

'Yes, sir, I took her a pot of tea afore the galley fire was put out. She didn't want no food, she said – had plenty of her own.'

'Was she seasick?'

'No, sir, not as I could see. Reading a book, she was.'

The steward scuttled off and Lamb buried his chin in his jacket and stared forward, his legs flexing and his body swaying easily to the movement of the deck with the unthinking habit of long years. It was absolutely dark beneath the thick, dense, unseen cloud cover; he could not see the lee rail but at the bow, as it plunged, the white burst of water flung high showed dimly. He pondered on the cutter's progress; she would be making no headway, facing into this wind, but her leeway was a source of concern. The only comfort was that to the east there was no land to threaten them, no hostile lee shore onto which they could be driven, only the vast expanse of the Atlantic Ocean.

The dark hours ground slowly by, the constant, malevolent, enveloping sounds of wind and bursting seas cocooning him with his thoughts. Mrs Brett – Charlotte, he thought of her now – played a large part in his musings, her beauty growing in precedence over her acid tongue, the memory of the humiliation he had suffered shrinking in proportion. He found he could picture her face quite distinctly in his mind – something he had never achieved when thinking of Mrs Mainwaring – and his inner eye dwelt lingeringly on the fine, broad sweep of her forehead, the slim, arched brows above the cool blue eyes, the soft lips, full and wide above the small, determined chin. Occasionally he would be wrenched back to the reality of the moment as the ship gave an alarming lurch or a huge wave burst inboard.

'All's well there, the helm?'

'Aye, sir, all's well. Helm's a-lee, sir.'

He would wipe the salt water from his face and settle into his thoughts again, half his mind on his ship, the other half roaming free, dwelling on his duel with Fox and the man's threats at Clarence House; the condition of the spare mainsail; Mrs Mainwaring; Guadeloupe to starboard, in French hands since '94; his leaking shoes; and Charlotte. She returned to his thoughts again and again, until towards midnight she was gazing intently into his eyes and her lips were rich and red, softening and pouting, drawing very close to his, sweet and sensuous.

'For'ard starboard gun's on the loose, sir,' yelled Snow as he ran past, moving confidently and easily on the cavorting deck with one hand brushing along the man-rope.

Lamb darted after him, troubled that his ears had not picked up those noises that had alerted Snow, and which sounded again now: the squeal and rumble of a gun's unwedged wooden trucks sliding on the wet deck. The bow trembled on top of a crest and dropped into the trough as Lamb caught up with the boatswain and he clung grimly as thunderous, leaping spray and solid water burst over them. The right-hand ring-bolt, one of the two through which the breeching rope passed to fasten the gun tight and snug against the side, had broken or come adrift from its timbers. Only the thin lashings which pulled the two sides of the breechings firmly together had prevented the rope from snaking through the pommelion and the gun was now tethered by its left-hand ring-bolt and free to slide and swing. Soon it would snap its remaining shackles and charge about the heaving deck like an unloosed, mad bull.

'I've got the end, sir,' snapped Snow, and Lamb fumbled for the boatswain's arm and took his own grip on the rope. The deck tilted to starboard, the gun ran back to hit the side with a jarring thud, and the two men leaned back hard on the breeching to hold the gun in its place. The bow plunged, water roared and swirled waist-deep about them, and the bow began shudderingly to rise. Snow leaped over the gun, pulling the rope beneath the barrel and securing it while Lamb snatched the flexible, rope-handled sponge from its brackets and kicked it hard beneath the little wooden wheels.

'That should hold it for a while, sir,' bawled Snow into Lamb's ear. 'I'll get a length of good hemp and make a proper job of it.'

The boatswain disappeared into the darkness and Lamb crouched beside the gun, gripping the breeching and leaning back hard, bending his head to the solid smash of water as the bow dropped and the ship rolled. Snow was back within the minute to finisn the task and Lamb left him to fuss over the wedges and lashings and made his way to his post aft, as wet beneath his tarpaulin jacket as if he had never worn it.

Midnight came and went, bringing with it the carpenter to stand his watch and fresh helmsmen to relieve the wet, exhausted men at the tiller. The wind and sea were as wildly menacing as ever and the wind howled about the streaming ribbons of the mainsail with a deep, resonant roaring that seemed to Lamb to carry a baleful, threatening note of malignant fury. During the long hours of the middle watch, the rigging of the inner jib tore free from the mainmast, leaving the sail writhing, lifting and streaming aft, lashing at the mainmast shrouds like a live thing, tethered by its foot at the bowsprit and clew. Ten minutes of furious, wet, dangerous work followed, often one-handed and submerged, with Snow determined that the sail should be saved. Eventually it was lashed in a shapeless bundle to the side with no more than a gashed hand for Mee and a torn finger-nail for Lamb.

The helmsmen were changed again, Jamieson arrived to relieve the carpenter, and an eternity later the darkness began to lift. Suddenly Lamb could see across to the other side of the deck and then the grey and white desolation of the water, massive, glassy escarpments lifting from a wild, confused sea, towering high above his head and swooping beneath the hull, lifting the cutter to the full force of the wind as if she were no more than a storm-blown leaf.

But the daylight brought a stirring of new life to numbed senses and Lamb stretched his aching limbs and scrubbed a hand over his bristled face, glad beyond measure that the long night was over. Was it blind optimism, the lifting of hope with the arrival of the new day, that made him sense an easing of the wind, a diminution of its incessant, malevolent howling? Two hours later he was certain; the sea was still very high, a depressing desert of grey, torn, ragged crests and deep hollows, but the wind had dropped dramatically, its menacing roar reduced to a gusting thrust from the south-east. Overhead, the clouds were still thick and heavy, the colour and texture of ashes, but far to the south Lamb could see a whiteness in the sky, a thinning in the dense cover, and by the time the forenoon watch had tumbled up from below shafts of weak sunlight were slanting down from its edge many miles ahead; from the galley chimney thin wisps of white smoke were whipped off to leeward as Harrison began to heat up his copper pans and Snow, looking as fresh and alert as if he had spent the night in a soft, warm bed, was hustling the hands to the tasks of removing the remnants of the shredded mainsail and replacing the rigging of the inner jib.

Lamb rubbed his salt-stiff face and stretched his aching spine. His eyes felt raw and dry and every bone and muscle in his body protested as he moved away from the side. He stifled a huge yawn. By rights he should be relieving Jamieson for the forenoon watch but that young man would be unlucky; after twenty-four hours on deck Lamb's pressing needs were coffee, breakfast and sleep, and if he could summon up sufficient energy he might even wash and shave.

'I shall leave the deck to you, Mr Jamieson. Bend on the new mainsail as soon as you can and maintain your present heading for the time being. See that I am called before the end of the watch – with a little luck we may get ourselves an observation.'

'Yes, we'll have made a fair bit of leeway, I reckon, sir.'

'Very likely,' said Lamb and made his way stiffly below. He was not too concerned about the leeway; it was far better to have been pushed eastwards into the clear ocean than westward towards the Leeward Islands. In any case, any leeway they might have made would have been much reduced or even balanced by the flow of the great, circular northern equatorial current, and if his noon observation showed the *Heron* to have made too much easting then the wind and the current were in his favour to enable him to easily make good his westing.

Sylvester met him at the foot of the companionway.

'Coffee and shaving water just coming up, sir,' he reported cheerfully. 'I'll have your breakfast ready by the time you've shaved, sir. Your clean linen's laid out ready for you.'

'Well done,' said Lamb wearily, rubbing his hand over his bristled chin and thinking that if he was not to lose ten minutes of precious sleep at the end of the morning he had best find the energy to make use of his shaving water now. 'How is our passenger? Have you seen her this morning?'

'She is a little bruised and buffeted by the motion of her bed but otherwise she is fine, thank you, captain.'

Charlotte stood in the doorway of her cabin clad in a plum-coloured dress. She was smiling slightly, her face exactly as Lamb had pictured it during the night, down to the very curve of her cheek and the level, faintly mocking gaze of her eyes. For a moment Lamb found himself gaping, almost stunned by the fresh, clean, wholesome beauty of her.

'I, er, I am pleased to hear it, ma'am,' he said, bitterly aware of his unshaven face, unkempt hair and damp, dishevelled clothes. 'It has been a nasty blow but the worst of it is over now. You should sleep more peacefully tonight.'

She looked at him a little curiously, her head endearingly to one side, and stepped a pace or two towards him.

'You look quite exhausted, sir. Have you been on deck all night?'

Lamb felt enormously pleased at the touch of concern in her voice. He found himself smiling.

'Yes, for my sins. Perhaps you will find that reason enough to excuse my appearance.'

'Tut, captain, a few whiskers are of small account; they are soon removed. You must not think I am unused to the sight of an unshaven chin. Does that little elf of a man look after you as well as me?'

'Sylvester, ma'am?' Lamb looked around. He did not remember seeing the steward slip away. 'Yes, he looks after us both, in his fashion. Just tell him what you need in the way of hot water, tea or whatever, and you will find him fairly accommodating. If he is not, let me know.'

124

'Oh, I am sure there will be no need. He has already brought me tea and hot water this morning and if he did not insist on smiling so much . . . but I am keeping you from your bed, I am sure.'

'Oh, I am quite used to that, ma'am,' said Lamb, aware that he was beaming like an idiot. His weariness had left him completely and he would have been more than happy to have given up every hour of his morning sleep to stand here and talk and listen and feast his eyes. 'A cup of coffee and a shave and I shall be as . . .'

'Par'n me, sir,' said Sylvester, squeezing between them, bearing a coffee-pot in one hand and a jug of hot water in the other. 'It's all hot, sir,' grinned the villain. 'Don't let it get cold now.'

Charlotte smiled and turned away. 'I must not keep you from your shaving water, captain,' she murmured over her shoulder and vanished into her cabin.

Lamb grinned cheerfully into his mirror and busily lathered his face between sips of coffee, thinking what a wonderful thing nature was when two minutes of an attractive woman's attention was sufficient to banish a man's weariness and make his spirits soar. He wondered if this magical action worked both ways but a glance at his bloodshot eyes, bristles and matted, salt-stiff hair convinced him it was extremely unlikely. Even so, he thought, even so . . . He chuckled at his enormous conceit and spat and cursed as his shaving brush lathered his tongue. His last thought as he laid his head on his pillow, feeling pleasantly clean and comfortably full, was of Charlotte's smile as she had turned away. Little sign of a distraught woman there, he reflected, and fell instantly asleep.

The sea was blue but still unsettled and the sky covered patchily with white, broken cloud when Lamb and Jamieson took their midday observations. Lamb took the readings to his cabin, where he found that Jamieson's altitude gave a longitude that differed from his own by half a degree west; this was an error of some thirty miles, but as it also placed the *Heron* firmly on the dry ground of Guadeloupe, Lamb decided that he could safely ignore Jamieson's reading and take his own as being more realistic. This put the cutter more or less where he had expected to find it; if the sky was clear this evening he would take a few lunars and calculate his longitude again. He entered his position in the log and went up to the deck.

He strode past Jamieson with a concerned expression on his face, leaned out over the side and peered down at the sea.

'This is damned peculiar,' he said, turning round with a puzzled frown. 'There is something seriously wrong here, Mr Jamieson.'

Jamieson raised his eyebrows and hurried to join him at the side.

'Wrong, sir? How do you mean?' he asked, looking anxious, switching his gaze between Lamb and the sea.

'Look there,' said Lamb, pointing over the side. 'Not a trace of a tree or a bush or even a blade of bloody grass. Where has it all gone? Has someone snatched Guadeloupe from under our keel?'

'Ah,' said Jamieson, suddenly comprehending. He blushed guiltily. 'My noon observation, sir?'

'Yes, Mr Jamieson. Either that or Guadeloupe has sunk.'

Jamieson looked very sheepish. 'I am very sorry, sir. I cannot understand how that happened.'

'That is only too apparent,' said Lamb, with a sad shake of his head. He relented, amused at Jamieson's hangdog expression. 'Go and have your dinner and ponder on it.'

'Aye aye, sir,' said Jamieson and hastily escaped.

The upper deck was almost empty, deserted by the hands for their dinners and grog. Lamb strolled back and forth along the weather side of the quarterdeck, enjoying the sunshine after two days of cloud, feeling its cheering warmth on his back. The new mainsail, its creases almost gone, bellied proudly in the brisk breeze; the inner jib reached up once more to the top of the mainmast and the topsail, braced hard round to catch the easterly wind, was free of reefs and sweetly curved. Three hours of dreamless, death-like sleep had left Lamb with gritty eyes, an uneasy stomach and a sense of numbed weariness, but he knew that an hour or so in the cleansing air of the upper deck would sweep away these familiar discomforts. He paced slowly between taffrail and mainmast, hoping that Charlotte would

126

decide to take a breath of fresh air on deck and carefully rehearsing in his mind a selection of greetings from which to choose, depending on the mood she displayed. The realization had come to him earlier, as he dressed, that he thought of her with a certain nervousness, an edgy wariness, as if she was in some way a shade dangerous. He was not sure why this should be, but after a little musing, he put it down to her barbed, unpredictable tongue. She was like a spirited cat, he thought; beautiful, aloof, made to be caressed, but apt to sink her claws into the stroking hand.

He had taken great pains over his appearance, within the limits of his wardrobe, and was quite confident that the close-shaven, clean-shirted, well-brushed officer of the afternoon was a vastly superior person to the dirty, dishevelled officer of the morning. Should he ask her to take supper with him this evening? It was, after all, not unusual for a captain to entertain his passengers at his table; she could scarcely see anything improper in it. He would drop the invitation casually in the course of conversation, as if it were of no great import to him one way or the other. He smiled and continued his pacing.

Charlotte made no appearance on deck that afternoon or during the evening and Lamb took his supper on his own, his confidence of the afternoon quite gone, convinced that she had no more thought for him than she had for the ancient, ugly Sylvester. He ate without appetite, his mood glum, with a book on gunnery propped before him. Shortly before eight o'clock he went up on deck to take the first watch.

The night sky was brilliant and beautiful, even to his jaded eye. The sea and wind had dropped and the air was soft and warm. A vast spread of stars glittered icily from a clear, black sky and a low moon, half full, huge and white, hovered in a thin halo of suffused, silver light, illuminating the deck of the cutter almost as if it were day and polishing the black surface of the sea. Lamb relieved Jamieson, had a word with the new lookout before he went aloft, checked the *Heron*'s course, and took up his customary, slow, night-time walking of his area of the deck with his hands clasped behind his back and his chin sunk onto his chest. From time to time he would glance up to sweep an eye around the quiet, deeply shadowed deck and at the silent

127

helmsman and the patient, motionless figure of the quarter-master standing by the tiller. The ship's bell sounded twice, marking the passing of the first hour of the watch, and suddenly Charlotte was at the companion hatch and walking lightly across the deck towards him.

'Good evening, Mrs Brett,' he smiled, his heart lifting.

'Good evening, Captain Lamb.' She turned slowly round with her head towards the sky until she faced him again. 'What a beautiful, beautiful night. I have never seen such a sky, not even on Antigua in all my time there. It – it touches the heart, don't you think, in some sad way?'

'I know what you mean, ma'am. We should be grateful, I think; we never see such nights in England, not even in the best of summers.'

'No, we do not.' She tilted her head again and gazed in silence at the huge majesty of the sky for several long moments. 'Oh, it really is magnificent! I feel I must drink it in and absorb the sight into my memory so that when I am suffering the grey English winters I can close my eyes and bring all this back to me.'

Lamb stared at her, entranced by the delicate perfection of her uplifted profile. She turned her head and caught his steady gaze, the whites of her eyes glinting in the shadowed curves of her face. She gave a light laugh and looked away.

'I am sorry, sir. I was carried away by the spell of the moment. Such sights are all too common for your eyes, I don't doubt.'

'That may be so, ma'am, but I never lose my sense of wonder at it all. Where in England is your home, may I ask?'

She looked down at her feet and paused for a moment before answering. 'I have the choice of two. My late husband's parents live at Plymouth, while my own mother lives in Kent – a little village by the name of Locksbottom, not too far from London. I intend to go back there. My father is dead and my mother will be pleased of my company.'

'I, too, come from Kent,' said Lamb. 'I was born and brought up in Maidstone. Do you know it at all?'

She flashed a quick smile. 'I have passed through it once or twice.'

'I have never been to Locksbottom, I am afraid.'

'No, it is a very small place.'

They fell silent, leaning side by side against the rail, looking across the bright deck marked with slowly shifting patterns of black and white. Lamb was aware of the quick beat of his heart and a strange, pleasurable sensation, almost of exhilaration, singing within him. He was suddenly, unaccountably, nervous; his fingers trembled slightly on the smooth oak of the rail and his armpits prickled with sweat.

'Sylvester is not neglecting you, ma'am?' he asked, anxious lest she became weary of the silence and returned below.

'No, no, he has been very attentive. He brings me tea and coffee, quite unbidden, six or seven times so far today; asks if I am peckish, would I like a boiled egg or a beef sandwich. He is most concerned that I have had none of his meals but Mrs Mortimer sent such a hamper on board that I am sure I could feed the entire crew for a week.'

'He is quite right,' said Lamb sternly. 'You will do your stomach a mischief if you give it nothing but cold food. You should have at least one hot meal a day. Perhaps – perhaps – it would be an honour and a pleasure, ma'am, to have you share my table. It is quite the normal thing,' he added hastily.

She turned her head and studied his face, the strange mix of faint puzzlement and slightly mocking smile showing again.

'That is most kind of you, captain; but I do not have a large appetite. I have almost nothing for breakfast and a bowl of soup and a little fruit is enough at midday. However, I shall be happy to take supper with you occasionally, and I thank you for asking.'

'Shall we say tomorrow, then?'

She dipped her head and smiled. 'Tomorrow, sir. And now I must say good night. I have trespassed on your time for too long.'

'Good night to you, ma'am. Sleep well.'

Lamb bowed, she smiled prettily and was gone, leaving a faint fragrance of lilies hanging in the air. He turned and gazed out over the moon-streaked sea, his mind in a buzz, excitement tingling within him. Never, never, never had he met such an attractive and disturbing woman! Mrs Mainwaring, for all her clinging lust, paled into insignificance beside her. Such beauty! Such quiet, mature intelligence! And what was she – twenty? Twenty-two? And already married and widowed and on her way home from an affair with a married post-captain. Would that she would start an affair with a certain unmarried, penniless lieutenant. He stared blindly out to sea, smiling at his thoughts.

The *Heron* sailed on through the lustrous night, the watches changed, the stars wheeled imperceptibly across the vast bowl of the sky, and paled and died, and the sun thrust its blazing, orange eye above the edge of the sea to larboard. The two islands of Guadeloupe lay far astern; Dominica, now in British hands again, had been passed in the dark hours and Martinique, birthplace of Bonaparte's Josephine, lay a hundred miles or so off the starboard beam. The boatswain's whistle and his baleful voice had drawn the hands in frowsty hurry from their hammocks to the upper deck and Jamieson strode the damp, scrubbed planks with the arrogant energy of youth and the eagerness of a hungry man knowing that breakfast was but a few minutes away. His voice sang out and his finger pointed to several minor imperfections in the way of rope ends and stowed hammocks. Snow sent men running to put these evils right and Jamieson made his way aft, happy in the knowledge that he could hand over the watch to the captain with little fear of criticism. Below his feet, in the captain's cabin, Lamb drained his coffee cup, leaned back in his chair and narrowed his eyes at his steward.

'Are you on good terms with the cook, Sylvester?' he demanded.

The gnome paused in the act of loading his tray and gave his awful grin. 'There ain't no one on good terms with that villain, sir. Cut his own mother's throat for amusement, he would. Still, I suppose I ain't on no worse terms than anyone else. Want a little favour done, do you, sir?'

'You could put it that way. I shall be entertaining our passenger to supper this evening and a little extra effort on his part would be most welcome – and on yours, too, come to that.'

Sylvester closed one eye. 'I get your drift, sir. Don't you worry, sir, I have ways of sweetening the bugger. I'll see he does

130

you proud, sir. Now what about wine? You've still got some white left but you ain't got no red. How about having the loan of one of Cap'n Pardoe's bottles, sir? You can always leave a note of hand in its place. He has a very nice claret in his cupboard, sir – or so I believe.'

The steward's hasty rider brought a grin to Lamb's face. He had already turned the same thought over in his mind and now that he had the official sanction of Pardoe's steward he would broach the captain's wine store with an easy conscience.

'I shall think about it,' he said, looking doubtful. 'I will leave Harrison in your hands, then. Nothing too elaborate, mind. I have no wish to strain his good nature.'

Sylvester gave a cynical chuckle. 'Not much fear of that, sir,' he said and departed with his tray.

'And I shall want a clean shirt!' Lamb shouted after him as he reached for his hat and prepared to go on deck.

'Good morning, sir,' said Jamieson as Lamb stepped aft and the ship's bell sounded the first of the eight strokes that marked the end of the morning watch.

'Good morning to you, Mr Jamieson. Reports?'

The lieutenant passed on the morning reports of the carpenter and the boatswain and Lamb nodded.

'And the last log?' he asked.

'Five and a half knots, sir. Six and one fathom before that.'

'Very good.' Lamb pointed to an inch or so of rope fibre which had blown against the truck of the starboard gun. 'There are sweepings beneath that gun, Mr Jamieson. Kindly attend to it before you go below.'

'Aye aye, sir. Sweeper to the quarterdeck!'

Lamb gave a little inward smile as he walked aft to check the compass course against the sailing instructions. He was quite sure that if he had been in Jamieson's shoes he would now be uttering a few curses beneath his breath at his captain's niggling eye. Jamieson was a pleasant enough youngster and a reasonably efficient officer but their forced closeness made for problems in the way of discipline. It was not easy to strike a balance between icy aloofness, which made life uncomfortable, and a too easy, over-familiarity, which could bring a lack of respect with all its attendant ills. An odd sweeping was a small enough thing but it was one of the little pegs on which Lamb could hang his authority from time to time without being constantly overbearing.

Jamieson disappeared below for his breakfast and Lamb took up his position by the weather rail and surveyed the quiet activity before him with a sense of supreme contentment and well-being. Snow had laid out the spars' battle chains on a length of old canvas and was supervising their annointing against rust while his mate was in the rigging with a couple of hands busily applying slush to the cordage. A boatswain's list of tasks to be done was never completed, mused Lamb; but all thoughts of boatswains vanished instantly from his mind as Charlotte stepped daintily on to the deck.

'Good morning, Mrs Brett,' he said, raising his hat as he advanced to meet her.

'Good morning, captain.' Her face was grave, her expression cool, unsmiling. 'Is there somewhere I can stand without finding myself in the way of your men?'

'Of course, ma'am.' Lamb led her to the spot where Mrs Skinner had sat with her embroidery. 'Can I send for a chair for you?'

'No, no, thank you for the thought. I shall only be here for a few minutes, just for a breath of air. I have letters to finish. Should I be able to send them from Barbados, do you think?'

'I am sure you will, ma'am. Let me have them later and I will see they are put into the proper hands, although you might well reach England before they do.'

'Thank you. I have a couple for Antigua, too. Is Barbados a very large island?'

'Middling large, yes. I have never been there but from all accounts it is a fairly busy place. The outward bound convoys make for it, using the Trades, and then separate for their different destinations. Most of them are shepherded from Port Royal in convoy on the homeward bound passage. That is how you will be going, ma'am, through the Windward Passage and on across the Atlantic, snug and safe in company with a dozen or so others.'

'I see.'

Something in her tone caused Lamb to give her a wary,

furtive glance. She stared fixedly at the wake, her chin set firm, her hands tight on the rail. Rigidity and tight control was in her every line, as if tears were pressing hard. She gave him a brittle smile and looked about the deck.

'So this is your little world, captain. It is a very small one, is it not? And your guns? What would they be – six-pounders?'

'Four-pounders, ma'am. But we also have two carronades – the shorter guns, there. They fire a much larger shot.'

'Yes, I have heard of carronades.'

She turned and looked over the taffrail again. Lamb hesitated, unsure whether he should go or stay. To his horror, he saw a large, glistening tear form at the corner of her eye. His immediate instinct was to stand close, to put his arms around her, to comfort her; instead he glanced away, feeling acutely awkward and very much in the way.

'Your pardon, Mrs Brett,' he said carefully, 'but if there is anything . . .'

'Gunpowder, Captain Lamb,' she said, cutting him off quickly. 'Tell me about gunpowder. It is a substance about which I know absolutely nothing. Is it difficult to make?'

'Well, it certainly requires a good deal of care.' Lamb hesitated, certain that her interest in gunpowder was on a par with his own for dressmaking or embroidery; but recognizing that a short monologue from him might give her time to collect herself, he leaned on the rail beside her and continued.

'Gunpowder is made from a mixture of saltpetre, charcoal and sulphur. In British powder, in every hundred parts, seventy-five will be saltpetre, ten will be sulphur and fifteen will be charcoal. The French, I understand, use a little less sulphur and a little more charcoal.' A movement from her caught his eye and he shot her a quick glance in time to see her dash the tears from her eyes with the tips of her fingers. He hurried on, trying to resist the temptation to gabble. 'It is all ground fine, mixed together and moistened with a, er, a little human liquid, pressed into tiny cakes and then when they are dry, broken up again into their individual grains. Sometimes they are polished with a small amount of black lead, and then sieved to separate the fine grains from the coarse. The finest grains make the very best powder; the coarse-grained stuff we use for salutes and gun-practice and the like. Then it is taken to the ships by a vessel flying a red flag, all lights and galley fires are extinguished, and the gunner stows it below in his magazine, a little room in the heart of the ship where no one is allowed to enter unless they are wearing felt slippers. A spark from one small nail in a shoe could blow a ship apart in the twinkling of an eye. And there you have it, Mrs Brett; your knowledge of gunpowder now matches mine exactly.'

She blew her nose daintily into a tiny scrap of a handkerchief. 'Thank you, captain. That was most interesting. It is amazing that we take so many of the things we use and have about us for granted, without a thought as to how they came to be there.' She sniffed and dabbed the handkerchief to her nose again. 'I think I have caught a cold in the head. Thank you for your kind attention, sir. Now I must go and finish my letters or they will never be ready for tomorrow.'

Lamb gazed after her trim, retreating figure with a frown of concern. Perhaps Admiral Upton had been right; she was far from happy today, at any rate. The thought crossed his mind that her letter writing might have been the cause, penning a farewell note to Captain Mortimer, possibly. Would it be a very shabby act to glance at the addresses on her envelopes tomorrow? Yes, it would, he decided – and in any case, what would he learn? No, he would be far better employed in trying to brighten her mood. A glass or two of wine tonight might bring the warmth back to her smile. He walked slowly forward, disturbed by her unhappiness but with his mind already turning to the plans for the day.

'Mr Snow,' he called. 'Kindly make haste with those chains. You will not have forgotten we are exercising the guns in ten minutes. Blackett, nip below and present my compliments to Mr Jamieson – I should be grateful for his presence on the gundeck within the minute.'

Whatever the nature of the influence exerted by Sylvester on the tender susceptibilities of the cook – probably bribery and not unconnected with rum, Lamb suspected – the effect was sufficient to bring the steward bustling into the cabin with an air of pride and a look suggesting that wondrous things were to follow.

'Pea soup, sir,' he beamed gappily. 'Eat it while it's hot. Main vittles coming up sharp.'

'A glass of wine, Mrs Brett?' suggested Lamb. 'I have a passable white here, or perhaps you would prefer the claret?'

'Oh, the claret, I think,' she said eagerly. 'I do love the colour. Do you know, captain, I was thinking earlier how pleasant a glass of wine would be. I am quite saturated with Sylvester's tea and lemon-water.'

Lamb studied her covertly as he filled her glass. She was a different woman entirely from the one of the morning. Her eyes shone and her skin glowed in the soft, yellow lamplight, giving her a warmth and animation that coupled with her closeness across the little table, he found almost overwhelming. She was wearing an ivory-coloured dress adorned with a scarlet sash around the waist, the neck cut very low and square and, in the French fashion, unprotected by a tucker. The view he received of her breasts was tantalizingly magnetic but with an effort he averted his gaze, remembering the acid comment she had made at Clarence House.

'Did you finish your letters, ma'am?' he asked as he picked up his spoon.

'Yes, all finished and sealed and ready. Please, captain, do not call me "ma'am". It makes me feel so old – quite fat and matronly. "Mrs Brett" is a little better but I much prefer my friends to call me Charlotte. I can think of you as a friend, can I not?'

'You can indeed, ma'am – Charlotte – and I thank you for the compliment,' said Lamb happily. He lifted his glass to her. 'And I insist that you call me Matthew. Your very good health, Charlotte.' How beautifully the name rolled off the tongue!

'And yours, Matthew.'

They drank, their eyes smiling over their glasses. Lamb was suddenly stricken with shyness and he turned his attention to his soup. If Charlotte was similarly afflicted, she gave no sign of it. 'This is very good soup, Matthew – and hot, too! I must admit I was getting a trifle weary of cold food. How kind you are to let me share your table.'

'Here we are, sir,' announced Sylvester, giving the doorpost a kick by way of a knock. 'Hot beef-and-onion puddin' with the cook's best wishes.'

He placed the steaming dish in the centre of the table and gathered up the soup plates, taking the opportunity to leer down the front of Charlotte's dress. Lamb gave him a warning glare, to which the steward raised a questioning, innocent eyebrow.

'Duff and fruit and cheese to follow, sir,' said the little man, giving Charlotte the benefit of his smile as he left the cabin.

'I shall serve,' said Charlotte, seizing the spoon. 'I am sure you would give me far too much, otherwise.'

She heaped a great mound of the pudding onto Lamb's plate and placed a tiny portion onto her own. 'There! And there is a little left if you are still hungry when that is gone.'

Lamb refilled their glasses, pleased that Charlotte was keeping pace with him glass for glass. She was clearly not one of those women who could stretch half a glass over an entire evening as if sipping from a brew of the devil.

'This claret is quite delicious,' she said as she put down her glass and reached for the salt. 'Have you been serving long in this part of the world, Matthew?'

'Not as long as some.' Lamb talked for a while of himself as they ate, and she listened with silent interest, studying his face in a searching way, spurring him on with an occasional question or a laughing comment. The atmosphere between them became very easy and informal, and Lamb, now happy and relaxed, found himself wishing that the evening would never end, astonished that he had the attention of this lovely woman entirely to himself.

The duff and fruit and cheese arrived. Lamb put the empty claret bottle to one side and filled the glasses with white wine.

'Oh, this is sharp!' Charlotte cried, wrinkling her nose. 'I am sure if I'd had this first I would have not drunk so much.' She laughed and took another large sip.

The wine had clearly taken hold of her. She giggled merrily at Lamb's slightest witticism, her eyes sparkled and a pink flush had spread over her face and down the soft whiteness of her throat and breasts. Lamb, too, was not unaffected by the wine and he allowed his eyes to linger with increasing warmth at the neck of her dress.

'I am pleased to see that your cold is so much improved from this morning,' he remarked mischievously.

'Oh, fie, Matthew! You know very well I was in tears. I was very low this morning, very low; but I have spoken to myself very firmly and I am quite reconciled to going home to cold, grey England. The past is past, Matthew; let us drink to the future, whatever it may bring.'

'I willingly drink to that,' said Lamb and they drained their glasses.

Charlotte belched daintily behind her hand. 'Oh, dear me! I do beg your pardon.'

Lamb chuckled and poured more wine. His own head was beginning to sing and he felt comfortably and pleasantly at his ease, almost boneless, as he leaned back in his chair with his ankles crossed; even the tumescence that had been plaguing him for the past hour had finally wearied. He recognized the signs; it would not take more than two or three more glasses before he reached that stage where unsteadiness was followed by incoherence and he decided that his present glassful must be his last.

Charlotte leaned across the table, giving his delighted eyes a sight of hitherto hidden areas, and patted his hand. She gave him a crooked smile; she was quite drunk, he realized, and he grinned in return, leaning closer.

'Do you know, Matthew, you have very kind eyes. I like men with kind eyes.' She shook her head sadly. 'My husband did not have kind eyes – no, nor a kind nature. Someone else I know sometimes had kind eyes, but he kept his kind nature for his wife. He disappointed me, Matthew; he had no courage, no backbone, when I needed it. So much man and so little spirit.'

Tears filled her eyes and ran down her cheeks. She lowered her head and sobbed, her shoulders shaking. Lamb, aghast, pushed back his chair and crouched beside her, fumbling for his handkerchief, thanking God that it was clean. She turned and clung to him like a child while he awkwardly patted her shoulder, murmuring: 'Now, now, Charlotte, now, now,' and revelling, in spite of the moment, in the closeness and softness and womanly feel of her, the delicate perfume and the brush of her hair against his cheek. Her sobs eased and she drew back, taking the proffered handkerchief and dabbing at her eyes.

'I am sorry, Matthew, so sorry. I promised myself I would be strong. It must have been the wine. What must you think of me?'

Lamb placed his hands on her shoulders and drew her close and kissed her salty lips, quite without conscious will and with no more thought of a rebuff than if he had patted her hand. She gripped his arms and pressed herself close, kissing back surprisingly hungrily. For a few moments Lamb's spirit soared high on wings of joy and wonder.

Charlotte released her grip and pulled away. She gave a breathless, tremulous smile. 'Oh, Matthew, Matthew, you are so nice, so very nice. But it is too soon – I must not . . . Oh, what am I trying to say? My head is swimming.' She stared at him closely for a moment and then abruptly pushed back her chair. 'I must go.'

Lamb rose with her and stood, tall and solemn with his head bowed beneath the low beams, unable to think of a single word that would not jar, filled with a deep and fierce tenderness for her and the faint stirrings of reawakened lust.

She reached up and kissed him lightly on the cheek. 'It was a lovely supper, Matthew. Goodnight.'

'Goodnight, Charlotte. Sleep well.'

Lamb stood without moving for a few moments, staring thoughtfully at the door through which she had passed, and then lowered himself into her chair and sipped at the remains of her wine. Jamieson's slow, heavy footfall sounded overhead from the quiet deck and the ship's bell gave four melancholy notes, signalling that the first watch was two hours old.

Lamb smiled. 'Matthew, my boy, if you are not very careful, you may find yourself in love,' he murmured aloud to his empty chair, and then left his cabin, making his way up to the moon-bright deck to clear the mists of wine from his head.

A flying fish slapped onto the deck beside his foot and thrashed, desperate to fly back to its own element. Flushed with new tenderness, Lamb picked it up and dropped it gently over the side.

Chapter 8

The *Heron* glided gently under reduced sail through the ruffled water of Carlisle Bay and turning into the wind, backed her topsail and lost way.

'Let go the best bower,' called Lamb from beside the tiller.

'Let go!' snapped Snow from beside the mainmast, turning his head to glare at the men waiting at the cat-head.

The anchor plunged sullenly into the water beside the starboard bow and the cutter came to rest, tugging at the cable in the slight chop of the bay.

There was very little shipping in the bay; a merchantman tied to the wharf, a two-decker moored under bare poles and a handful of assorted small craft suggested to Lamb that this was hardly the busy, crowded rendezvous for convoys he had expected to find. It may be, he thought, that he had arrived at a quiet time between arrivals and departures. He turned his attention to the town as Jamieson and the boatswain supervised the lowering of the boat and the stowage of the mail-bags. Bridgetown lay bathed in morning sunshine, a low sprawl of white-painted buildings split in two by the narrow finger of Carlisle Bay thrusting inland. There was no soaring backcloth of mountain peaks or rocky heights typical of the curving chain of islands to the west; the town was set at the edge of countryside as gentle and serene as that of England's rolling downs. Inland he could see half a dozen scattered windmills, their arms forever circling in the unfailing winds of the Trades.

'The mail is stowed and snug in the boat, sir,' reported Jamieson, condescending to give Lamb a touch of his hat.

'Very good. Tell me, where will I find. . . ?'

An appreciative glint came into Jamieson's eye and Lamb turned to see Charlotte approaching, her face grave and demure beneath a white bonnet. The two officers swept off their hats.

'Good morning, ma'am,' said Lamb, his heart leaping.

'Good morning, ma'am,' said Jamieson, his square young face broadened by a huge grin.

'Good morning, gentlemen. Captain, would you be so kind as to set me ashore?'

'Of course, ma'am. Have you in mind to do a little shopping?'

'Yes, but I thought I would take myself a room at an inn for the night. I long for a bath and a steady bed, and firm ground beneath my feet for a while. When do we sail?'

'At noon tomorrow,' said Lamb. He was loath to see her leave the ship. 'You will not be late? I should hate to sail off and leave you marooned with those savages ashore.'

She did not smile. 'I shall be waiting for the boat at eleven o'clock, precisely where you put me ashore,' she promised. 'Could you let me have a man to carry my bag and see me to an inn?'

'Mr Jamieson here knows the town, ma'am. He will be delighted to look after you.'

'Yes, indeed, ma'am,' said Jamieson joyfully and he took up her bag and skipped into the boat so that he might have the chance of touching her as he helped her down.

'Charlotte,' said Lamb quietly, using her name with a degree of shyness, 'are you sure you wish to spend the night ashore? You know nobody here – it might . . .'

'I am not a child, sir,' she snapped, with a touch of her old spirit. 'I just wish to get away from that damned cell of a cabin for a few hours.'

'Yes, of course,' muttered Lamb, taken aback by her sudden sharpness. 'Let me see you down into the boat.'

Jamieson reached up his hand and settled her down beside him, leaving Lamb separated from them by a heap of mail-bags and listening to Jamieson's cheerful talk as he described the town to the attentively nodding Charlotte. The pair of them walked away from the wharf with Jamieson stepping close and his tongue as busy as ever, and watching them Lamb reflected gloomily that he might have been wiser to have sent the ancient Sylvester as escort to her.

It was Sunday; Lamb found the Harbour Captain's office

140

locked and deserted, the mail-office shut up, and the Navy Yard closed. War or no war, the officials, administrators and shore-based officers were today bowing to the needs of their souls or the demands of their flesh and were anywhere but at their offices. Lamb returned silently raging to the boat, where Jamieson, who had it in mind to request a few hours shore leave for dark reasons of his own, took one look at his captain's furious expression and sensibly held his tongue. Back on the deck of the *Heron* Lamb was immediately approached by the boatswain, a man of considerably less sensitivity than Jamieson and to whom Lamb's dark scowl might not have existed for all the effect it had on his stolid nature.

'Shore leave for the hands, sir?' he demanded, with a touch of his hat.

'Yes, why not?' replied Lamb, a trifle savagely. 'There will be damn all work for them today, by the look of things. Watch and watch, Mr Snow, four hours apiece.'

Jamieson seized his chance and put in his own plea and was rewarded with a nod. Lamb went below and the boat pulled shorewards again, bearing the starboard watch intent on whatever devilry they could find and afford, and Jamieson, eager to renew the close acquaintance he had made on his last visit with a dark lady of extraordinary stamina whose practice was hard by the rum shops of the wharves. Lamb spent a quiet day with the ship's books and papers, a great deal of time slumped in silent contemplation of the bulkhead, and retired early to his cot.

Monday morning brought a wan and drained Jamieson back to the *Heron* and sent Lamb and the mail-bags ashore. At the mail-office he collected bags for Port Royal and at the Harbour Captain's office he was given orders to postpone sailing for twenty-four hours in order to embark two officers and twenty Marines for Jamaica.

'Twenty Marines, sir?' echoed Jamieson hotly. 'The ship will burst at the seams. Where shall we put them all?'

Lamb looked down at the youth's indignant frown and resisted the temptation to snap. Had Jamieson been serving on a rated ship he would never have dared to express his feelings so bluntly – if at all. On a small cutter, however, a certain amount of leeway was to be expected and tolerated.

'The lieutenants can go into the two spare cabins,' he said patiently. 'The sergeants can mess with Mr Snow and Mr Mee and for the remainder, I will allow you to exercise your undoubted initiative. They will not be coming aboard until tomorrow morning, so you will have plenty of time to get all their little cots made up.'

'Cots, sir? They will be lucky to have one hammock between four, standing on end.'

'I leave it all in your very capable hands, Mr Jamieson,' said Lamb, cheerfully unhelpful. 'I shall be going ashore for a few hours. The water-hoy is due alongside shortly and I want you to take on board every drop you can. With an extra twenty-two men we may well need it all.'

'Aye aye, sir,' muttered Jamieson morosely, squinting his bloodshot eyes against the stabbing agony of the morning sunlight.

Lamb dived below to his cabin, gave himself a hasty wash, fretted over an obstinate pimple and counted the money that was left to him from his purchases at Antigua. It ought to be enough, he thought, and ran up to the deck with a sudden lightening of his spirit, eager to be ashore.

It wanted at least five minutes to eleven o'clock when Lamb picked out the slight figure on the quay with a quickening of his heart while the boat was still a couple of hundred yards off. He would dearly have loved to wave a hand but curbed his eagerness and managed to maintain a stern, expressionless face quite at odds with his bubbling feelings.

'Back to the ship, Timms,' he ordered as he stepped from the boat. 'Pick me up at six.'

'Aye aye, sir, six o'clock it is,' growled Timms with a knowing leer as he pushed off from the steps.

Charlotte met him at the top of the steps with a puzzled frown at the receding boat. 'You have sent the boat away!'

Lamb smiled down at her, drinking in her clean freshness, itching to touch her. He was struck by a sudden nervousness – he was being far too presumptious, he thought. 'We have had a change of orders. We do not sail until tomorrow. I was thinking

142

that you might care to see a little of the island. We could hire a trap, perhaps.'

She clapped her hands together. 'Oh, what a kind thought! That will be delightful. But what about my things?'

Lamb glanced at the bags and parcels piled at the feet of a young black boy whose skin shone like polished marble and whose eyes and teeth flashed with the joy of living. 'Your footman can leave them where we hire the carriage. I saw a place when I was ashore earlier. It is this way.' He nodded at the little black boy. 'Pick them up and tag on astern, youngster.'

Charlotte fell into step beside him, taking two steps to his one, her fingers resting lightly on his arm. They threaded their way along the busy wharf with Charlotte's parcels bringing up the rear, passing the merchantman whose gangplanks bounced to lines of trotting men carrying enormous sacks on their shoulders, and weaving in and out of stacks of barrels and sacks and boxes. Lamb felt enormously happy.

Charlotte laughed suddenly. 'You were very sure of yourself just then, were you not, sending the boat away like that. What would you have done if I had said no?'

Lamb glanced at her face and grinned. 'Such a thing never entered my head,' he lied.

'Such conceit!'

The trap was hired, the boy sent happily on his way clutching far too many of Lamb's coins, and the horse hitched. Lamb lent his arm for Charlotte to lean on as she climbed lightly up and he sprang up beside her and took the reins, feeling a sense of bubbling anticipation that he had not experienced since he was a schoolboy at the start of the holidays.

'She won't need any hard driving, sir,' called the ostler. 'She works better without the whip.'

'Very good,' said Lamb and clicked his tongue and shook the reins.

'Don't forget the brake, sir,' said the man, hiding his grin.

The trap rattled and swayed along narrow Broad Street, the knowing horse picking its way between the roadside stalls and the heedless pedestrians with room to spare, in spite of Lamb's

143

awkward, inexperienced twitches at the reins.

'Where are we heading?' asked Charlotte as the houses thinned and rolling fields of green young canes opened out before them.

'North. There is another port there, Speightstown, an hour or so's drive, I understand. It is not too far for you?'

'No, no.'

'We could eat there, I thought.'

'Mmm, I am famished. I had little breakfast. Look, Matthew, have you ever seen so many windmills all at once? It is just like Holland, I am sure.'

The narrow, tree-lined road swung left to follow the sparkling sea. The horse made its own steady pace, refusing to be hurried, and Charlotte laughed at Lamb's growls and threats and shakings of the reins as he tried without success to induce an extra knot from the stubborn beast. Charlotte was very gay, sitting close to Lamb and pressing his arm as they laughed together. The road headed due north, straight as an arrow, with the blue sea to the left and neat, cultivated fields to the right. The black field workers leaned on their hoes and waved and grinned beneath their straw hats as the trap made its slow way past and Lamb and Charlotte raised their hands in reply. They rattled through little Holetown and on along the straight road, the sun striking hot and Charlotte's bonnet ribbons flying in the warm breeze.

At Speightstown Lamb put the nosebag on the horse and left it in the shade of a tree while they ate in a small, dark inn – baked ham, yams and coconut bread. They lingered over a second pot of strong, rich coffee, talking lightly and easily – nothing very deep – comfortable in each other's presence and with Lamb, for his part, happily entranced. The town was quiet and sleepy in the hot, afternoon sunshine as they wandered slowly around the little forts, down to the old quay and then back to the town to rouse the nodding horse. The sun hung low over the sea as they made their way south, blinking through the tall trees on their right and flooding the road and fields with orange light and deep, violet shadows. The horse, knowing it was homeward bound, quickened its pace at last without encouragement and the trap swayed and bounced along the hard, rutted road.

144

Charlotte leaned close and sighed, gripping Lamb's arm and causing him to almost burst with happiness.

'It has been a perfect, perfect day, Matthew,' she murmured. 'Thank you so much. It has quite taken me out of myself. I felt so low and wretched yesterday, and so guilty about my tears in your cabin. I am sorry, it must have been very embarrassing for you.'

It was the first time she had mentioned the previous evening; Lamb glanced at her a little warily.

'Nonsense,' he said stoutly. 'It was . . .'

The horse, startled by a rat or a snake, shied, swerved and pulled the trap onto the grass beside the road. The trap tipped sharply sideways, Charlotte gave a short scream of fright and Lamb flung out an arm to hold her in her seat. There was a sharp crack of timber and the hard earth rose up and hit him on the head and shoulders. Charlotte's anxious face swam above him and there was a moment of blank unknowing. Then memory returned and he sat quickly upright. The world rocked and steadied but he gave her a reassuring grin although something hammered busily inside his head.

'Are you hurt?' he asked, touching her shoulder.

'No, I fell on top of you. You look very pale, Matthew. Are you sure. . . ?'

'Yes, yes. Perfectly.'

The trap was on its side in the deep ditch, one wheel was lying a dozen yards further on and the perfidious horse was quietly cropping at the coarse vegetation at the edge of the road, still tethered to the broken shafts.

They were some two or three miles from Bridgetown, Lamb guessed, and there was nothing to do but set off along the rutted, darkening road side by side with the horse snorting and champing behind them and the cut traces in Lamb's hand. They walked in silence for some ten minutes, the pain gradually easing in Lamb's head, and then suddenly, wonderfully, Charlotte's slim fingers had crept in to his hand and entwined themselves with his. He said nothing, not daring to break the quiet joy of the moment, and they walked on through the violet dusk without so much as a look or a word to acknowledge the shared warmth of their clasped hands.

At the point where the road turned away from the sea, just north of the town, the trees to their right had been cleared and here, as if to a signal, they halted and gazed at the magnificence of the setting sun. The whole sweep of the sky to the west was hugely washed with rich pink and streaked with a delicate green, merging overhead into the darkening blue of the encroaching night. The sun was a mere sliver balanced on the far rim of the sea, sending its orange light flooding over the serene water; it blinked and was gone and the orange sea faded to the deepest of deep blues, the smallest step from black.

'It makes me shiver,' said Charlotte quietly. 'It is like standing in an enormous cathedral.'

Lamb turned his head towards her. She looked at him, her eyes wide, her skin flushed with the warm glow of the pink sky, her expression quiet and grave. He bent his head and kissed her very gently, his mind quite free from passion, and she responded in the same way, her lips soft and yielding. She stroked his cheek and turned away, the horse nuzzled at his shoulder and they walked on into the town hand in hand.

'Andrew Crouch,' said the larger Marine lieutenant in a loud, genial voice, extending his hand.

'Matthew Lamb. Welcome aboard, Mr Crouch.'

'Jack St John,' said the other. 'How do you do?'

'Welcome aboard, Mr St John. Mr Jamieson has cabins ready for you. Your two sergeants will mess with my warrant officers but your men will have to make the best of things in the hold, I am afraid. Our space is a trifle limited.'

Crouch laughed. 'That will not do them any harm. They will rather enjoy the passage, I fancy; your deck space is so small that we won't be able to drill the buggers. Careful with that bag there, fellow!' he shouted angrily at the seaman at the side. 'If you bump it like that again I shall bump your bloody arse over the side! My hunting guns,' he explained to Lamb. 'Cost me a bloody fortune.'

Lamb watched the scarlet file of Marines clamber onto the deck, each burdened with musket, blanket roll, haversack and pouches, and move forward to disappear below, hastened on their way by the impatient shouts of their sergeants.

146

He turned to Crouch. 'You are the senior, sir?'

'Yes, for my bloody pains.'

'Then with your permission, once we are at sea, I will employ the Marines at the guns. The exercise will be beneficial all round.'

'Capital notion, sir. Fresh air and honest sweat will soon shake the stink of the bloody rum shops and brothels out of 'em. Use them as you will, captain – it will save me the bother of trying to keep the buggers healthily occupied.'

Crouch chuckled, pleased at having rid himself of a tiresome chore. He was a large, beefy man a year or two older than Lamb, with a loud, confident voice redolent of wealth and privilege and a pampered youth. Lamb had taken an instant dislike to him.

'Thank you, Mr Crouch,' he said with a smile. 'Have you any preference for one side to the other?'

The Marine looked about him, puzzled at the question. 'No, they both look much of a muchness to me.'

'In that case you may take charge of the starboard guns at practice, and Mr St John the larboard. We shall make a start this very afternoon; there is no point in wasting time.'

Crouch goggled, struck dumb at the idea. St John laughed and clapped him on the shoulder.

'Fresh air and honest sweat will soon shake the stink of rum shops and brothels out of you, Andrew!' He turned his laughing face to Lamb. 'We shall both be delighted to make acquaintance with your guns, sir.'

'Splendid,' beamed Lamb. He much preferred the look of the younger officer, his slim figure and boyish face a marked contrast to Crouch's corpulent, indulged appearance. He nodded at Jamieson, conversing with the sergeants. 'I do not know how familiar you both are with four-pounders, but may I suggest that a word with Mr Jamieson there might be to your advantage? He will be pleased to show you over them.'

'Of course, of course,' said Crouch, determined not to allow his junior to take control of the arrangements. 'They do not come new to either of us, as it happens.' He changed tack abruptly. 'Have you any other passengers, sir?'

'Only the one; a young woman by the name of Mrs Brett.

147

You will meet her later, I don't doubt.'

Crouch's face showed immediate interest. 'A married lady, eh? Joining her husband in Jamaica, is she?'

'No, she is a widow. She is on her way home.'

'A widow!' Crouch gave St John a wink of massive significance. 'We must do our best to make this part of her journey a happy one, eh, Jack?'

Lamb's dislike of the man became several degrees stronger. He caught sight of Sylvester heading for the companion hatch with a heavy bag over his narrow shoulder and gave him a hail.

'Sylvester! Show these officers to their cabins, if you please. You must excuse me, gentlemen. I have pressing duties to attend to.'

The *Heron* sailed sharp on noon, heading north-west out of Carlisle Bay into the Caribbean Sea with a fine, brisk following wind. Two hours later Barbados was a blue smudge far astern and the Marines, many of them no more than boys, were spread about the guns on both sides of the deck, their naked backs and chests considerably paler than those of the *Heron*'s nut-brown seamen. Their officers and sergeants, clinging resolutely to the splendour of their coats, paced restlessly beside the guns, anxious that their men should not put the Royal Marines to shame before the cutter's small sample of the Royal Navy. Lamb nodded to Jamieson, to whom he had given the honour of conducting the practice and who was delighted to see full gun-crews to starboard and larboard for once.

'When you are ready, Mr Jamieson.'

'Open ports!' roared Jamieson. 'Run out the guns!'

For half an hour the deck rumbled and vibrated to the rolling of the squealing gun-carriages on their wooden wheels as the Marines and the sprinkling of seamen amongst them ran the guns in and out and wielded the worms and sponges and rammers. Lamb strolled up and down the deck, looking benignly on and saying nothing, leaving everything to Jamieson and the Marine lieutenants. He was pleased at the speed with which the young Marines became familiar with their tasks and, in spite of his dislike for the man, impressed by Crouch's professional, economic bark and his quick eye for the awkward or the stupid. When he was satisfied that the new gunners knew their duties well enough to handle powder and shot without killing themselves, he passed the word to Jamieson and watched from beside the tiller as, first on the starboard side and then on the larboard, the guns crashed and flamed, sending gunsmoke billowing about the deck and whipping off to leeward, and the sea-birds wheeling high in squawking fright.

'Secure the guns, Mr Jamieson.'

'Swab out!' shouted Jamieson, striding up and down with a ferocious scowl, thoroughly enjoying himself. 'Secure the guns! Close ports!'

Crouch was sweating hard, his large, red face awash with moisture that dripped freely from his nose and chin. 'Well, let us have your opinion, sir,' he boomed as Lamb approached. 'We did not disgrace ourselves, I think?'

'Far from it, Mr Crouch, far from it. For green hands they far exceeded my expectations. They would be welcome on any self-respecting ship of the line,' said Lamb, laying it on a trifle thick. 'We just need to add a little speed and polish, and we can make a start on that tomorrow. I was most pleased with the enthusiasm you gentlemen both showed; that can make all the difference, as you well know. I saw that there is little we can teach you about gunnery, Mr Crouch. It was a pleasure to see you at work.'

A little butter went a long way with Crouch, as Lamb had shrewdly guessed, and when Lamb left he was deep in earnest discussion with Jamieson about the next day's practice, gesticulating from gun to gun, showering the unfortunate youth with perspiration and impatiently chopping short St John's tentative contributions.

Lamb glanced at the sky as the cutter heeled to a wayward gust. Clouds were building up from the north-east, slow-rolling, snowy billows where they met the blue of the sky, stained with grey below. They were in for a bit of a blow, he thought, nothing very serious, probably more rain than storm. He paced the deck abaft of the mainmast, his eye alert to the sails and sky, hearing Crouch's loud laughter come up from below, his thoughts mainly concerned with Charlotte. Apart from a brief moment after breakfast when he had extracted a

149

promise from her to sup with him that evening, she had kept
to her cabin throughout the day, as she had on the southerly
run from Antigua. Lamb had gently chided her about this
while they were drinking coffee in Speightstown but she had
laughed, assuring him that she was happy enough with her
books and diary and letter-writing and when she was weary of
those there were always Sylvester's pots of tea or a catnap; in
any case, she much preferred the quiet of the evening deck to
the crowded activity of the day and the curious eyes of the
seamen.

Lamb was quite besotted with her; whether this was the
same as being in love, he was unsure. She certainly occupied
many of his thoughts and his dreams, but his yearnings were as
physical as they were emotional, and he was far from certain
that lust did not outweigh his purer feelings. It may be, he
mused, as he walked slowly back and forth, that the two feelings
always went hand in glove; he knew that lust unencumbered by
love was possible, but was the reverse also true? He did not
think so, at least, so far as he was concerned; his urges were
never far below the surface and his frequent tender thoughts of
Charlotte were sometimes attended by involuntary stirrings of
quite another nature. Her feelings towards him were a constant
source of conjecture in his mind. He was not so conceited as to
imagine that they were as strong as his own towards her, but it
had become clear that she found his company amusing and
acceptable. Did she, too, suffer from lustful imaginings, he
wondered? Until recently he had always considered women to
be free from such demanding urges but his weeks with Mrs
Mainwaring had opened his eyes. Charlotte was not inexperienced and he suspected that below that cool, grave demeanour
lay a woman of some passion. The clouds rolled higher and
darker and the deck increased its slope to larboard as the wind
gained in strength. The first drops of rain began to fall while the
hands were shortening sail and Lamb leaned over the companionway and bellowed for Sylvester to bring up his
tarpaulins.

'You'll not want the trousis, sir?' enquired Sylvester, peering
up from below and careful not to show a grin.

'Just get a damned move on,' snapped Lamb, in no mood for

150

the steward's humour as the rain began to lash at the back of his neck.

Sylvester scampered up with the tarpaulin coat and, as Lamb struggled into it and vainly tried to pull the cuffs to somewhere approaching his wrists, the steward said: 'A message from the lady, sir. She sends her regrets but she can't take supper with you tonight. She said to say she's undispersed, sir.'

Lamb savagely jammed down his sou'wester. 'Indisposed, you mean, you fool.'

'That's it, sir,' agreed Sylvester cheerfully. 'Retiring early, she said. Asked for a dish of tea, she has.'

'Give her my best wishes when you take it to her.'

'Aye aye, sir.'

The rain lashed harder, the sky grew darker and Lamb stood hunched beneath it, his mood as bleak as the weather, convinced that Charlotte's indisposition was a polite invention in order to save her from the tedium of his company. Perhaps he had been too pressing, too demanding of her time – had become a damned nuisance, in fact. His cheeks grew warm at the thought. Well, that was soon mended; he would keep a cool distance from now on, friendly but impersonal. The resolution did not cheer him.

The rain passed over as suddenly as it had arrived, the clouds rolled away and the *Heron* sailed on into the evening under a warm breeze and clear skies. Lamb took his supper alone with the familiar words of Moore's *The Complete Navigator* propped up before him, shutting his ears to the loud laughter and the sound of Crouch's booming voice coming from the Marine's cabin forward. Later two masculine voices raised themselves in drunken song and Lamb shut his door on the noise and took Moore to his cot. He fell asleep half-way through the chapter on double altitudes.

The same low pensive mood was with him during the long, quiet hours of the morning watch, but daylight and a serene blue sky, coupled with thoughts of breakfast, lightened his temper considerably, and when Jamieson relieved him at eight o'clock, he greeted him with a cheerful grin.

'Good morning, Mr Jamieson.'

'Good morning, sir. A clear, fine day.'

151

'Your keen eye is a source of constant wonder to me.'

'Thank you, sir.'

Lamb's shaving water was waiting for him when he ducked into his cabin and he was standing before his mirror, lathering his face, when Sylvester bustled in with a loaded tray.

'Here you are, sir,' said the wrinkled elf as he laid the dishes on the table. 'Eggs, ham, toast and coffee, all hot. Don't let it get cold, now.'

'I shall finish my shave first, with your kind permission,' said Lamb, stropping his razor. 'Be so good as to pour me a cup of that stuff you call coffee before you go.'

He took a sip of coffee, pursing his lips so as not to dislodge his lather, and took up his razor. A shout, an angry bellow and the sound of running feet above his head made him pause before he had taken his first stroke. More shouts followed and he swore, seized his towel and ran up to the deck hastily wiping his soapy face. A small group of men was standing by the forward hatch, two of them held in the firm grip of the boatswain and his mate and thrusting their chins at each other as they snarled and struggled.

'Belay that, you two!' snapped Lamb, striding forward. 'What the devil is going on here, Mr Jamieson?'

'A fight, sir – or the start of one, at least.'

'Fighting, is it? I'll give them bloody fighting! I'll have them fighting for breath under the keel!' Lamb gave the men a hard glare. 'Blackett, isn't it? And you, the Marine, what's your name?'

'Bennett, sir,' said the man sulkily. He was still angry and full of fight; he glowered at Blackett, who returned the look, no less angry.

'Right, what was it all about?' asked Lamb. 'Blackett?'

''E started it, sir. Called me names, 'e did, and pushed me.'

'It were him first, sir,' protested the Marine, hotly. 'Just standing quiet, I was . . .'

'Bloody lyin' bullock!'

'I'll bloody show you who's a bullock!'

'Hold your damned tongues,' snapped Lamb. 'Another lying word and I'll have the grating rigged and the skin off your backs.'

He would never get to the bottom of it, he knew. Bringing them up for punishment would do little good; he would have to punish both of them and the thing between them would simmer and boil over again. The last thing he wanted was bad blood between his seamen and the Marines. Better by far to let them get it out of their systems in the time-honoured way, but he would give them half an hour for their blood to cool a little. That would give him time to finish his shave and eat his breakfast before it congealed on the plate. He gave them both a hard stare and nodded.

'Very well. If you want to fight, then fight you will. You can settle your differences with your knuckles. Keep them apart until nine o'clock, Mr Snow, and then call the hands to form a ring.'

He flung his towel over his shoulder and walked aft, thinking that he had the choice between warm shaving water and a warm breakfast. He ran a hand over his chin and opted for the warm breakfast.

Charlotte appeared at her door as he reached the foot of the companionway. She gave him an uncharacteristically shy smile.

'Hello, Matthew.'

'Charlotte!' He stepped closer. 'Are you feeling better this morning?'

She gave a slight shake of her head. 'There was nothing really wrong with me. I had much thinking to do and being with you would have – would have disturbed me. You have soap in your ear.'

Lamb scrubbed at his face with the damp towel. Disturb her? What did she mean?

'And is all this deep thinking over now?' he asked, thinking how delightful she looked in her pale blue wrap, with her curls fetchingly tousled.

'Yes, I think so.' She raised herself on her toes and dabbed a quick kiss on his cheek. 'You taste of soap,' she said with a pretty grimace and stepping back into her cabin, gently closed the door.

Lamb touched his cheek and stared for a long moment at her door, a happy grin of wonder and joy spreading wide. He walked slowly into his cabin and taking up his shaving brush, re-lathered his face from the tepid water and thoughtfully shaved himself with many pauses while his breakfast grew colder on its plate.

The ship's bell sounded the hour as Lamb emerged onto the deck. The entire ship's company was gathered abaft the mainmast, forming a rough ring of men discreetly using their elbows to gain a better viewpoint. Crouch and St John had cleared a free space for themselves and the larger Marine turned a huge grin towards Lamb.

'You know what is about to happen here, Mr Crouch,' said Lamb. 'I take it you have no objection to your man taking part? It is either that or formal punishment.'

'Objection? Not I. I only hope they put on a bloody decent show.'

Lamb made his way into the centre of the ring and beckoned Snow to bring the two contestants before him. Both men were stripped to the waist; Blackett thin, wiry, as hard and brown as tanned leather, Bennett larger, heavier, his pale body well muscled. They stared to their front, neither man looking at the other.

'Now I want this to be a fair fight,' announced Lamb, speaking loudly to include the watching seamen and Marines. 'I want no one crippled by it, do you understand? You will use your knuckles only – no elbows, feet, knees, heads, teeth or nails. Clear?'

Both men nodded.

'Aye, sir.'

'Yes, sir.'

'If one man goes down the other will stand back until he rises. You will fight until one of you has had enough or I decide to put an end to it. Mr Snow, you will see to the observance of these rules, if you please.' Lamb stepped back and motioned the two men to face each other. 'Go to it.'

He rejoined the two Marine officers and stood watching as the two men circled warily. Bennett swung a large fist at the seaman's head and Blackett ducked out of its way.

'Two to one the little 'un,' said Crouch.

'There will be no gambling on this ship, Mr Crouch,' snapped Lamb.

154

Crouch raised an eyebrow. 'Figure of speech, sir. I was merely stating his chances, not the odds.'

Blackett danced in close and struck hard, once, twice, at the bigger man's ribs. He reeled back as a fist landed heavily on his forehead. He shook his head and grinned as the Marine sucked his bruised knuckles and flexed his hand, and sprang forward again to drive Bennett backward with quick blows to his head, throat and chest. Bennett came up against the men forming the ring, who pushed him off, and he lunged forward roaring like a young bull, striking aside Blackett's darting fists and rocking his head back with a wild blow that split the seaman's lips. Blackett staggered, spat blood and came forward again, straight into another punch that caught him below the ear and dropped him instantly to the deck.

'Stand back, stand back!' roared Snow as Bennett bent over the seaman with his fist raised to strike. The boatswain rushed at the Marine and pushed him away with the thrust of one massive arm. 'Stand back when you're fuckin' told!' he snarled. He bent over Blackett and bellowed into his ear. 'Get on your feet, you idle bugger!' An enormous hand plucked the seaman to his feet and held him steady as he shook the mists from his brain and firmed his limp legs. The boatswain's lips moved beside Blackett's ear as he muttered something and with a reassuring slap on the seaman's shoulder, Snow strode away.

Blackett swayed, blood dripping from his mouth onto his chest, and Bennett, sensing victory within his grasp, stepped forward and aimed a careful, powerful blow at his opponent's head. Blackett dropped to a crouch and as the Marine's fist whistled over his head, punched his adversary heavily in his tightly-bunched groin, a wicked, crunching blow that brought a shrill scream of agony from Bennett's gaping mouth and bent him double.

'Now, Jem, hit the bastard hard!'

'Now's your chance, Jem; flatten the bullock!'

Shouts of excited advice arose from the *Heron*'s men as the Marine staggered backwards, one hand clutching at his groin and the other held up to ward off the seaman. Blackett gave a bloody grin and went after him, his weathered, teak-hard fists smashing again and again at Bennett's face and chest. The

Marine was young and big and strong, and he took all that Blackett gave him without going down, backing away all the time and striking out wildly in return. A swinging blow from a forearm caught Blackett in the throat and he backed off, choking for air through his bruised windpipe. For several seconds the two men held off, swaying, panting and glaring at each other, their bodies gleaming with sweat and blood. Bennett's face was now also badly marked; blood welled from a split eyebrow into an eye swollen and half-closed, and more blood streamed from his battered nose. The ring of watching men was silent and enthralled, staring fixedly at the two protagonists, waiting for them to clash once more.

They went for each other with a rush and met toe to toe exchanging blows by the dozen, the seaman ducking and dodging, escaping some of the Marine's heavy punches but still hit hard; Bennett, slower, less experienced in brawling, taking vicious blows to the head but landing some wild and heavy fists. They backed away from each other again, desperately sucking in air through bloodied lips, shaking their heads and scattering sweat and blood over the white, scrubbed deck planks.

'Evens now the little 'un,' murmured Crouch, giving Lamb a sly, sideways grin.

The two men staggered close again, their punches slower and weaker now, not bothering to guard themselves but concentrating on hitting each other, both men grunting with effort and pain. Suddenly Bennett dropped to his knees. His face was a mask of blood, his open mouth struggling for air. Blackett stood over him raining blows down at his head until the boatswain stepped leisurely forward.

'Stand back now, Blackett,' he said disapprovingly. 'You know the rules.'

Crouch gave Lamb an indignant frown. 'Your bo'sun would not have any money on your man, by any chance, would he?'

'Of course not,' said Lamb; 'he knows that gambling is quite illegal.'

'Yes, of course,' said Crouch in a tone of deep unconviction.

The watching Marines were bellowing at their man to get off his knees, he'd rested long enough, what the bloody hell was he playing at? Bennett raised himself valiantly to his feet and stood swaying like a drunk pawing at the air. Blackett, his strength and wind almost gone, his knuckles split and bleeding, stumbled forward with his fists raised, and for half a minute the two men exchanged a dozen weak punches, staggering on legs which threatened to buckle beneath them. They fell against each other, clutching for mutual support, and suddenly they were on their knees, forehead against forehead, their arms still moving in vague, punching motions.

'Enough!' cried Lamb, striding into the ring. 'No more! It is an honourable conclusion. We have neither winner nor loser here. Mr Snow, have some sea water drawn up for these brave men.'

He stood back as the two men were doused with water and pulled to their feet, held upright by their friends. They were a sorry sight, dripping with water and blood, peering through eyes almost closed, their lips puffed and torn. Lamb ordered them to shake hands and reminded them firmly that their disagreement was now at an end. Blackett and Bennett appeared to be of the same opinion; they grinned horribly at each other as they gingerly clasped battered hands and patted at shoulders before being led away to have their wounds treated with vinegar and their strength revived with illicitly hoarded rum.

Crouch fell into step beside Lamb as he walked aft. 'A bloody fine show they put up, the pair of 'em,' said the Marine. 'But my man should have won, you know.'

Lamb laughed. 'Nonsense. He had his chance, the same as Blackett, but neither won.'

'But what about that wicked punch to Bennett's balls? Hardly bloody fair, that. And that boatswain of yours . . . Hello! This must be our fair passenger, who has been hiding her charms from us all this time.'

Charlotte had stepped from the aft companionway and was looking vaguely about her. She was dressed in a pale grey dress and dark blue velvet spencer, topped by a bonnet of the same colour as her dress. Her face lit up at the sight of Lamb approaching with Crouch at his side.

'I am delighted to make your acquaintance at last, ma'am,' boomed Crouch, bending over her hand. 'You have been teasing our imagination, hiding yourself away in your cabin – keeping your light under a bushel, so to speak, ha! ha! ha!'

'I have been a little indisposed, sir,' said Charlotte gravely, gently pulling her hand free from his clinging grip.

St John came hurrying aft, anxious not to be left out. Lamb introduced him and stood a little to one side as the two Marines outbid one another in the way of charm, wit and flattery, and he noted with pleasure the quiet, unsmiling way in which Charlotte responded. They are pushing at a locked door there, he thought, hugging to himself with a glow of pride his own warm relationship with her.

Four bells sounded, marking the middle of the forenoon watch and Jamieson approached with a touch of his hat and a sly glance at Charlotte.

'Four bells, sir,' he said to Lamb. 'Hands to gun practice?'

'If you please, Mr Jamieson. I am sorry to intrude, gentlemen, but I would be obliged if you went to your stations. Would you care to step below, ma'am? I am sorry that your sojourn on deck has been cut short.'

The two Marines bowed to Charlotte and hurried away as their men came pouring up from below and Lamb took Charlotte by the elbow and escorted her to the companionway, delighting in the touch of her and the provocative scent of her perfume.

'I am sorry I have to chase you from the deck,' he murmured, 'but it is no place for you to be during gun-drill. I fear for your eardrums.'

'It is scarcely less noisy in my cabin,' she laughed, 'or so I thought yesterday.'

Lamb leaned closer. 'Would you take pity on a poor, lonely sailor and give him the pleasure of your company at supper tonight?'

'And which poor, lonely sailor would that be?' she whispered, smiling. 'The quartermaster, perhaps – or Mr Jamieson?'

'Little tease,' growled Lamb, scowling.

She giggled. 'Oh, did you mean yourself? In that case, captain, how can I dare refuse?'

Lamb turned away and hid his grin while he waited for the gun-crews to settle themselves at their stations, his skin tingling with pleasure. So much for his resolve to be cool and distant. What a splendid, wonderful day it was!

During the afternoon watch, Crouch brought his hunting guns and fowling-pieces from his cabin and invited Lamb to join him and St John at a little target practice. For an hour the three blazed away at empty wine bottles and scraps of timber thrown from the taffrail. Crouch, no mean marksman, employed the quick, instinctive aim; St John took more time and care but, even so, fared less well; Lamb, perhaps because of a keener eye and a steadier hand, outshot them both, to his great delight.

The bright, burning day ended in an awesome, shrinking blaze of orange and pink and green to the west. Lamb leaned on the larboard rail, his warm thoughts given to love and sex, with no clear demarcation between them, when a hail from aloft interrupted his pleasant abstractions.

'Deck there! Sail ho!'

Lamb seized hold of Jamieson's telescope and striding quickly to the mainmast shrouds, pulled himself up the ratlines to the mast-head.

'Where away?' he demanded.

Selby's hand pointed to the north-east. 'On the starboard quarter, sir. I caught a glimpse, but then I lost her in the darkness, sir.'

The daylight was almost gone, the sea to starboard a black glimmer merging into a blue-black sky. Lamb raised his telescope and slowly swept the sea to the north-east. For the briefest of instants something tall and white trembled ghost-like in his vision, far to the east, and then it was gone. He searched again, caught a grey shadow for a moment, and then lost it.

'You were right, Selby.' he murmured. 'There was certainly something there. Keep your eyes alert for lights.'

'Aye aye, sir.'

Lamb made his way slowly down to the deck, deep in thought. The momentary glimpse he had snatched of the distant sail had suggested something larger than a schooner, perhaps a brig or a sloop, but almost certainly a privateer; and heading north, probably on her way from the Spanish Main to Hispaniola.

'Man the tops'l weather brace!' he called as his feet touched the deck. 'Starboard the helm! Steer due west!'

Jamieson had come up on deck, alerted by the lookout's hail, and when the cutter was settled on her new course, he raised an enquiring eyebrow to Lamb.

'A brig or a sloop, I think,' said Lamb. 'It's unlikely that she saw us but it's best to act on the assumption that she did. If she recognized us as a mail-packet, it would not take a very clever master to deduce where we are bound or what course to lay to pick us up. If we keep on this heading until daylight we should lose her, I think.'

'Yes, sir,' said Jamieson. 'Will you be wanting the men standing by the guns at first light, just in case the Frenchman is a little cleverer than we give him credit for?'

It was a sensible suggestion and tactfully put. Lamb nodded. 'Yes. It may be a needless exercise but it will be useful practice for the hands. Send Mr Snow aft, if you please.'

A tiny shower of rain dampened the deck at the end of Lamb's watch and he ducked into his cabin shaking the water from his hat. Sylvester was at the table, polishing a spoon with a cloth that once might well have been white.

'Break out a clean shirt for me, there's a good fellow,' said Lamb, stripping off his damp coat.

'Laid out ready on your cot, look, sir, such as it is. It won't stand many more washes, that one. I nearly had to pass it on to the sailmaker to make it presentable. It's got more patches than a fair-weather jib.'

'Stop your bloody blethering and hand me the towel,' said Lamb, lifting his dripping face from his basin. 'What's for supper?'

'Soup, cold beef, carrots and cheese, sir,' said the steward, making it sound like a feast fit for Belshazzar.

Lamb grunted through his towel. 'Out of favour with the cook, are you? What soup is it?'

'Pea, o'course.'

'Again? Does Harrison never make any other kind of soup?'

'No, sir.'

Lamb buttoned his shirt, tied his stock and bent to the mirror to brush back his hair. It was almost time he paid a visit to a barber, he thought. Was that a grey hair he saw? He peered close, frowning, fingering his torn, still tender ear.

'Good evening, ma'am,' said Sylvester. 'I'll bring in the soup, sir.'

Lamb jerked hastily away from his mirror. She looked radiant, her hair and skin and eyes shining in the soft lantern light, her shoulders and bosom gleaming above the pale blue gown in which he had first laid eyes on her in Clarence House. The sight of her almost took his breath away.

'Good evening, Mrs Brett.' He stepped close and taking her hand, bent to kiss it. 'May I say . . .' He faltered, his courage almost failing him.

'Yes?' Her eyes were wide and lustrous, her voice barely a whisper.

' . . . how beautiful you are?' His heart was thudding hard, loud enough to be heard, he was certain.

She gave a light laugh and stretching up, kissed him quickly on the cheek. 'You may, Matthew, you may, as often as you care to.'

Sylvester's quick step sounded. Lamb pulled back Charlotte's chair and she settled into it as the steward rapped the doorpost with his foot and entered with the soup.

Lamb spoke little during the meal. He felt tongue-tied and nervous; his opening burst of candour had drained him of the ability for small talk. Charlotte was gaiety itself, smiling and laughing a great deal although she took little of the wine; her talk was light and inconsequential: her childhood, her mother's quaint ways, the silly novel which she was reading. She giggled over the accident with the trap and its owner's fearful indignation when they returned with only the horse. 'That 'orse ain't never been known to shy, no, not once, not never, it ain't, no,' she growled, mimicking the man's London voice, and Lamb chuckled at her performance.

Sylvester brought in the coffee, cleared the dishes and closed the door behind him. The cabin was suddenly very quiet. Lamb sipped his coffee and held Charlotte's smiling gaze over the top of his cup; it seemed to him as if the very air was tingling.

'You are very quiet tonight, Matthew,' she said softly. 'Are you not happy?'

'On the contrary, I have never been happier than I have been these last few days.' He glanced down and fingered the edge of his cup. 'I am quiet because – because I have been trying to find the courage to ask you something.'

She nodded, as if she had been expecting this moment. 'Am I such an ogre?' she smiled. 'Ask away.'

'Charlotte, when I get back to England – it may be a year or two yet, I know, but when I do, may I call on you?'

'Oh, Matthew, Matthew!' She reached across the table and gripped his hand. 'What a coward you are in some things! Of course you must call on me; I should be deeply hurt if you did not. I shall write my mother's address down and you must promise not to lose it.' She released his hand and leaned back in her chair, her face suddenly solemn. 'And now I have something that I must say to you. You know very well, I am sure, that my name was linked with John Mortimer's on Antigua.' Lamb nodded. 'Well, I do not intend to say anything of that. It is a closed chapter now. But when I parted from him, I vowed to myself that I would shut out all men from my life from then on; I would play the virtuous widow to the hilt. And I was quite determined to do so – and then I met you, and you were so kind, so sweet . . . but it is too soon, do you see? Much too soon. Oh, I am not expressing myself at all well, I know, but you understand what I mean, Matthew, I am sure. I am confused at the moment. I thought I had things all settled in my mind but now I feel unsure again. Forgive me, Matthew, but I can promise you nothing, nothing at all, even though I ask you to call on me. Can you understand? Oh, I am a silly, stupid woman. Please lend me your handkerchief.' Her eyes filled with tears.

Lamb silently passed his handkerchief and Charlotte wept a little. Then she folded the handkerchief and ran her fingers over Lamb's initials.

'I shall steal this from you,' she said firmly, quite composed again. 'It will make sure that you visit me in England, if only to claim it back again.'

'I shall make a point of it,' said Lamb.

'And you must call on me while I am in Kingston, too, providing you do not sail off again straight away.'

'I shall make a point of that, too. I remember you mentioned once you had relatives in Kingston. Do you know them well?'

She pouted. 'Not really. Fanny is my second cousin – or third, I can never remember – but she is a good deal older than I am and I have not seen her since I was quite young. I have never met her husband. His name is Mainwaring, Captain Mainwaring. I understand he is in charge of the Navy Yard, or some such. She will be astonished to see me, no doubt, when I turn up after all these years, begging for lodging.' Lamb was aware of his smile becoming frozen. 'And now I must go,' Charlotte went on briskly. 'But first you must kiss me goodnight.'

She leaned across the table and closed her eyes. Lamb kissed her gently on the lips, his mind numb with disbelief.

'Goodnight, captain. God bless you.'

'Goodnight, Mrs Brett. Sleep well.'

The door closed gently behind her and Lamb stared at it for some minutes, occasionally giving a disbelieving shake of his head.

'Cousins!' he muttered at last, reaching for the wine. 'Hell and bloody damnation!'

Chapter 9

The darkness was almost absolute, without the faintest glimmer of moonlight or a single star to relieve it. Jamieson's solid bulk, no more than six feet away, was visible to Lamb only as a slightly denser blackness against the black night air. The *Heron* hissed quietly through the easy swell, heeling a little to the warm, south-easterly wind that came across her larboard quarter. Lamb, restless as always, walked aft, glanced at the dimly-lit compass in the binnacle and moved further aft, resting his hands on the taffrail as he stared out into the soft blackness; below him, the dim whiteness of the cutter's track extended back no further than ten feet before it was lost to the night. He felt a curious, undefined sense of expectancy, a feeling which had been with him since he awoke with a start in his cot an hour before he was due to take over the watch and which had brought him to the deck long before eight bells. It was a vague sense of unease, of something shortly due, a feeling which was almost physical, lodged just below his breastbone. The Frenchman of last night was, he was certain, not above a couple of cables distant, out there in the darkness, waiting for daylight. He moved to the tiller and spoke quietly with the helmsman, a bald, jolly little man who put him in mind of Friar Tuck in miniature.

'How is your foot now, Fletcher?'

'Oh, bearable, sir, bearable, thank you kindly.' Fletcher had suffered from the clumsiness of a Marine during practice at the guns and was now missing a toe-nail and nursing a nasty bruise to his foot. 'It had one blessing, sir: it took my mind off my toothache for an hour or two. Now I hurt at both ends, like.' He chuckled, apparently finding humour in his pains.

'Have you tried a lump of tobacco on it? That can ease it, I'm told.'

'What, on my toe, sir?'

'No, on your tooth, you bloody fool!'

'Ah, I see, sir. Well, I'm a chewin' man anyway, sir, but I could try chewin' a bigger quid, I daresay.'

Lamb shook his head at the man's obtuseness.

'The quarter, sir,' reported the quartermaster with his eye on the glass.

'Very good,' said Lamb and raised his voice to the unseen boatswain and his mate waiting by the forward hatchway. 'Stand to, Mr Snow!'

The shrill keening of the boatswain's pipe and the loud roar of the boatswain's voice shredded the quiet air. 'Stand to, stand to! Rouse out, rouse out! Rouse yourselves and show a leg! Stand to the guns! Move, move, move!'

'Mr Jamieson,' said Lamb, suddenly mischievous, 'be so good as to present my compliments to our Marine officers and inform them that I would be grateful beyond measure if they were to join their men at the guns.'

'I shall do so with enormous pleasure, sir,' chuckled Jamieson, clattering noisily below.

The seamen and Marines swarmed up from below and ran or groped their way to the guns, the seamen as light and sure as cats and the Marines heavy-footed and bewildered by the darkness of the deck. Lamb heard one plaintive call: 'Eh, Sam, is this my gun?' and smiled at the snarled reply: 'No, it fuckin' ain't and my name ain't fuckin' Sam!' The deck shook to the travel of the gun-carriages as they were hauled inboard and loaded; Crouch and St John appeared and stumbled blindly to their stations.

The ship was suddenly quiet. Jamieson loomed up out of the darkness. 'Guns loaded and ready, sir.'

'Very good,' said Lamb. His sense of uneasy expectancy was gone, swept away in the bustling noise and activity from the guns, and he knew, with calm conviction, that daylight would reveal an empty sea.

Jamieson, not being privy to Lamb's easy thoughts, hailed the lookout. 'Mast-head there! Keep your eyes open now – it wants but a minute or two to daylight.'

His estimate was not far out; the darkness was suddenly a little less dense and the men and guns the length of the deck became indistinct, black shapes. A hint of greyness suffused the air and Lamb could see Jamieson's face almost clearly; it was wearing a frown of concentration as the lieutenant stared anxiously to starboard.

'Sail ho!'

The lookout's shout shattered Lamb's composure and he jerked his head up. 'Where away?'

'Square on the starboard beam, sir, about five mile off. But she ain't no privateer, sir. A little brig, Spanish, by the cut of her jib.'

A little brig? Lamb and Jamieson glanced at each other, the same hungry thought passing unspoken between them. Jamieson cupped his hands and yelled aloft. 'What else do you see?'

'Nothing, sir. Just the brig.'

'Take your glass to the mast-head, Mr Jamieson,' said Lamb, and took a thoughtful turn round the deck. A little brig? And Spanish at that. He stroked his morning bristles. A mail-packet was no man-of-war and had no business chasing after brigs, little or no, but he had six long guns and two carronades, and by good fortune enough crew to man them and to form a sizeable boarding party. He would be taking a risk, he knew, not only from the brig, which might have very sharp teeth, but also from the Commander-in-Chief for risking the King's mail. Well, life was one long risk, he told himself, and had made up his mind to take it by the time Jamieson hailed the deck.

'A small brig, all right, sir, flying Spanish colours and heading east – no, she's going on the larboard tack. She's heading north.'

'Larboard the helm!' snapped Lamb. 'Mainsheet haul!' Brace in the tops'l! Midships!'

The deck heeled as the cutter came on the starboard tack and put the wind on her starboard quarter. Dawn had arrived in a rush in the last few minutes, showing a clear, pale sky with a few stars stubbornly clinging far to the west. To the north, some five or six miles off, was a two-masted, square-rigged, fat little merchantman.

Jamieson descended to the deck. 'She's just set her t'gallants and royals, sir, but she's a round little tub, no match at all for us in the way of speed. Four hours should see her under our guns, sir.'

'I shall hold you to that,' said Lamb. 'Stand the hands down, if you please, and inform our scarlet friends of our intentions. And Mr Snow can pipe to breakfast.'

When Lamb went back up to the deck after his breakfast, Snow was standing at the side with Jamieson's telescope trained on the brig; he gave a little start when he suddenly sensed Lamb's tall presence beside him.

'Beg pardon, sir, was you wanting this?' he asked, proffering the telescope. 'Mr Jamieson invited me to take a look, sir,' he added hastily.

'Please carry on, Mr Snow,' said Lamb politely. 'I am in no great hurry.'

He bitterly regretted the loss of his own fine telescope, gone for ever with many of his other possessions to the bottom of the Caribbean Sea; it had been a part of him for so many years that it had been like losing an old, well-loved friend.

'I've seen enough, sir, thank-ee,' said Snow, to whom the idea of keeping his captain waiting was unthinkable, and handing Lamb the instrument with a touch of his fur cap, rolled his way forward to find some urgent task with which to expunge his moment of idleness.

Lamb swung himself into the mainmast shrouds and hooking an arm through the ratlines, levelled his glass at the brig. The great golden flag of Spain, red, yellow and red with the flaming crown at its centre, flew majestically from her gaff end. She was a dumpy, rotund vessel, rather burdened with too much sail, in Lamb's opinion, to make the best of the wind. It smacked of a touch of desperation on the part of her master and he grinned, happy to see it. She was some four or five miles ahead, which meant the *Heron* had shortened the distance between them by a mile or more in a little over half an hour; Jamieson's estimate of four hours would not be far out, he thought, and leaping to the deck, made his way aft with the early sun already striking warmly through his thin shirt.

He stepped forward again to greet Charlotte as she emerged from the companionway, neat and fresh and pretty, clutching at her bonnet in the fresh breeze. She thought she might have a breath of fresh air – and what was that ship she could see ahead? Was the *Heron* trying to catch up with her? Lamb gave her a fond smile, led her to the side and allowed her to use Jamieson's telescope, holding her arm as she leaned out to look past the bow.

'It is a Spanish brig, a merchant ship,' he said. 'Do you see her flag? We should be up with her shortly, and there may be a little gunfire – but not too much, I think. It will be best, though, if you keep to your cabin until she heaves-to, in case she decides to make a fight of it.'

Charlotte handed him the telescope and shook her head disapprovingly. 'It does not seem right to me, to pursue and rob innocent merchant ships. It is no better than the behaviour of footpads or highwaymen.'

Lamb laughed at her innocence. 'Taking a prize is a legitimate act of war, a long established custom on all sides. There would be a great deal of indignant seamen if the Admiralty ever declared it otherwise. Prizes are the plums in the pudding, the only hope we poor sailors have of ever making a shilling or two. There has been many a fine house built with prize money and if I am lucky enough, I shall build one of my own one day.'

She gave him a strange look. 'Then I hope you are lucky, sir.'

The wind snatched at her bonnet, she made a desperate clutch as it was whipped from her head, and Blackett, passing behind them, leaped high and caught it.

'Well held there, Blackett!' cried Lamb.

'I've played a bit in my time, sir,' said Blackett, handing Charlotte her bonnet with a shy smile on his bruised face.

At four bells, half-way through the morning watch, the *Heron* was half a mile astern of the brig. The men were once more at their guns; Crouch and St John, splendid in their scarlet, paced up and down on either side and Jamieson stood between the forward guns with his eye on Lamb, waiting for the order to run out. Lamb studied the brig through his glass, looking for signs of activity at her guns. She carried only three, one at each side and the other at her stern, three-pounders, he thought, brass by the look of them, apt to overheat after a short while. There was not much chance of their being used long enough for that to happen today, he reflected, looking at the deserted guns at her sides and the men staring anxiously astern from the after gun. He could see a small group of men standing aft of the wheel, some of them wearing swords, several of them with telescopes directed at the *Heron*. We must give them something to look at, Lamb decided, and snapped shut his glass.

'Run up the colours, quartermaster,' he ordered, and lifting his voice, bellowed: 'Open your ports! Run out the guns!'

The ports swung up on their hinges and the guns rumbled on the deck as their muzzles reached out over the water. The ship became still and silent again, the men glancing at the brig and at Lamb as he waited beside the tiller. The sight of the *Heron*'s colours and her threatening guns had evidently not been enough; the brig continued on her course with her flag still bravely snapping to leeward.

'Give her spars a crack with your starboard gun, Mr Jamieson,' called Lamb.

The forward guns were trained hard round and ready and they banged and recoiled, sending smoke sweeping across the deck and low over the sea. Lamb had his telescope to his eye and saw the brig's mainsail twitch and streamers of torn canvas appear at the leech. A shout of triumph went up from the cutter's deck, followed by a louder roar as the great red and yellow flag began to slide down its halyard and the Spaniard turned into the wind.

'Put us under her lee, quartermaster,' cried Lamb with a huge grin.

A score of Spanish seamen and a handful of ship's officers and civilians gazed forlornly from the brig's deck as Jamieson and a dozen armed seamen and Marines pulled across and climbed her side. Lamb looked down at Charlotte, who had refused to go below, and grinned.

'There, you see, scarcely a bit of damage, apart from the torn mainsail. Just the one roundshot and no blood spilled. Her master is a sensible man.'

'I still feel it is unjust,' said Charlotte firmly. 'To steal a ship which offers no harm to anyone is wrong, I am quite convinced of that. And her poor captain – he must be in agonies.'

'Well, you can judge for yourself in a moment. He is climbing down into our boat, do you see?'

The Spanish captain was tall, thin and elderly, with a shock of white hair which tumbled forward as he removed his hat and gave a courteous bow.

'Captain Francis Ignatius Velantes at your service, señor,' he said in strongly accented English. 'Master and owner of the ship *Virgen del Asturias*.'

Lamb touched his hat in salute. 'Lieutenant Matthew Lamb of His Britannic Majesty's packet *Heron*, sir. Where are you from and where are you bound?'

'First, from La Vera Cruz, then last from Cartagena, bound for Spain, señor. I and some friends, on our way home after many years. It is very bad that you stop us, señor.'

'It is something that I very much regret, sir,' said Lamb. He became aware of the creeping advance of the *Heron*'s men as they edged and sidled their way aft with their ears cocked, greedily curious. 'What are you carrying?'

'Your pardon, señor?'

'What is your cargo?'

'Cochineal, señor, in bales.'

A low murmur of excitement rose from the eavesdropping men. 'Cochineal, eh? That was worth a fair old penny, mates.'

Lamb turned and glared. 'Silence on deck!' he snapped. 'I beg your pardon, sir,' he said to Velantes. 'Cochineal, you say. Any other cargo, sir?'

The captain hesitated. 'A little indigo,' he said at length.

The hesitation had not been lost on Lamb. 'And that is all, sir? I have men searching your ship at this moment.'

Velantes sighed and spread his hands in a gesture of despair. 'Twenty years of work, señor, all we have in the world. Gold dust and dollars.'

A great shout went up from the *Heron*'s deck. Gold dust and dollars! The cook sent his greasy hat spinning high into the air and even Snow unbent so far as to grin and slap his thigh.

'Silence on deck!' shouted Lamb again with a ferocity he was far from feeling. 'Mr Snow, clear the deck aft. Mr Timms, step here, if you please.' He gave Velantes a brief bow. 'Captain, I must ask you to be my guest until we reach Jamaica. My quartermaster here will show you to my cabin.'

The Spaniard bowed deeply in return. 'You are very kind, señor,' he murmured with enormous dignity and was led away by the quartermaster.

Charlotte stepped close to Lamb and squeezed his arm, looking up at him with shining eyes. 'Gold dust and dollars!' she whispered. He smiled down at her, astonished at the excitement in her eyes and voice.

The gold dust was in eight small, leather sacks, each heavy enough to be a good load for one man. Lamb, mindful of the danger of keeping all his eggs in one basket, transferred four of them to the mail-room of the *Heron* and left the remainder on the *Virgen del Asturias*, together with Jamieson, the carpenter, four seamen, the two Marine lieutenants and twelve of their men. The dollars were packed in canvas bags inside a large, brass-bound chest. Lamb hefted a bag in his hand, shook his head in wonder and re-locked the chest, refusing to hazard a guess at its value. It could wait until they reached Port Royal, he decided; there would be no capstan-head share-out of this fortune. He saw it man-handled into the mail-room, locked the door and placed a Marine outside with a musket in one hand and a bayonet in the other, there being insufficient headroom for the two to be fixed together.

'Keep to leeward of me and stick close, Mr Jamieson,' yelled Lamb as the *Heron* moved away.

'Stick close, aye aye, sir,' shouted Jamieson, wearing a huge, happy smile. He lifted his hat high in the air. 'Goodbye to you, ma'am.'

'Goodbye, Mr Jamieson,' called Charlotte, with a wave of her hand.

'Helm a-lee,' ordered Lamb. 'Steer nor'-west by north.' He looked down at Charlotte by his side. 'I must go and settle our new guest. Dare I ask you once more to have supper with me tonight?'

'Oh, I would love to,' she replied, surprising him by her eagerness. She leaned close, almost laying her body against him. 'I shall wear my new dress.' She smiled up into his eyes, slyly stroked his hand and made for the companionway, leaving him in a state of utter astonishment.

'Mr Snow, you have the deck,' called Lamb. With Jamieson gone, the boatswain would have to take over his watch if Lamb was not to spend the greater part of each twenty-four hours on deck. He gave a last glance at the brig and the Marines moving about her deck as they were introduced to the art of sail-handling and went below to his cabin, the excitement of his prize still bubbling and seething within him.

Captain Velantes was a man of infinite courtesy and he sat and drank wine with Lamb and talked and smiled gravely as if the loss of his ship and his life's earnings were of absolutely no consequence. Lamb learned that Velantes was only part-owner of the brig; it had been bought by him and several of his friends as an investment and as a means of transporting themselves home to their retirement in Spain. Velantes was captain only by virtue of his seniority; he knew almost nothing of the sea and he and his partners had hired a sailing-master to navigate for them.

'He was not a good master,' said Velantes sadly. 'He always knew better than us and he was in love with his bottle. Yesterday we had to strike him to the deck and put him in chains for his insolence. Today I think we were lost and there was talk of putting back to Cartagena when you came along.'

Lamb shook his head and restrained a smile. 'It would have been better for you to have suffered the faults of your navigator – bottle, insolence and all, I think. Better still, perhaps, not to have sailed alone in a small, slow brig. Did you not know of the dangers?'

Velantes smiled. 'We knew of the war, of course, but it touched us little until today. And danger is with us always, even in our beds. Does not each day bring us one step nearer to our deaths? We had our faith and our prayers and our love of Spain to give us courage. It was not enough, I know now, but we are still in the Lord's hands, are we not, señor?'

'You are, sir, but not in His alone, I am afraid,' said Lamb. 'Come, sir, I will show you to your cabin.'

'Good evening, Mr Snow,' said Lamb, bestowing on the boatswain the pleasantry of one watch-keeping officer to another, the *Heron*'s only two now that Mee and Jamieson had been transferred to the brig.

'Evenin', sir,' said Snow with a touch of his hat.

'The course is nor'-west by north. Keep the lantern burning at the mast-head for the sake of Mr Jamieson and if you should lose sight of his, call me immediately. Heave the log at two bells and six bells and if it comes on to blow, call me. If you think it at all necessary, call me anyway, for any reason.'

'Aye aye, sir,' murmured Snow patiently, as if all this was quite new to him and he was the greenest of green midshipmen with the letters L and S inked on different hands.

Lamb gave a last look at the distant, yellow light of the *Virgen del Asturias* to larboard and went below, his thoughts rather more on Charlotte than the brig. As he washed and changed, he felt again the discreet stroke of her hand on his and the affectionate squeeze of his arm. Her behaviour had been a marked change from the tears of the evening before, from which he had deduced that she found him kind but no more than that. The thought came into his mind that the change in her was not unconnected with his own suddenly altered prospects. Did she look upon him with different eyes now that he was no longer penniless? 'Gold dust and dollars!' she had whispered excitedly. Surely she did not gauge a man by the depth of his pocket? He shook his head angrily as he adjusted his stock, disgusted at his unworthy thoughts. No, it was quite impossible – it was transparently clear that she was too honest a person, too true, too thoroughly beautiful.

'Here we are, sir,' announced Sylvester, giving a polite kick to the doorpost as he entered. 'Spanish chicken, fresh killed, with Spanish cheese to follow and a bottle of Spanish wine to wash it all down.'

He placed the steaming dish on the table and tugged the bottle from his pocket.

'A good wine, is it?' asked Lamb casually.

'Ah, well, that I wouldn't know, would I, sir?' replied the steward artlessly. 'Never have been one for strong drink, sir. But I think you'll find it to your taste, sir – perhaps a bit on the sharp side.'

The wine was excellent and a few minutes later Charlotte

173

pronounced it so, smacking her lips in appreciation and emptying her glass before she had taken a taste of her chicken.

'You seem very happy tonight,' remarked Lamb as he refilled her glass. 'I was beginning to think that I had a depressing effect on you and had almost decided that we should discontinue our little suppers together.'

'Oh, Matthew, do not be so cruel, reminding me of my silly tears!' she said, leaning forward and smacking his knuckles with her fingers. 'One would think that I was forever in floods, hearing you talk. No, I am happy for you with your prize. Will you be promoted now?'

Lamb laughed. 'For taking a little brig? No, small chance of that. If it were not for its cargo, it would pass quite unnoticed. And in any case, what is this? I thought you were quite opposed to the notion of taking prizes?'

'I am, but when a thing is done, it is done; and you looked so happy, grinning like a boy – and the men, too – that I could not but help being happy with you. Will you get a large share, do you think?'

He looked at her over his glass. 'Certainly my prospects are improved. But your supper will be cold; you have scarcely taken a bite.'

'Oh, I am not at all hungry.' She laid down her knife and fork and pushed her plate to one side, resting her elbows on the table and leaning forward provocatively. Lamb felt an immediate urgent stirring. 'Let me fill your glass,' she said and smiled fondly at him as she poured.

'I find I am not very hungry either,' he said, aware of the sudden thumping of his heart as he raised his glass. 'You will not think it too forward of me if I say that you are a truly beautiful woman?'

'I am sure I would not, if you were to say so,' she said softly, laying her hand on his, her touch light and warm and thrilling.

He leaned across the table, bringing their faces very close. 'Very well, then,' he whispered. 'You are a truly beautiful woman.' He kissed her. Her lips were soft and clinging and her grip tight on his hand.

The swift clatter of Sylvester's shoes warned Lamb an

instant before the door catch rattled and he drew hastily back and took up his glass.

'Cheese, sir,' announced the steward, laying the dish on the table. He gave a disapproving frown at their plates. 'Chicken not to your liking, sir?'

'No, it is like leather,' said Lamb. 'Quite inedible.'

'Ah, 'cause it's Spanish, I expect, sir. Ready for your coffee, sir?'

'No, we shall not need any coffee. Goodnight to you, Sylvester.'

'Goodnight, sir,' said the steward, tactfully expressing no surprise at Lamb's unexpected courtesy and shut the door behind him.

Their lips were together again almost before Sylvester had gone. Charlotte mewed gently and clutched at Lamb's arms and he half rose out of his seat in order to press himself closer. Her wine glass toppled and a thin puddle of red wine ran across the table and into her lap.

'Oh!' she cried, pushing back her chair and leaping to her feet. 'Look what you have done! All over my new dress! It will stain, I know it will! Oh, how could you be so clumsy?'

'I am sorry, Charlotte,' said Lamb, taken aback by the sudden change in her. 'Here, take my napkin.'

'It is too late to be sorry, sir. Oh, just look at it!' She dabbed furiously at the dark red stain spread across the skirt of her pale lemon dress. 'It is ruined, ruined, and I have never worn it but the once before. And I put it on tonight just for you.'

'I am very sorry,' repeated Lamb feebly. 'Will it not wash out?'

'Red wine on pale yellow? Hardly! I must take it off and sprinkle salt over it. That may help a little but I know it is quite ruined. I shall never be able to wear it again.'

'Do not take it so badly, Charlotte,' said Lamb, putting on a mollifying smile and stepping round to her side of the table, anxious to return to that happy state that had prevailed before he spilt the wine. 'I will ask Sylvester to soak it in sea water for you.' He reached out and took her by the shoulders. 'It is such a trifling thing to come between . . .'

She wriggled free, pushing his hands away. Her eyes were

175

furious. 'I am pleased *you* think so little of it, sir! A ruined dress is a trifle to you, is it? If you knew what it had cost me you would not think it so trifling. Let me pass, sir. I have things to do. Goodnight!'

'Goodnight,' said Lamb to the quivering door. He sighed, shook his head and dabbed ineffectually with his napkin at the spilled wine on the table and her chair. Bloody clumsy oaf, he told himself, and drained the last of the bottle into his glass. He cut himself a hunk of cheese and sat munching and sipping from his glass, thinking that Charlotte's reaction had been a little extreme, but vaguely aware that dresses were high on her list of priorities. He chuckled aloud; she certainly had a sharp temper, and a tongue to go with it; he had been left gaping like an idiot.

The cheese, he decided, was not to his taste, and rinsing his mouth with the last of the wine, he rose and prepared himself for his bed. Bloody clumsy oaf, he told himself again as he punched his pillow and stretched out on his cot but he grinned wryly, dismissing the evening from his mind and turning his thoughts instead to gold and dollars and cochineal, safer and happier ground altogether. He drifted off into sleep, dreaming of a column of gold coins reaching far above his head, swaying alarmingly on the deck of the cutter.

The click of the catch of the door brought him instantly awake, thinking that midnight had come amazingly quickly. 'Right, I am awake,' he said to the dark figure in the doorway and swung his feet to the deck. 'What is the weather like?'

There was a soft laugh and the patter of bare feet on the deck. Lamb was immediately aware of the scent of lilies and he reached out to feel naked flesh beneath a thin peignoir. She let that fall to the deck and stretched out beside him, skin against skin, warm and glowing and alive. He gripped her, stunned and wondering, not certain that he was awake.

'Oh, Matthew, Matthew!' Charlotte breathed, kissing his face and straining close, pressing breasts and bush and thighs tightly against him. 'Forgive me. I was so horrid to you over that silly dress. I had such plans for the evening and I ruined it with my nasty temper. Please say you forgive me.'

'There is nothing to forgive, nothing at all,' he whispered

176

hoarsely, running his hands over the wonderful, yielding mysteries of her flesh. He kissed her hungrily and she responded eagerly, holding his head between her hands, murmuring his name and opening her body to him in an explosion of panting kisses.

'Darling, darling Matthew,' she sighed as her knees drew up and she enfolded him. 'Yes, yes!' she cried as he entered her and he put his fingers lightly over her lips, fearful that her cries would be heard by the watch on the quiet deck above their heads.

She was sleeping when he crept from the cabin shortly before midnight, cursing himself for having transferred the carpenter to the brig. When he returned at the end of his watch she had gone, leaving him the faint scent of lilies on his pillow.

He stretched out on his cot but felt quite unable to sleep and lay staring into the darkness, filled with an exuberant happiness. Was this love, he wondered, this bubbling mixture of tender yearning and pride and lust and joy? Certainly, words of love had passed between them, engendered by their mutual passions, but there had been no commitment to love, no grand confessions. Lamb had been tempted, but a tiny sense of caution or fear had held him back. He smiled at the deck beams, thinking that if he was not in love then he was as near to it as he was ever likely to get. Mrs Mainwaring came into his mind and his smile vanished. Now there was a problem to which he must give some thought before they reached Kingston; if he did not tread very carefully, Charlotte would be lost to him.

Chapter 10

Lamb stirred as the distant sound of gunfire entered his dream and opened his eyes as the urgent shouts of the boatswain sounded above his head. The noise of running feet brought him sitting up and out of his cot, striding naked to his door and brushing past Lipton, the diminutive messenger sent down to wake him. The grumbling roll of gunfire came again as he emerged onto the deck, the yellow flashes flaring and fading in the half darkness to larboard. The deck quivered and groaned to the squeal of gun trucks as the men hauled them inboard and prepared to load.

'Starboard the helm!' snapped Lamb, peering out over the dark water at the dim, ghostly shape of the brig a mile to leeward. He could see a tall, indistinct mass beyond her, lost instantly as bright gun flashes reduced his vision. 'Put us to leeward of the brig, Mr Snow,' he called as the rumble of the gunfire reached his ears. He gripped the rail, staring out in a fever of impatience as the deck heeled and the cutter bore down on the brig.

'Sylvester!' he shouted, turning his head to the steward's station at the carronade.

'Sir?'

'Nip below and get my clothes. And my sword and pistols, while you are at it.'

Snow approached and touched his hat, modestly averting his eyes from his captain's unclothed body. 'Break out the boarding weapons, sir?'

'Yes, please do, Mr Snow.'

The light was growing stronger by the minute and as the *Heron* drew closer to the *Virgen del Asturias* the stranger beyond her resolved itself into a large brig, her colours obscured by her canvas but the narrow yards and black-painted masts stamping her as French as a pair of wooden sabots. The gap between

178

the two vessels was very narrow but the guns of both continued to fire as the Frenchman bore down on the smaller ship. The *Heron* would not arrive in time to prevent the privateer grappling, Lamb realized, and he dare not use his guns for fear of hitting his prize. He could make his presence felt, though, and as Sylvester emerged from the companion hatch with his weapons, he gave a shout along the deck.

'For'ard guns! Aim wide and fire!'

The two guns banged almost together while he was scrambling into his clothes, and the familiar, bitter stench of the smoke filled Lamb's nostrils. They would achieve little, he knew, but they might put some heart into the little brig's defenders, if nothing else. The two vessels were side by side now, their yards touching, and he could see stripe-shirted seamen and red-coated Marines thronging the far side of the Spanish brig while a mass of Frenchmen rose up above them.

'Lay me alongside the Frenchman, quartermaster,' snapped Lamb over his shoulder to Timms at the tiller, and in a great roar: 'Leave your guns! Stand by to board! Stand by to board!'

He buckled his sword belt and drew the weapon from its scabbard, crossing to the starboard side while Timms brought the cutter round in a long, sweeping curve to lay her alongside the privateer's unencumbered side. He could see a confused mass of struggling men on the Spaniard's deck as the *Heron* crossed her stern and he glanced along his own deck at the armed men crowded at the starboard bow, with Snow standing on the bulwark with a boarding axe in one hand and a grappling iron in the other.

The *Heron* swept down towards the Frenchman's stern. The dull grey sea suddenly became alive, sparkling and blue at the touch of the first rays of the sun. Lamb wondered vaguely what the precise time might be; his watch was ticking in his waistcoat pocket inches from his hand but he dared not take his eyes from the privateer for a single second. Tiny red flashes showed from the Frenchman's taffrail and musket balls began to thud into the cutter's timbers and viciously split the air above her deck. A ball plucked at Lamb's sleeve, another sung past his ear; there was a loud grunt from behind him and the *Heron* slewed sharply to larboard and then swung back again. Lamb turned his head, seeing Timms on his knees with his face a mask of blood but still clinging grimly to the tiller with one hand while he tried to steer, and Charlotte standing beside the aft companionway, staring in shock and horror at the activity on the deck and the locked brigs a hundred yards away. Lamb was aghast and he flung himself at her as a musket ball burrowed into the deck beside her foot. The privateer's stern-chaser flamed and thundered and he folded her tightly against his body as the roundshot struck and splinters flew and Timms screamed.

'Oh, God, God, what is happening?' she cried into his chest. He seized her by the arm, brutal in his desperate haste, thrusting her towards the companionway.

'Get below!' he snapped. 'Get to your cabin and stay there. Go now!'

He caught a last glimpse of her white, horrified face as she scrambled below and he ran to the tiller. Timms was still clinging determinedly to the helm, his face chalk-white beneath the blood from his ruined mouth and his side laid open from armpit to hip by the razor-like slash of a timber shard.

'Right, Timms, I have her,' Lamb cried as he seized the tiller, sticky from the quartermaster's blood. Timms gurgled something through his smashed teeth and bent his head to the deck, cradling his face in his hands.

The privateer was fifty yards off but Timms had inadvertently swung the helm away from her and Lamb pushed it hard to larboard, setting the jib-boom at the Frenchman's stern. She was named the *Lejoille*, he saw, as a musket ball ripped a splinter from the tiller an inch from his hand. The bow crashed against her hull with a shock that jarred his teeth and brought a rending crack of protest from the topmast yard as it caught at the brig's mainmast shrouds. He snatched up his sword from beside the kneeling Timms and ran forward to join the confused jostle of men struggling to clamber across to the privateer. Snow was already there, he noticed, the short, solid slab of muscle sitting astride the brig's rail and striking down one-handed with his boarding axe. More men were swarming across the narrow gap to join him and Lamb forced himself into the crowd of men packed into the bows, desperate to be among the first to board.

'Stand aside!' he roared, furious at being impeded. 'Let me through! Stand aside, I say!'

He thrust aside the boy Spooner, elbowed his way past an indignant, black-eyed Blackett, and using the forward gun as a step, sprang on to the rail and leaped across to the mainmast chains of the *Lejoille*. He scrambled up the shrouds and on to the side, pausing for an instant to take in the scene before him. There were two or three small groups of his men and Frenchmen fighting on the privateer's deck; the giant Selby and the boatswain were standing back to back swinging their axes at half a dozen Frenchmen closing in on them with short pikes and cutlasses; and immediately below him was Sylvester, grinning hideously as he ducked beneath the thrust of a pike and slashed two-handed with a cutlass almost as long as he was tall. The Spaniard's deck at the far side was lower than that of the Frenchman but he could see the heads and shoulders of a confused mass of men and their busy weapons, their shouts and curses an indistinct roar of sound. The bright coats and crossed belts of the Marines at both ends of the ship showed that Jamieson's force had been split into two by the wedge of boarding Frenchmen and he sprang to the *Lejoille*'s deck with his sword raised high, knowing that it could only be a matter of moments before Jamieson's men were overwhelmed.

Sylvester gave a last, unnecessary hack at the Frenchman on the deck at his feet and turned in time to cut at the neck of another running at Lamb with an axe raised in both hands. The man screamed and dropped and Lamb jumped over his body with a quick grin of thanks at his steward. The last of the *Heron*'s men tumbled over the side on to the deck and Lamb raised his voice in a shout: 'To me, *Herons*, to me!' He had no more than two dozen men all told, if he counted Spooner, and he knew that if he was to fight his way on board the Spaniard with any hope of success he must keep them together as one force.

His men gathered round him and he led them at a rush to the Frenchmen surrounding Snow and Selby, the circle smaller now, with two men lying still and bloody on the deck. The remainder were cut down in a moment, hacked and beaten to the planks in five furious seconds, and Lamb lifted his stained sword above his head.

'To the Spaniard, my lads! Our shipmates are in need of us!' he roared, his blood singing with excitement. His men gave a loud shout of enthusiasm, shaking their weapons high, and he turned and led them at a run for the starboard side, aiming to cut his way in to the centre of the French boarders amidships.

He sprang up onto the side, taking in the mad scene below him at a glance. The deck of the *Virgen del Asturias* immediately before him was almost clear of men, but fore and aft the two small groups of Jamieson's men were fighting desperately, pressed close by larger groups of Frenchmen. He caught a quick glimpse of Crouch, standing tall in the centre of his men forward, his mouth gaping as he roared and swung his sword.

'Give our mates a shout, my lads!' screamed Lamb, and carried forward by the rush of his men and his own wild blood lust, sprang across the gap and on to the rail of the Spaniard without a thought for the terrible drop below him and with the shouts of his men ringing in his ears.

'*Heron! Heron! Heron!*'

Lamb teetered on the rail for one horrible moment, steadied himself with a clutch at the mainmast shrouds and leaped to the deck as the first of the Frenchmen turned their startled heads and ran at him with their weapons raised. One of Lamb's pistols had found itself unbidden into his hand and he thumbed back the hammer and fired into the bearded face that loomed up snarling before him. He dropped the pistol to the deck, transferred his sword to his right hand and struck out at another Frenchman. He missed and a blade stabbed at him, passing beneath his arm, bringing fire to his ribs; he brought the hilt of his sword down onto the man's head with all his strength, grunting with the effort, and the man dropped at his feet. Snow was beside him, crouched low, smiling faintly as his axe jabbed and swung and chopped, and to his other side was little Sylvester, striking out with his cutlass and swearing without pause in a low voice: 'Bastid, bastid, bastid.'

Suddenly Frenchmen were all round them, a swirl of dark, moustached and bearded faces and woollen caps, red and blue, crowding in from both sides and forcing Lamb's small group close together, shoulder to shoulder. Lamb found himself echoing Sylvester – 'Bastard, bastard, bastard,' – as he was

182

pressed backwards, cutting and hacking at the faces and bodies before him. Out of the corner of his eye he saw Sylvester go down, falling almost to his knees but held upright by the press of men around him. A red-shirted Frenchman, huge gold earring flashing beneath dark curls, lunged forward to stab down at the steward and Lamb slashed savagely sideways, feeling his blade bite deep beneath the gold earring. A flash of bright steel caught his eye as he turned his head and he ducked, feeling the wind of the whirling axe-head brush his hair. From beside him Snow leaned forward and gave an economical chop with his boarding axe, a delicate little blow that cleaved the man from ear to jaw. There seemed to be no end to the Frenchmen; Lamb felt a moment of black despair as they pressed closer and he struggled to keep his feet and ward off the shouting, surging mass around him, striking aside a jabbing pike with his left arm while he hacked with his sword. Faintly, above the shouts and yells and curses and clash of steel, he heard a cry from the bows, and he took it up, his heart swelling at the sound. '*Heron! Heron!*' His men around him followed his example – '*Heron! Heron! Heron!*' – and Lamb sprang forward, careless of his skin, his blood pounding madly, cutting and slashing, driven on by fury and desperation, scarcely feeling the weight of his sword, driving like a wedge into the solid mass of Frenchmen. Something slammed into his ribs, something else tore at his thigh, and suddenly Crouch was before him and he was through, with Snow at his side, and the Frenchmen were streaming aft in disorder.

Blood coated the side of Crouch's face and neck, mingling with the sweat that poured from him. He gripped Lamb by the shoulder, grinning and panting. 'I am delighted to see you, sir. You arrived in the very nick – at our very last gasp.'

'Your work is not finished yet, Mr Crouch,' said Lamb breathlessly, looking at the body of St John curled up in ugly, grinning death. 'Mr Jamieson has need of us.'

Snow was rounding up the *Heron*'s men and Marines, pushing and cuffing them into a group, callously indifferent to their wounds and weariness.

Lamb set off at a stumbling run towards the knot of struggling Frenchmen and Englishmen aft of the mainmast, picking his way through the corpses on the deck, feeling the squelch of blood in his left shoe from the throbbing wound in his thigh. A number of the privateer's men broke away from the group aft and began to scramble across to their own vessel. The sight incensed Lamb – to slink away like rats, deserting their comrades! Rage took hold of him and he swung round to Crouch, pointing at the fleeing men. 'Mr Crouch, take some men and cut down those cowardly bastards!'

Snow and his men ran past him and he set off after them, his leg stiffening, but there was little left for them to do. The few Frenchmen that had not broken and run had thrown down their weapons and Snow's men drove them to the taffrail with a few encouraging jabs and cuts from their cutlasses. Jamieson leaned on his sword, panting, bleeding from a dozen wounds on his arms and ribs, his head bowed in pain and weariness.

'Stir yourself, Mr Jamieson,' snapped Lamb mercilessly. 'We still have much to do. The Frenchman has yet to be taken. Get your men together and follow me. Mr Snow, toss those fellows' weapons over the side and leave them . . .'

'They are cutting the bloody grapples!' roared Crouch from the side.

Lamb whirled, horrified. 'Aloft with you, Mr Snow! Lash the yards together or we shall lose the cutter.' He felt sick at his stupidity, leaving the *Heron* unguarded. Charlotte! My God, he had completely forgotten her! 'Come, my lads!' he bellowed, frantic with worry, and ran along the littered deck. 'Over you go, Mr Crouch,' he snapped. 'Don't stand there waiting for the bloody side boys!'

Frenchmen were hacking at the grapples from fore and aft as he sprang onto the side and launched himself across the gap, gripping the privateer's shrouds and leaping to her deck without a pause. Crouch and Jamieson landed hard on his heels and Lamb grabbed Crouch by the arm. 'Guard the cutter! Mr Jamieson, see to those Frenchmen for'ard!'

There were Frenchmen running at him from the wheel and in a second his sword was in action again, cutting and slashing as more of his men poured over the side. He found himself facing a tall, slim man, hatless and silver-haired, his white, lace-ruffled shirt open at the neck and splashed with red, a long, slender,

184

flashing blade in his hand. Lamb lunged at him with his sword raised high and the man bent his knee and extended his sword. His arm moved slightly as Lamb brought his weapon down to beat the blade aside; a needle-sharp point scored fire along Lamb's jaw. He jerked his head back from the sting of the cut and sprang at the man with his sword flailing, endeavouring to get in close. The Frenchman backed, side-stepped and circled, his black, deep-set eyes hard and a thin smile of contempt for Lamb's swordsmanship showing on his dark face. His blade flashed like quicksilver, avoiding Lamb's lunges with ease, darting at Lamb's throat and stomach and chest, keeping him at the length of his sword. He drew blood again, the lightest touch from his point slicing through coat sleeve and shirt and into the flesh of Lamb's sword arm. For a moment Lamb experienced a moment of black, hopeless terror, feeling like a child before this master of the sword, and he sprang forward again, hacking and slashing. The man eluded his blade with contemptuous ease, and as his point circled threateningly at Lamb's throat there came a flash of scarlet at the edge of Lamb's vision. The Frenchman grunted and collapsed to the deck as if pole-axed. Crouch jerked his sword from the man's neck and grinned sweatily at Lamb.

'This is no time to fight like gentlemen, sir,' he said, changing his grip to wipe his damp palm along the leg of his breeches. He waved his hand towards the bow. 'The ship is ours. Mr Jamieson has secured t'other end.'

'Very good,' said Lamb breathlessly, resting his sword point on the deck, certain he would not have the strength to lift it again. He dashed the sweat from his eyes and looked about the ship. The French seamen aft had been herded into a sullen group under the watchful bayonets of a couple of grinning Marines and a smaller group forward were squatting in the bows with Selby and his wicked axe standing hugely over them. Jamieson was limping aft, using his sword as a stick with a huge smile of triumph on his filthy, blood-smeared face, and a few of the *Heron*'s seamen were moving about the deck looking for their mates and turning the corpses of the Frenchmen over on to their backs to make sure that they were dead.

Lamb turned to Crouch, extending his hand. 'I thank you for

185

the stout efforts of you and your men, sir. You were all magnificent. I am truly sorry that we lost Mr St John.'

'Thank you,' grunted Crouch as he shook Lamb's hand. 'It is particularly painful for me – he owed me seventy pounds.'

Jamieson came hobbling up and exchanged handshakes with Lamb and Crouch, grinning with happiness and excitement in spite of his wounds. Lamb cut short his expressions of wonder and delight.

'How the devil did you let the bloody Frenchman get so close?' he demanded. 'Was the watch asleep?'

'No, certainly not, sir,' protested Jamieson indignantly. 'I was on deck myself. It was pure bad luck. At the first hint of light she was there, not above two cables off the larboard quarter. I think we did very well to get the guns into action so quickly.'

'No quicker than the Frenchman,' said Lamb pointedly. He was taking the edge off Jamieson's moment of glory, he knew, but the thought of how near he had come to losing the brig and the cost in lives to secure her, let alone the danger to which he had exposed Charlotte, bit deeply. He could not be sure that the blithe youngster had been so carefully alert as he himself would have been; but this was not the time or the place to go into that. There was much to do.

'But never mind that now,' he said. 'Mr Crouch, would you be so good as to round up the Frenchmen and secure them below? Make sure their knives are removed from them – and do not overlook those few we left on the Spaniard. How are your wounds, Mr Jamieson?'

'They are not too bad, sir. No worse than your own, I think.'

'Good,' said Lamb, glancing down at his bloodstained shirt and the bloody rip in the leg of his breeches. His wounds were smarting like the devil, particularly his ribs and jaw. 'You will transfer to this brig and hand over the Spaniard to Mr Snow.' He glanced at the *Virgen del Asturia*'s sails. 'He will have to find some new canvas for her – the French guns have chewed them up somewhat. I think it will be best to move our Spanish prisoners in with the Frenchmen and you can have Mr Crouch and most of his Marines. Right, Mr Jamieson, let us to work. We shall have the corpses over the side first, I think.'

186

He moved to the side and looked down to the deck of the *Virgen del Asturias* and the ugly sight of sprawled bodies. Sylvester was bending over one of the dead Frenchmen and he gave him a hail. 'Sylvester, you rogue! Come across. There are more important things to do than rob the dead.'

'Just the odd earring or two, sir,' said Sylvester as he scrambled on to the *Lejoille*'s deck. 'It'd be a waste to throw them over the side still in their owners' ear-'oles.'

'I thought you were dead,' said Lamb, eyeing the blood-stained rag around the steward's forehead. He had been relieved to see the elf-like man on his feet; he would have missed his cheerful, near-insolent banter. 'I am sorely disappointed. Take your useless body to the *Heron* and present my compliments to Mrs Brett. You may tell her that the fighting is over and it is quite safe for her to leave her cabin. She would appreciate a cup of tea, most likely, but wash the shit and blood off you first.'

'Aye aye, sir. A wash and a change of shirt wouldn't come amiss with you, sir, by the look of things.'

'Nor would a little civility from you,' said Lamb. 'Be off with you.'

The work aboard the two brigs proceeded slowly throughout the long, hot, weary morning. There were very few men who had not been wounded at least once and it took a double issue of grog and much savage growling from the boatswain to get them creeping about the decks and crawling painfully aloft. In addition to St John, the *Heron* had lost three Marines and two seamen; one of these was Timms, who was found kneeling in death beside the cutter's tiller in a vast pool of blood and had to be straightened before he could be sewn into his canvas shroud. The British dead were transferred reverently to the deck of the cutter and the French dead tossed unceremoniously over the side where they floated for some time, face down and arms wide, slowly drifting astern, trailing pink tendrils in the clear water.

The Spanish seamen were brought blinking into the light of day and herded across to the privateer and down into her hold, from where they sent up bitter protests at being lodged with murdering corsairs – and Frenchmen, at that.

Lamb explored the captain's cabin, wrinkling his nose at the smell of strange food and scent and stale cigar smoke that permeated its dark interior. The captain had evidently been something of a dandy and Lamb's eyes gleamed as he piled a dozen lace-bedecked shirts, a pair of new breeches and a handful of flawless silk stockings on to the table. He also took possession of a superb sextant and a silver-hooped telescope, and followed a loaded Blackett across to the cutter, eager to wash the blood from his body, bandage his wounds and dress himself in his new finery.

The cutlass thrust beneath his arm had left a long, shallow score over his ribs, the bruise more painful than the cut; the stab to his thigh, from a pike head, he thought, had gouged out a lump of flesh and his stocking and shoe were saturated in blood. He stood in his basin, the water turning a deeper shade of pink by the second as he washed his body and gingerly dabbed at his wounds. One of his old shirts, the cause of Sylvester's constant complaints, was cheerfully torn into strips and with his wounds bound and his body dressed more expensively than it had ever been before, he gazed into his mirror and adjusted his shirt with a murmur of thanks to the dead donor, wincing as the movement pulled the flesh on his scored forearm. He peered at the sword cut along his jaw; it had bled a great deal but it was not deep and with luck, he thought, he would be left with a distinguished scar gained with not too much hurt.

He left his cabin and moved quietly along to Charlotte's door. 'Charlotte?' he murmured, giving the door a gentle tap.

The door opened a crack to reveal a blue eye. 'Matthew!' she cried, opening the door wide. 'Come in quick; I am not decent.'

She was indecent only in so far as under-bodice and layers of petticoats would allow but Lamb felt his body stirring at the sight of her underclothes and the closeness of her in the small cabin.

Her hands flew to her mouth. 'Oh, Matthew, your poor face! Does it hurt very much?'

'No, it is only a scratch,' he smiled, delighting in her concern. 'I came to apologize for my roughness earlier. I was frightened that you might be hurt – there were musket balls flying everywhere.'

She shuddered. 'I did not know what was happening. I awoke and heard the noise and the shouting and I dressed and went on deck and I could not believe my eyes. It was terrifying, terrifying.'

Lamb folded her in his arms and kissed her hair. 'I am sorry, Charlotte. There was not time to warn you. But it is all over now, and we have a fine, new brig to take into Port Royal.'

'Yes, but poor Mr St John is dead, and those other men. Sylvester tells me that you will be burying them soon. I have been trying to decide which dress to wear – I have a dark bonnet and black gloves but I cannot decide between my dark blue dress or the plum. Which do you think?'

Lamb laughed. 'Now there's a question of some enormity! The plum, I think. There will be enough dark blue on deck.'

She buried her head in his chest, her voice muffled. 'Matthew, you do not think too badly of me after last night? You do not think me wanton? I am not at all –'

He raised her chin and silenced her with a kiss, a long lingering kiss that reawakened the passions of the night before. 'My darling girl,' he murmured.

Charlotte searched his face. 'You will not forget me when I am in England? You will write to me? You promise?'

'I promise, my love. I have your address safe.'

He kissed her again, straining against her, aflame with lust. 'Charlotte, Charlotte,' he murmured.

She laughed lightly and pushed him gently towards the door, dabbing a quick kiss on the tip of his nose. 'Off you go and let me finish dressing. I have my hair to do yet.'

In accordance with his rank, Lieutenant St John was buried first and separately, the grating on which his canvas-wrapped body lay held at the side by Crouch and Jamieson. As Lamb intoned the solemn words over the bare heads of the seamen and Marines, he caught sight of Charlotte emerging from the companionway, her curls hidden beneath a dark grey bonnet and a small Bible clasped between her hands. She was wearing a dark blue dress, he noticed with an inward smile. St John slid from beneath the flag and plunged to the bottom standing on a French roundshot. Lamb completed the last few words of the service and Selby and Blackett took over the grating for the honour of tipping the other dead men into the sea. The final splash sounded, the last words were spoken. Lamb closed his book and stood for a moment with his head bowed, listening to the quiet hush on the deck, moved as he had always been by the words of the service and the solemn, respectful attention of the men – villains all, perhaps, in one way or another, but with not a face amongst them that did not show due reverence for the occasion.

'On hats,' said Lamb, replacing his own.

'Careful with that flag now, Blackett,' growled Selby, promoted to acting-boatswain's mate and determined to make the most of it. 'Johnson, clap hold of this here grating. Look sharp, now.'

'Steady there, mate,' muttered Johnson, the acting-boatswain's mate's brother-in-law and best friend. 'Just watch your bleedin' gob, give yourself airs, get your fuckin' 'ead punched, toot sweet.'

'Mr Jamieson, Mr Snow, take your men and get to your commands, if you please,' ordered Lamb. 'We will get under way immediately we have cast loose.'

He walked aft and removed his hat as he halted beside Charlotte. 'Hello, my love,' he murmured quietly, aware of the keen ear of the helmsman close by. 'You wore the blue dress after all, I see.'

'Yes, I thought the plum would not look its best beside the Marines' coats. It was a beautiful service, Matthew.'

'I am glad you came. I am sure the men appreciated your presence.'

She smiled. 'I am glad you did. How many days now, to Port Royal?'

'Three, perhaps, if this wind holds.'

She leaned close. 'We must make the most of them then,' she whispered, her smile full of promise, and made her way to the companionway.

Lamb smiled fondly after her and was still smiling when he looked up and saw the *Lejoille* lined with curious faces and Jamieson looking down at him with a carefully bland expression as he waited for the order to cast loose.

'Cast loose!' he snapped, feeling the colour rise to his face.

'Starboard the helm. Shove off for'ard. Loose the tops'l.'

The three vessels slowly drew apart from each other and Lamb put the *Heron* to windward of the *Virgen del Asturias*, leaving the little brig snug and safe between them. The sun was sliding coyly behind the small, scattered clouds and Lamb leaned his hands on the rail as he watched his prizes sail in and out of patches of sparkling blue water, the darting sunlight catching with sudden brilliance at their white, bellied canvas. It was not until that moment that the enormity of his achievement came home to him, welling up within him like a burst of summer heat, and he filled his lungs and gave a huge grin of supreme, sublime happiness. Wealth and promotion stretched before him, a golden, untrodden road, and he chuckled aloud, intoxicated by the thought, his wounds and weariness shrinking to nothing. It was the happiest, the most wonderful day of his life and he spread his arms wide, grinning up at the sky in pure joy.

'Land ho! Fine on the starboard bow!'

Lamb heard the hail from the mast-head as he emerged from his cabin and he felt a small glow of satisfaction regarding the accuracy of his navigation. His pleasure was less than it should have been; the immediacy of the *Heron*'s return to Jamaica brought the problem of Mrs Mainwaring very much to the fore, a question to which he had devoted a great deal of thought in the past few days but had found no easy answer. He gave a glance at Charlotte's cabin door and smiled; she would not be astir for a couple of hours yet, not having gone to her own cot until nearly midnight. Lamb was quite convinced that he was in love and although neither he nor Charlotte had put it into words, he was certain that she felt the same way.

The deck was still damp from its morning scrub and the low sun was warm on his cheek as he gazed lovingly at the two prize vessels to leeward before moving aft and acknowledging the salute of the officer of the watch.

'Jamaica's in sight, sir, fine on the starboard bow,' reported Selby.

'So I heard.' Lamb forbore to mention that he should have been informed of the sighting some two minutes ago; the acting-boatswain's mate was a very large man with stern, rough-hewn features but Lamb had discovered that for all his size he was inordinately shy and would blush like a young girl beneath his tan at the slightest hint of criticism. Lamb glanced at the vane and the set of the sails. 'We'll keep the weather helm for a while. You may go to your breakfast, Mr Selby.'

'Thankee, sir.'

Selby put a knuckle to his forehead and moved purposefully forward, the deep frown which he considered appropriate to the authority of the quarterdeck slowly lifting as he left his burdensome new area of responsibility behind him. Lamb took a slow turn about the deck to satisfy himself that all was as it should be and took up his station at the lee rail beside the tiller, from where he could see the other two vessels without peering beneath the low boom.

His thoughts returned immediately to Mrs Mainwaring and he cursed himself for the hundredth time for ever becoming entangled with her. She and Charlotte under the same roof would present him a pretty problem; even if the two women did not discover that they had shared the attentions of the same man, which seemed extremely unlikely, he would not dare to call on Charlotte while she was staying there. He would fare better sticking his head into a hornets' nest. Mrs Mainwaring's rage at being thrown over for a younger woman would be a frightening thing, he was sure, and Charlotte's injured pride at the knowledge that she was in the house of a rival – and her own cousin, no less – would undoubtedly lose her to him for ever. She had already shown him that she was a woman of strong and sudden passions, who would not suffer humiliation lightly.

He became aware that the mountains of Jamaica were now visible from the deck as a hazy blue smudge on the horizon and that he had been gazing at them deep in thought for some moments. He shook himself alert.

'Come east a point,' he ordered.

'East a point it is, sir,' murmured the helmsman and the distant smudge slid along the hard edge of the horizon a fraction to line up with the bowsprit.

Lamb made up his mind. He had shirked the thing for long enough. He would inform Charlotte of his past acquaintance with Mrs Mainwaring – a slight acquaintance, no more – the moment he went below, even if he had to wake her to do so. She would not be happy about his silence over it for the past few days and she might well suspect that the acquaintanceship had been more than he was telling. As to his silence, he would claim that it had been quite unintentional, a failure on his part to connect her cousin with the Mrs Mainwaring he had known, and which had only occurred to him that very morning; any suspicions that she might have he would shrug off with a disarming chuckle. His confession would be, at best, only a delaying tactic, he was sure, but it would clear his decks so far as a future accusation of deceit was concerned.

Selby's hesitant voice broke into his thoughts and he turned to see the giant standing beside him.

'I've – er – had m'breakfast, sir,' said Selby, politely implying that Lamb was now free to go below for his own.

'Very good. The course is north by west.'

'North by west, aye aye, sir.'

Lamb remained where he was, finding, for reasons that had much to do with his recent resolution, that he was reluctant to go below, a feeling which he acknowledged with wry amusement but pandered to it, nevertheless.

'Did you have a good breakfast, Mr Selby?' he enquired conversationally, as if the boatswain's mate had been given any degree of choice in the way of food.

'Aye, sir, thankee.'

'What did you have?'

Selby did his best not to look surprised. 'Just the usual, sir, burgoo and beer, with a mite of cheese what I'd put by, like.'

Lamb nodded. 'Really?' he commented, in a tone which suggested more than passing interest. 'I like a bit of cheese myself, at breakfast.'

The seaman did not know how to answer this and made do with a 'Yes, sir.'

Lamb rocked on his heels for a few moments, thinking that he was showing craven qualities unbecoming to an officer, while Selby frowned at the topsail. 'Well,' said Lamb at last, nerving himself for his ordeal, 'I suppose I had better find out what delights Sylvester has laid out for me in the way of breakfast.'

Selby was relieved of the burden of finding an answer by a hail from the mast-head.

'Sail ho! Fine on the starboard bow! Make that two sail – and two more! It looks like a convoy, sir!'

Lamb craned his neck and cupped his hands to his mouth, feeling a sudden glow of hope.

'What's their heading?'

There was a long dragging silence of several seconds while Jackson studied the distant ships.

'East, sir!'

Lamb swung round to the helmsman, the glow giving way to a rush of gleeful excitement. A homeward-bound convoy, by God! It was like a gift from heaven. 'Larboard the helm! Steer north by east! Ease the sheets, Mr Selby!'

He waited until the *Heron* was slicing through the blue water with her bowsprit pointing to the east of the island and the wind on her larboard quarter, laying her over at a moderate angle.

'Stand by to run up a weft, Mr Selby,' he ordered. 'I must go below for a moment.'

He cast a quick glance astern to make sure that the two prizes were on the same tack as the cutter and rattled hastily down the companion ladder.

Charlotte was tousle-haired and blink-eyed from her sudden awakening. Lamb thought she had never looked so bewitching. He kissed her forehead.

'My love, you must dress yourself. There is a convoy in the offing, bound for England. Quickly now, there is not a moment to lose.'

'What? What? What do you say? She was still half stupified with sleep. His words suddenly reached her and she sat up, her eyes wide. 'A convoy? What do I want with a convoy? We have not reached Jamaica yet.'

'Nor shall you, my sweet. We must not let this chance go by. It might be weeks – months, even – before another convoy sails. Come, stir yourself. Do you want to be transferred in your nightgown?'

Charlotte folded her arms and set her jaw, suddenly wide awake. Her voice was sharp. 'I have no wish to be transferred anywhere! Do you think I am a barrel or some such, to be slung

194

from one ship to another without so much as a by your leave? Have you lost your mind, Matthew Lamb? Or are you so weary of me that you cannot wait to be rid of me?'

Lamb crouched beside her cot and stroked her hair. 'Of course not. How can you say that? But I have my orders. Admiral Upton was most specific. You are to take ship in the first available convoy.' He was stretching the truth more than somewhat and he went on hastily: 'Besides, I could not rest easy with you in Jamaica. It is a dangerous, fever-ridden place, quite different from Antigua – and swarming with handsome, unattached officers. I would be quite undone with jealousy, and who knows how long you may have to wait there, if you do not take advantage of this convoy?' She gave him a long, sideways look, her chin set firm. He kissed her temple. 'Charlotte, I have only your comfort and safety in mind. Please do not be stubborn.'

She cocked her head to one side and stared thoughtfully at the plum-coloured dress hanging in the corner. 'Well,' she said at last, drawing the word out to stress her reluctance, 'I am not altogether convinced of the need for such haste but if you really think it is for the best . . .'

'I really do, my love.'

She smiled. 'As I recall, cousin Fanny and I were never the best of friends. I shall not be altogether stricken for not seeing her again.' She threw her cover to one side and swung her legs over the side of the cot. 'Are you going to stand there while I dress, you shameless man?'

'Should I not?'

She gave him an impish smile. 'There was not a moment to lose, did you say?'

Lamb put his hand on her cambric-covered knee. 'Well, perhaps no more than two or three.'

The bright weft flying at the *Heron*'s mast-head caught the eye of the lookout on the sloop to windward of the convoy while there were still several miles of sea between them. Lamb gave a little grunt of satisfaction as he saw the sloop turn away from the convoy and into the wind, her yards and sails swinging as one. He lowered his telescope and turned to Selby.

'Put Johnson on the tiller, Mr Selby. I want to run alongside as close as we can without carrying away our spars.'

'Aye aye, sir.'

Charlotte looked up at Lamb with a slight frown, the ribbons of her bonnet dancing in the breeze. 'That looks to be a very small ship, Matthew. I am sure her cabins must be quite tiny. Can you not find me something a trifle larger?'

Lamb laughed. 'That is a ship-sloop, my dear, a naval vessel. Her officers would certainly be delighted to have a pretty face at the wardroom table but I would not put you aboard her, even if her captain allowed it. No, I shall find you something rather more comfortable, have no fear, but first we must beg permission to close the convoy.'

She gave him a curious look. 'You appear to be in high humour, considering I am about to leave you for heaven knows how long,' she said accusingly.

Lamb looked down into her eyes. 'Far from it, my love. I am putting on a brave face.'

She smiled, squeezed his arm and leaned close.

The sloop was the *Scimitar*, newly-built, lean and fast and armed with carronades. At close range, she would be capable of delivering a broadside of greater weight than that of ships twice her tonnage armed with long guns. The faces of her youthful commander, her officers and many of her crew looked down curiously at the little cutter as Johnson brought her into the sloop's lee, taking her as close alongside as he dared.

Lamb raised Jamieson's speaking trumpet to his mouth and bellowed over the narrow gap. 'I have a lady passenger who desires passage to England.'

'Would that I could take her!' roared the *Scimitar*'s commander, doffing his hat and grinning down at Charlotte.

'I'm sure we could find room, sir!' came a shout from one of the officers, nudging his grinning fellows.

The commander ignored the suggestion. 'Try the *Maid of Bath*, towards the rear of the convoy. She has cabins to spare, I believe. A large barque, green and white – Captain Bisco.'

'I am much obliged to you, sir,' called Lamb, raising his hat.

The commander nodded and barked an order over his shoulder. As the two vessels began to draw apart, he leaned

196

over the bulwark and smiled winningly down at Charlotte. 'A safe and pleasant journey to you, ma'am. Perhaps I might have the pleasure of a closer meeting before we reach England.'

Impudent sod! thought Lamb. He glanced down at Charlotte and felt a prickle of unease as she stared at the sloop with sparkling eyes, flushed cheeks and a bright smile.

'Down helm,' he growled to Johnson. 'Make for the rear of the convoy.'

Captain Bisco was brusque and barely courteous but after a little muttering into his beard, turned his ship out of line into the wind and braced his topsails aback, losing way and rolling slowly in the easy swell. Lamb carefully edged the *Heron* alongside with the mainsail lowered to the boom.

'Back the tops'l!' he snapped, judging the moment, aware of Captain Bisco frowning anxiously down as the two hulls drew near. 'Hook on for'ard! Hook on aft!'

The barque's master did not intend to waste a moment. A boatswain's chair came down at the end of its whip and swung invitingly a foot or so above the cutter's deck.

'Get the lady's gear aboard, Mr Selby,' ordered Lamb and took Charlotte by the arm. She looked askance at the chair as it rose and fell in Lamb's steadying hand.

'Is that contrivance safe?' she enquired anxiously. 'It looks a very thin rope.'

'It would bear a dozen little loads like you,' said Lamb reassuringly. 'Come, let me make you all snug and fast. There, put your back against this bridle and I shall make this rope fast around your waist. Now, put your hands just here, hold tight, and you'll be as safe as if you were in an armchair.'

She gave him a forlorn smile. 'I must keep one hand on my skirts,' she whispered. 'It would never do . . .'

'Hold fast below!' came a bellow from the deck of the barque.

'Oh!' said Charlotte as she swayed into the air past Lamb's head, her eyes shut tight.

Lamb silently cursed the damnable haste of the barque's master and managed to touch her hand just before it went out of reach. 'Goodbye, my dear, goodbye,' he called. 'A safe journey to you.'

The chair swung inboard and Charlotte vanished into a cluster of seamen, officers and solicitous female passengers. Captain Bisco leaned over the side.

'Cast off, sir, if you please. You have delayed me long enough.'

'I am much obliged to you for your kindness, sir,' called Lamb, but the master had already turned his back.

Lamb stood at the stern with one hand on the boom as the *Maid of Bath* made her way back towards the long, double line of merchant ships, attempting to pick out Charlotte from the throng of tiny figures beneath the towering masts and canvas. He stared until the figures were no more than an indiscriminate blur and then turned and made his way to the helm, the relief he had earlier felt now given way entirely to a sensation of loss, of a brightness suddenly gone from his life and a feeling of guilt. He stood in silence for several minutes, bleak and dispirited, certain that his precipitate haste had been unnecessary, that he had treated Charlotte very shabbily, that he had been a fool and had probably lost her for ever.

Sylvester came up from below to enquire cuttingly whether Lamb liked his bacon stone cold and stuck fast to the plate.

'No,' said Lamb. 'Eat it yourself, if you've a mind.'

The elf's lip curled. 'It'd take two good men to prize it off the plate by now, sir.'

'I'll have a mug of coffee, though. Bring it to me here.'

He sipped his coffee while Jamaica's dark green mountains rose slowly and massively out of the blue sea. The sun was warm on his back and his two prizes sailed safe and snug to leeward. Gradually, his spirits began to rise and by the time he tossed the dregs of his mug over the side his gloom was gone, replaced by a growing sense of excitement as his landfall drew nearer. The thought came to him that he had solved the problem of the two women in his life very neatly, very neatly indeed, and he grinned, amused by the image of one of them sailing east while he sailed west towards the other. You wicked dog, he thought, and chuckled aloud, vastly pleased with himself. He turned away from the side and caught the thoughtful gaze of the helmsman.

'It's a glorious, wonderful day, Johnson,' he said, beaming

affectionately at the seaman's square, brown, honest face.

Johnson cocked an eye aloft. 'Aye, t'ain't too bad, sir; a fair wind with a nice bit of sun,' he said, and raised a puzzled eyebrow as his captain threw back his head and laughed.